Word Frequency and Lexical Diffusion

Palgrave Studies in Language History and Language Change

Series Editor: **Charles Jones, Emeritus Forbes Professor of English, University of Edinburgh**

This monograph series presents scholarly work in an increasingly active area of linguistic research. It deals with a worldwide range of language types and presents both descriptive and theoretically orientated accounts of language change through time. Aimed at the general theoretician as well as the historical specialist, the series seeks to be a meeting ground for a wide range of different styles and methods in historical linguistics.

Titles include:

Panayiotis A. Pappas
VARIATION AND MORPHOSYNTACTIC CHANGE IN GREEK
From Clitics to Affixes

Betty S. Phillips
WORD FREQUENCY AND LEXICAL DIFFUSION

Daniel Schreier
CONSONANT CHANGE IN ENGLISH WORLDWIDE
Synchrony Meets Diachrony

Ghil'ad Zuckermann
LANGUAGE CONTACT AND LEXICAL ENRICHMENT IN ISRAELI HEBREW

Palgrave Studies in Language History and Language Change
Series Standing Order ISBN 978-0-333-99009-4
(outside North America only)

You can receive future titles in this series as they are published by placing a standing order. Please contact your bookseller or, in case of difficulty, write to us at the address below with your name and address, the title of the series and the ISBN quoted above.

Customer Services Department, Macmillan Distribution Ltd, Houndmills, Basingstoke, Hampshire RG21 6XS, England

---

Word Frequency and Lexical Diffusion

Betty S. Phillips

© Betty S. Phillips 2006

All rights reserved. No reproduction, copy or transmission of this publication may be made without written permission.

No paragraph of this publication may be reproduced, copied or transmitted save with written permission or in accordance with the provisions of the Copyright, Designs and Patents Act 1988, or under the terms of any licence permitting limited copying issued by the Copyright Licensing Agency, 90 Tottenham Court Road, London W1T 4LP.

Any person who does any unauthorised act in relation to this publication may be liable to criminal prosecution and civil claims for damages.

The author has asserted her right to be identified as the author of this work in accordance with the Copyright, Designs and Patents Act 1988.

First published 2006 by
PALGRAVE MACMILLAN
Houndmills, Basingstoke, Hampshire RG21 6XS and
175 Fifth Avenue, New York, N.Y. 10010
Companies and representatives throughout the world

PALGRAVE MACMILLAN is the global academic imprint of the Palgrave Macmillan division of St. Martin's Press, LLC and of Palgrave Macmillan Ltd. Macmillan® is a registered trademark in the United States, United Kingdom and other countries. Palgrave is a registered trademark in the European Union and other countries.

ISBN-13: 978–1–4039–3232–7 hardback

This book is printed on paper suitable for recycling and made from fully managed and sustained forest sources.

A catalogue record for this book is available from the British Library.

Library of Congress Cataloging-in-Publication Data
Phillips, Betty S., 1949–
  Word frequency and lexical diffusion / Betty S. Phillips.
    p. cm. — (Palgrave studies in language history and language change)
  Includes bibliographical references and index.
  ISBN 978–1–4039–3232–7 (cloth)
  1. Grammar, Comparative and general—Phonology. 2. Linguistic change.
  3. Neogrammarians. 4. Language and languages—Word frequency.
  5. Historical lexicology. I. Title. II. Series.
P217.3.P52 2006
414—dc22   2006040171

10 9 8 7 6 5 4 3 2 1
15 14 13 12 11 10 09 08 07 06

Contents

List of Tables	ix
List of Figures	xii
Preface	xiii

1	**Word Frequency and the Neogrammarian Controversy**	**1**
	1.0 Introduction: neogrammarian vs. lexically diffused	1
	1.1 Labov's treatment of lexical diffusion	7
	1.1.1 Labov's complementary distribution of regular vs. lexically diffused changes	11
	1.1.2 A central puzzle: Æ-tensing in Northern cities	13
	1.2 Optimality Theory and word frequency	18
	1.3 Usage-based phonology and word frequency	22
	1.4 Actuation versus implementation	26
	1.5 Conclusion and preview	28
2	**The Lexical Diffusion of Phonetically Abrupt Changes**	**31**
	2.0 Introduction	31
	2.1 Diatonic pairs in English: the least frequent words changing first	34
	2.2 Other product-oriented schemas	39
	2.3 Stress shift in *-ate* verbs: a case of the most frequent words changing first	41
	2.4 The role of lexical analysis	46
	2.5 Word frequency and the Rhythm Rule	49
	2.6 Forms in *-ate* versus *-ator*	52
	2.7 Motivation, actuation, implementation	55
3	**The Lexical Diffusion of Phonetically Gradual Changes**	**57**
	3.0 Introduction	57
	3.1 Gradual changes affecting the most frequent words first	58
	3.1.1 Vowel reductions and deletions	58
	3.1.2 Consonant reductions and deletions	63
	3.1.3 Assimilations	67

vi *Contents*

	3.1.4	Vowel shifts	71
	3.1.5	Summary	75
3.2	Gradual changes affecting the least frequent words first		76
	3.2.1	Glide deletion in Southern American English	76
	3.2.2	Other consonant deletions/reductions	81
	3.2.3	Middle English unrounding of /ø(ː)/	84
	3.2.4	Old English lengthening before -*ld*, -*nd*, etc.	87
3.3	Conclusion		93

4 Lexical Diffusion and Word Class — 96

4.0	Introduction		96
4.1	Function words		102
	4.1.1	Function words changing first and most frequent words first	103
	4.1.2	Function words changing first but most frequent words last	104
	4.1.3	Function words changing last but most frequent words first	108
	4.1.4	Function words changing last and most frequent words last	109
	4.1.5	Summary	112
4.2	Other word class effects		112
4.3	Frequency effects within word classes		116
4.4	Conclusion		123

5 Analogy, Borrowing, and Lexical Diffusion — 124

5.0	Introduction		124
5.1	Lexical diffusion and analogy		125
5.2	Lexical diffusion and borrowing		128
	5.2.1	Borrowings which affect the least frequent words first	135
		5.2.1.1 Reversed changes	136
		5.2.1.2 Other cultural borrowings based on prestige	137
		5.2.1.3 Ideologically motivated vs. ideologically free changes	141
	5.2.2	Borrowings which affect the most frequent words first	142
		5.2.2.1 The spread of broad /aː/ to the United States	143
		5.2.2.2 Old English *an* > *on* before nasals	148

Contents vii

| | | 5.2.3 | Phonetic discreteness vs. gradualness in borrowed changes | 155 |
| | 5.3 | Conclusion | | 157 |

6	Applications of Lexical Diffusion			158
	6.0	Introduction		158
	6.1	Lexical diffusion as a guide to scribal intent		159
	6.2	The *Peterborough Chronicle* diphthongs		165
	6.3	Lexical diffusion and competing analyses of sound change		172
		6.3.1	Description	173
		6.3.2	Evidence	173
		6.3.3	Explanations	175
		6.3.4	Ogura's hypothesis	176
		6.3.5	Görlach's hypothesis	176
		6.3.6	An alternative explanation	177
		6.3.7	Conclusion to /uː/ laxing	179
	6.4	General conclusion		180

7	Conclusions, Connections, and Implications		181
	7.0	Introduction	181
	7.1	Apparent time effects	182
	7.2	Child language	183
	7.3	Age of acquisition	186
	7.4	Discourse strategies	188
	7.5	"Neogrammarian" change as rapid dispersion through the lexicon	191
	7.6	Conclusion	196

Appendix A	Stress Patterns and the Suffix -ate	197
Appendix B	Prenasal /a/-Raising in the Old English *Pastoral Care*	200
Appendix C	Unrounding of OE Long and Short /ø(ː)/ in the *Ormulum*	203
Appendix D	Vowel Lengthening before Voiced Homorganic Consonant Clusters in the *Ormulum*	205
Appendix E	Spellings in ≪a≫ versus ≪o≫ before Nasals in the *Pastoral Care*	209

viii *Contents*

Notes   211
References   220
Topic Index   245
Author Index   248

List of Tables

1.1	Lexical diffusion of /u/ > /ʊ/ before /t/ – modeled on Wang (1979: 362), with frequency counts from Carroll et al. (1971)	4
1.2	Lexical diffusion of OHG consonant devoicing	13
2.1	Diatonic/shifted vs. oxytonic/unshifted stress in English noun–verb homophones	35
2.2	Stress patterns for C$C(C)-*ate* disyllables	42
2.3	British English, disyllables in C$C(C)-*ate*	43
2.4	American English, disyllables in C$C(C)-*ate*	44
2.5	British English trisyllabic verbs in -*ate*	45
2.6	American English trisyllabic verbs in -*ate*	45
3.1	Deletion of /t/ in double-marked pasts	64
3.2(a)	Deletion of [t] in final [xt] and [st] clusters in Dutch, present and past tense forms	64
3.2(b)	Deletion of [t] in final [xt] and [st] final clusters in Dutch, present and past tense forms	65
3.3	Preconsonantal diphthongization in the *Ormulum*, *c.* 1180	68
3.4	Word-final -*e(o)ww* in the *Ormulum*	69
3.5	Lexical diffusion of intervocalic voicing in the *Ormulum*	70
3.6	Development of Middle English /iː/	72
3.7	Development of Middle English /uː/ by phonetic environment and dialect	73
3.8(a)	Southern American English glide deletion	77
3.8(b)	Southern English glide deletion in apparent time	77
3.9	Phonetic gradualness of glide deletion by initial phoneme	80
3.10	*Rushworth 1* loss of /h/	82
3.11	*Lindisfarne* loss of /h/	83
3.12	*Rushworth 1* /hw/ > /w/ by word class	83
3.13	Development in the *Ormulum* of /øː/ > /eː/	85
3.14	Development in the *Ormulum* of /ø/ > /e/	86
3.15(a)	Average frequency in the *Ormulum* of nonauxiliary verbs containing changed (long) vs. unchanged (short) vowels before -*nd*	88

x *List of Tables*

3.15(b)	Average frequency in the *Ormulum* of nonauxiliary verbs containing changed (long) vs. unchanged (short) vowels before *-ng*	88
3.15(c)	Average frequency in the *Ormulum* of nouns containing changed (long) vs. unchanged (short) vowels before *-nd*	89
4.1(a)	Switchboard Corpus nouns	97
4.1(b)	Narrative Corpus nouns	98
4.2	Diphthongization of West German î in Dutch based on Goeman et al. (1993) and CELEX word frequency ( ) for Dutch	100
4.3	Percentages of innovative ≪on, om≫ spellings in the *Pastoral Care* (OE, late ninth century)	104
4.4(a)	Middle English long /øː/ unrounding	105
4.4(b)	Middle English short /ø/ unrounding	106
4.5(a)	Frequency effects of long /øː/ > /eː/ in the *Ormulum* by word class	106
4.5(b)	Development in the *Ormulum* of short /ø/ > /e/	107
4.6	Low-frequency words changing first in vowel lengthening before homorganic consonant clusters in the *Ormulum*, *c.* 1180	110
4.7	Precluster vowel lengthening in the *Ormulum* (*c.* 1180) by word class	111
4.8	Middle English /uː/ > Early Modern English /ʊ/ (> /ʌ/)	114
5.1	Borrowed pronunciations in north Jordan from Standard Arabic	138
5.2	Distribution of innovative "broad *a*"	145
5.3	Average frequencies by phonetic environment	146
5.4	"Eastern US" [æ] ~ RP [aː] in comparatively infrequent words	147
5.5	Progression of *a* → *o* before nasals in early Mercian glosses	149
5.6	Progression of WGmc. a → ≪o≫ before nasals in early Mercian glossaries (Toon 1983: 100–6), plus early West Saxon *Pastoral Care*	153
5.7	*Pastoral Care* progression of ≪o≫ before nasals by word class and phonetic environment	153
5.8	Word frequency and ≪on≫ spellings in the *Pastoral Care*	154
5.9	Percentage of ≪o≫ versus ≪a≫ in *Rushworth 1*	155

6.1	Reflexes of OE *ēo* in the *Peterborough Chronicle*, 1122–54	161
6.2	Reflexes of OE *ĕo* in the *Peterborough Chronicle*, 1122–54	162
6.3	Comparison of lexical diffusion by word class	164
6.4	≪ai≫ and ≪æi≫ in the *Peterborough Chronicle*, 1122–54	167
6.5	≪ei≫ and ≪eg≫ in the *Peterborough Chronicle*, 1122–54	168
6.6	≪au≫ and ≪aw≫ in the *Peterborough Chronicle*, 1122–54	169
6.7	≪ou≫ and ≪ow≫ in the *Peterborough Chronicle*, 1122–54	170
6.8	≪eu≫ and ≪ew≫ in *Peterborough Chronicle*, 1122–54	171
6.9	Summary	171
7.1	Acquisition of [b] "phone class" by T	184

List of Figures

2.1	Development of noun–verb homographs	37
2.2	Connectionist links in the mental lexicon	55
6.1	Tongue position of laterals and high back vowels	178

Preface

The recognition that lexical diffusion constitutes an important aspect of sound change has grown significantly since Wang introduced the term in 1969. In particular, Labov (1981, 1994) acknowledges the importance of lexical diffusion as a method of change, although he denies its central importance and fails to account for word frequency effects noted in Phillips (1984). Therefore, while many scholars are now aware of lexical diffusion as a possible explanation for exceptions to sound change, few consider lexical diffusion to be the underlying mechanism behind the implementation of change, and even fewer acknowledge the role of word frequency. This book started as a way to redress this situation by bringing together the work I had done on lexical diffusion and word frequency since 1984 and melding it into a coherent whole. In particular, I found that my 1984 article in *Language* was regularly cited, but my own understanding of lexical diffusion had grown since then and changed, as I investigated word frequency effects on different types of sound change. This book updates my earlier work, discusses how it relates to work others have done, and clarifies how it fits with modern theories of the lexicon. Fortunately, not only have other researchers begun to notice and report word frequency effects, but the importance of frequency in perception and production has enjoyed renewed interest in the field of psycholinguistics, findings which Bybee (2001) has used to support a usage-based model of phonology. Thus the time seemed right for synthesizing the findings on word frequency and sound change in one volume where the different threads could be connected. Therefore, I deeply appreciate Palgrave Macmillan and the editor of this series, Charles Jones, for giving me the opportunity to achieve this goal.

Acknowledgements

I would like to thank the many people who have helped and encouraged me in my work on lexical diffusion. Among others, I owe deep thanks to Bill Wang and John Algeo for supporting my early work, and I particularly want to thank Joan Bybee and Donka Minkova for encouraging me to write the current book. It was in Joan Bybee's class at the LSA Summer Institute in Oswego, New York, that I was first introduced to the notion

xiv *Preface*

that word frequency had an effect on sound change, and since then I have consistently found in her works answers (or intimations thereof) to questions I have confronted in my own studies. Donka Minkova has been a valued friend for many years, and beyond her own considerable accomplishments, I greatly appreciate her unfailing encouragement not only of my work but also that of many others in the field of English historical linguistics. Her detailed comments on the early chapters of this book proved invaluable. Previous versions of much of the work here have also benefited greatly from Robert Stockwell's incisive comments, as well as from anonymous reviewers for the journals in which they appeared.

Others who contributed comments to drafts of portions of this book include my colleague Cecil Nelson and my former student I-wen Lai. James Meyers offered me early advice about frequency in Optimality Theory. It would be impossible to list all the others whose work, comments, inspiration, and support have combined to make this volume a reality. Of course, all shortcomings in the final work are strictly my own.

I would also like to acknowledge the editors of the following journals who generously granted me the right to incorporate varying amounts of previous articles into the present work: *American Speech, Journal of English Linguistics, Language, Linguistics,* and *Word.* The publishers John Benjamins and Mouton de Gruyter also granted me the right to use all or part of book chapters that had appeared in their publications.

In addition, I sincerely thank my colleagues in the Department of Languages, Literatures, and Linguistics for supporting my sabbatical application and Indiana State University for granting me the sabbatical during which this book was written. Finally, I would like to thank my daughter Sara for her help in the final formatting of the book, and both my children, Sara and Larry, for their constant loving support. To my parents, Mary and Arthur Steedley, now deceased, I am too indebted to count the ways. To them and to my children I dedicate this volume.

Indiana State University   BETTY STEEDLEY PHILLIPS

The author has made every effort to contact copyright holders, but in the event that any have been inadvertently overlooked, the publisher will make amends at the earliest opportunity.

1
Word Frequency and the Neogrammarian Controversy

1.0 Introduction: neogrammarian vs. lexically diffused

Two positions articulated in the nineteenth century continue to reverberate in discussions of sound change today. At that time Gilliéron was working on his monumental *Atlas linguistique de la France* (1902–10), leading him to the conclusion that every word behaves independently (1918) – or, as formulated by Malkiel (1967), "Every word has its own history." The neogrammarians' work on unraveling the historical relationships between languages led them to adopt as axiomatic Osthoff and Brugmann's (1878) position that "all words in which the sound subjected to the change appears in the same relationship are affected by the change without exception" (as translated by Lehmann 1967: 204).[1] Most language historians today would consider both positions overstated, but the debate continues in search of a balance between the two positions.

The neogrammarian claim grew out of Karl Verner's (1876) discovery of phonetic explanations for seeming exceptions in the consonant shift known as Grimm's Law. Its most succinct declaration is expressed in the dictum "Sound laws admit of no exceptions," first expressed by August Leskien (1876), reiterated by Osthoff and Brugmann (1878),[1] taken as slogan by the *Junggrammatiker* (as the nineteenth-century neogrammarians were called), and used as a working principle even now by all serious students of sound change. The neogrammarian stance was adopted into structural linguistics from its beginning, namely, as early as Saussure's formulation of synchrony versus diachrony. Saussure's

2 Word Frequency and Lexical Diffusion

account of diachrony indeed specifically excluded individual lexical items from participation in sound change (1916 [1959]: 94):

> The real issue is to find out whether phonetic changes affect words or only sounds, and there is no doubt about the answer: in *néphos, methu* [sic], *ánkhō*, etc., a certain phoneme – a voiced Proto-Indo-European aspirate – became voiceless, Proto-Greek initial *s* became *h*, etc.; each fact is isolated, independent of the other events of the same class, independent also of the words in which the change took place. The phonic substance of all the words was of course, modified, but this should not deceive us as to the real nature of the phenomenon.[2]

Saussure elaborated by comparing words to a melody and phonemes to an instrument, such as a piano, which plays those sounds: "Our system of phonemes is the instrument we play in order to articulate the words of language; if one of its elements is modified, diverse consequences may ensue, but the modification itself is not concerned with the words which are, in a manner of speaking, the melodies of our repertory" (p. 94).[3]

Saussure's position influenced all structuralists who followed him, and foreshadowed modern modularist theories of language, that is, those that include an autonomous phonology. As Bakken (2001: 67) puts it, "A phonetically regular process is characterized by general productivity, and such productivity seems to be incompatible with lexical exceptions, i.e. lexical diffusion. Lexical diffusion and phonetic regularity are therefore truly mutually exclusive." Labov (1994: 542), for instance, accepts lexical diffusion as a method of change only for "lexical rules," which substitute one phoneme for another, and not for "postlexical rules," which are phonetically conditioned. The neogrammarian stance is also implied in Janda and Joseph's (2003a: 115) statement that "diffusionary effects in the spread of phonological change through the lexicons of speakers...are actually epiphenomenal, being the result of already-needed mechanisms of analogical change and dialect borrowing." Thus, students within the structuralist tradition of sound change still often treat exceptions to sound changes as marginal, with the primary focus of change remaining on the phonological system, not on the lexicon. Labov (1994) is certainly within this tradition. Optimality Theory also follows in this tradition by focusing on the system, and only as a reflection of universal and innate properties of language. Such a view contrasts with that adopted here, whereby sounds exist within words and the phonological system itself is epiphenomenal, being an extraction from pronunciations of the words and phrases of the language.

Lexical diffusion follows in the footsteps of Gilliéron, and more specifically in those of Schuchardt, who observed that more frequent words tend to change first (1885: 58):

> The greater or lesser frequency in the use of individual words that plays such a prominent role in analogical formation is also of great importance for their phonetic transformation, not within rather small differences, but within significant ones. Rarely-used words drag behind; very frequently used ones hurry ahead. Exceptions to the sound laws are formed in both groups.

In a number of publications, Mańczak has noted the influence of word frequency in and across languages (see Mańczak 2000, 2004 for a summary and bibliographical references), and Chen (1972: 470) gives a historical overview of other linguists who hinted at the lexically gradual nature of sound change:

> Sapir spoke of incomplete changes (1921: 180) and of how a 'drift' "gradually worms its way through a gamut of phonetically analogous forms" (p. 178); Karlgren (1954: 229) alluded to "retarded remnants" and "belated cases" (p. 275) which could be easily identified with "residues" in Wang's (1969) sense; while Martinet (1955: 187) speculated about "variantes synchroniques" (coexistent variants) as result [sic] of gradual replacement of lexical items by innovating forms.

He notes that the most specific example of lexical diffusion was made by Sommerfelt (1962: 75), namely, that the loss of the initial voiceless velar fricative [χ] (Old Welsh ch-) in some Welsh dialects first affected the word χwarę 'to play,' then χwanen 'flea,' and only later χwaːir 'sister.'

However, it was not until Wang (1969) revived the notion of change gradually spreading through the lexicon that the term "lexical diffusion" was used to describe this process and to ascribe to it the status of a regular method of the implementation of sound change. As Chen and Wang (1975: 256) explain, "a phonological rule gradually extends its scope of operation to a larger and larger portion of the lexicon, until all relevant items have been transformed by the process." Table 1.1, modified from Wang (1979: 362), gives an example of a lexically diffused sound change

4 *Word Frequency and Lexical Diffusion*

Table 1.1 Lexical diffusion of /u/ > /ʊ/ before /t/ – modeled on Wang (1979: 362), with frequency counts from Carroll et al. (1971)

Word	boot	loot	root	soot	foot
Frequency	5.6262	0.8000	58.060	1.8513	158.32
Unchanged	/but/	/lut/			
Variable			/rut ~ rʊt/	/sut ~ sʊt/	
Changed					/fʊt/

familiar to speakers of English, the laxing of /u/ to /ʊ/ before /t/ in words like *foot* (now changed to /fʊt/ for all speakers), *soot* and *root* (now variable between /u/ and /ʊ/ for many speakers), and *boot* and *loot* (still unchanged for all speakers).

Although this change is clearly phonetically conditioned by a following /t/, within the phonetic environment, individual lexical items have changed at independent rates. The typical pattern of a lexically diffused sound change seems to be an S-curve, as suggested initially by Wang and Cheng (1977: 154). A change begins in a few words, builds up speed in the middle of its course, but often leaves a residue of one or more words which resist the change (Ogura and Wang 1998: 322). At times further phonetic influences may play a role. But very often no such phonetic explanation can be found. For instance, there is no phonetic reason why the two fricatives /f/ and /s/ or the two liquids /r/ and /l/ should affect the following vowel differently. Within these phonetic environments, however, the influence of word frequency can be seen, even in this simple example. The word *foot* is used much more frequently than the word *soot*, and the word *root* more frequently than the word *loot*, an impression which is confirmed by the relative frequencies as reported in Carroll et al. (1971) – the estimated frequency per million tokens for *foot* being 158.32 versus *soot* 1.8513, and for *root* 58.060 versus *loot* 0.8000. This relationship between lexical diffusion and frequency is the focus of this book.

The role of word frequency in sound change was not mentioned, however, in Labov's (1981) review of the "Neogrammarian Controversy." Labov identified the larger issue in acknowledging lexical diffusion, that is, "In the evolution of sound systems, is the basic unit of change the word or the sound?" (p. 268). He placed sound change squarely in the phonology, with lexical diffusion being a variable that might affect only certain kinds of sound change. Labov (1994: 421–39, 502–43) investigated lexically diffused changes in more detail and admitted, "There are more than enough solid examples of sounds changing one word at a time to support the view that lexical diffusion is deeply rooted in the process of change. But where it is rooted, and where it flourishes, is more difficult to decide" (p. 471). Yet he comes to a conclusion very similar to the one he advocated in 1981, namely, that there are two diametrically opposed types of change: REGULAR SOUND CHANGE, which affects "a single phonetic feature of a phoneme in a continuous phonetic space," and LEXICAL DIFFUSION, which requires "abrupt substitution of one phoneme for another in words that contain that phoneme" (p. 542).

One version of this view of neogrammarian change is Hale's (2003: 344) suggestion that the neogrammarian hypothesis is "a claim about... the set of possible change events," with constraints on diffusion being part of sociolinguistics. Change he defines very narrowly in terms of first language acquisition, where "the core context for change is reanalysis during the acquisition period" (p. 358). But he dismisses lexical influence in this process, saying that "while chance distortion... may impact the acquirer's ultimate representation of a given lexical item..., they are too context-dependent to give rise to regular phonological change" (p. 349). Change in individual lexical items are, by definition, not considered part of sound change:

> One coherent way to limit the term "sound change" is thus by requiring that the environment in which the change takes place be specified in *phonological* rather than lexical terms. ... Neogrammarian theory was thus never intended to account for changes in the phonological representations associated with individual lexical items. (p. 347)

Therefore a change such as metathesis in a single lexical item is not considered a sound change, but merely a change in the phonological representation of a particular lexical item (p. 347). Yet there are problems with Hale's narrow definition of neogrammarian change, not the least of which is that studies on first language acquisition have found word frequency effects as well as neighborhood density effects (Morrisette 1999), the latter being the number of words similar to the word in question. That is, children do not acquire the adult pronunciation of phonemes across their entire lexicon at the same time but word by word (Berg 1995: 350–1; Beckman and Edwards 2000; Gierut 2001; Gierut and Morrisette 1998). In fact, even the frequency of sublexical phonological

6 Word Frequency and Lexical Diffusion

sequences influences the accuracy of children's imitation of novel word forms (Beckman and Edwards 2000: 217).

Another solution to the controversy has been the suggestion that "all phonological change starts with lexical diffusion and most ends up Neogrammarian, given enough time" (Lass 1997: 140–1; cf. also Andersen 1973: 787). This position is similar to Schuchardt's (1885 [1972]: 62) statement:

> I find it even more remarkable that the psychological bases of sound change, the social character of a language, the fluid borders of its spatial and temporal variations can be perceived with such lucidity and, at the same time, that unexceptionability of the sound laws can be defended so staunchly. The neogrammarians confuse "the very simple concept of law with that of the complex effects that are produced by many laws that variously operate simultaneously together" (Merlo [1885], p. 159).

Schuchardt's observation is echoed by Krishnamurti's (1998) suggestion that lexically diffused sound changes, especially those based on typological universals, may well eventually affect all the phonetically pertinent words, making their end result neogrammarian. Nevertheless, some sociolinguists – accustomed to looking at change in progress – hesitate to adopt such a strong lexical diffusionist view; Milroy (1999: 181), for instance, responds to such suggestions by saying, "I too am reluctant to distinguish two opposites in the implementation of sound change, but when we get into sociolinguistic detail it does appear that some changes diffuse lexically whereas others appear to affect all relevant lexical items equally."

Just as Milroy hedges his statement with the word *appear* in "others appear to affect all relevant lexical items equally," one problem is that it is impossible to prove a negative. That is, it is impossible to prove that a change has been truly neogrammarian, affecting all the pertinent words at once, because perhaps the observation of the change has taken place after the change has ever so rapidly affected all the pertinent words. To expropriate Wang's (1969: 21) metaphor, "We cannot prove that a platypus does not lay eggs with photographs showing a platypus NOT laying eggs."

The primary aim of this book, therefore, is not to prove that neogrammarian changes never occur but to demonstrate which kind of changes affect the most frequent words first and which affect the least frequent words first. By so doing, the provenance of neogrammarian changes will be shown to be so restricted and their likelihood so remote that it seems preferable to treat them as very rapidly (lexically) diffused changes.

Proponents of various theories of phonology, including Lexical Phonology and Optimality Theory, have attempted to incorporate word frequency effects into their models, and this book hopes to benefit all who are interested in doing so. At present, however, frequency effects can most easily be described within a usage-based network model such as that espoused in Bybee (2001). This book will assume such a model and will demonstrate how lexically diffused sound changes fit within and support a usage-based model. To the extent that other theories accept its basic tenet of the importance of perception and production to the structure of the lexicon, they too should benefit from our findings, especially if they are also interested in accounting for diachronic tendencies. Our definition of lexical diffusion will be same as that proposed by Ogura (1995: 32): "In lexical diffusion, diffusion from word to word in the language progresses from speaker to speaker in the community.... The three processes of diffusion from word to word, diffusion from speaker to speaker and diffusion from site to site progress side by side." Lexical diffusion is, to Ogura, "the fundamental mechanism of change," and neogrammarian regularity is shown when diffusion from word to word proceeds "so fast that it is difficult to observe it" (1995: 32). This stance was apparently first expressed by Oliveira (1991: 103), when he declared: "My position is more radical than Chen and Wang's, and I will say that *all* sound changes are lexically implemented, that is, there are *no* neogrammarian sound changes (although we can have neogrammarian long-term end results)." The following sections will demonstrate why Labov's (1994) characterization of lexical diffusion is not just inadequate but also inaccurate. And because so much of the debate has been framed in terms of Lexical Phonology, reference will be made below and in the ensuing chapters to the shortcomings of that model in particular.

1.1 Labov's treatment of lexical diffusion

Labov acknowledges instances of lexical diffusion and gives his fullest treatment of the neogrammarian controversy in the first volume of his *Principles of Linguistic Change: Internal Factors* (1994: 541), where he tries to answer the neogrammarian paradox; that is, "If Wang and his associates are right about lexical diffusion, and the Neogrammarians were more right than they knew about sound change, how can both be right?" He notes that "one group has asserted that 'Phonemes change,' the other that 'Words change.' Neither formulation is very useful as it stands; they are abstract slogans that have lost their connection with

8 *Word Frequency and Lexical Diffusion*

what is actually happening" (p. 541). Labov's answer to the paradox, worded in terminology from Lexical Phonology, is that

> we have located Neogrammarian regularity in the low-level output rules, and lexical diffusion in the redistribution of an abstract word class into other abstract classes. . . . The whole array of sound changes will undoubtedly show many intermediate combinations of these properties of discreteness, abstractness, grammatical conditioning, and social conditioning. (pp. 541–2)

He mentions "other dimensions" which might affect changes, including the suggestion that fortitions might be more likely to be diffused than lenitions (on which see Chapter 4), or that there might exist "some lexical irregularities within subsystems" (p. 542). Despite these reservations, he nevertheless suggests the following divisions:

> **Regular sound change** is the result of a gradual transformation of a single phonetic feature of a phoneme in a continuous phonetic space. It is characteristic of the initial stages of a change that develops within a linguistic system, without lexical or grammatical conditioning or any degree of social awareness ("change from below").
>
> **Lexical diffusion** is the result of the abrupt substitution of one phoneme for another in words that contain that phoneme. The older and newer forms of the word will usually differ by several phonetic features. This process is most characteristic of the late stages of an internal change that has been differentiated by lexical and grammatical conditioning, or has developed a high degree of social awareness or of borrowings from other systems ("change from above"). (p. 542)

This bipartite division of sound change is no doubt influenced by Labov's adherence to the theoretical model of Lexical Phonology, with its crisp division between lexical rules and postlexical rules. But even adherents to the Lexical Phonology model have noted problems that require adjustments in that model if it is to accommodate mounting evidence of lexical diffusion. Carr (1991), for example, finds that the Tyneside Weakening of /t/ to /r/, a postlexical rule, exhibits lexical diffusion. Harris (1989: 37), in looking at the history of æ-tensing, argues that the grammatical level at which a change occurs is in principle independent of the phonetic or phonological feature involved. In other words, we can track the progress of a change along two independent dimensions; through phonological or phonetic space (involving alternations to feature specifications) and through different levels of linguistic structure.

Pandey (1997: 130) too notes that it is impossible to predict at which level lexical diffusion may be found: "cyclic or level I lexical rules must undergo lexical diffusion; word-level lexical rules may undergo exceptionless change; and although it is typical for postlexical rules to undergo exceptionless change, they may also lead to diffusion." Tone sandhi in Beijing Mandarin may also present a problem, since it is both postlexical, affecting phrasal constructions, and lexical, of necessity applying before tone deletion, which is lexically idiosyncratic (Chen 2000: 384–5).

Bybee (2000a: 266) also explains how Lexical Phonology makes incorrect predictions concerning changes such as /d/ reduction and deletion in Spanish, which

> is disappearing faster in the non-alternating environment of the Past Participle suffix, -ado, than in stems. Stems would be subject to the reduction or deletion rule both at Level 1 and at Level 2, but -ado, since it is a part of regular inflection, would not be available to undergo the rule until Level 2. It would thus have *less* reduction and deletion than a stem, rather than more.

As Bybee concludes, "This example shows that the Lexical Phonology approach is fundamentally the wrong approach, for it is a fact of usage, not structure, that is accelerating the change." Other researchers have documented changes which are both phonetically gradual and lexically diffused – an impossibility in Labov's model, where phonetically gradual rules supposedly affect only postlexical rules (affecting low-level output) and lexical diffusion only applies to lexical rules (involving phoneme substitution). Bybee (2000a: 262), for instance, in her discussion of the lexical diffusion of /t, d/ deletion in English, notes that Lociewicz (1992) found that "on average the -ed suffix on low frequency verbs is 7 msec. longer than on high frequency verbs." Bybee (2000b: 69) also notes that schwa deletion in English involves subphonemic detail since words like *memory* may vary at least three ways – as in [mɛmri] ~ [mɛmr̩i] ~ [mɛməri],

10 *Word Frequency and Lexical Diffusion*

yet "/r/ and syllabic /ɹ̩/ are not distinguished phonemically, nor are syllabic /ɹ̩/ and /ər/." Other studies documenting the lexical diffusion of phonetically gradual changes include Yaeger-Dror (1994) for a chain shift in Montreal French, Phillips (1994) for glide deletion in Southern American English, and Hansen (2001) for the raising of nasalized vowels in French. In a similar vein in synchronic phonology, Steriade (2000) has demonstrated that noncontrastive features such as the durational difference between [t] and [ɾ] are grammatically relevant to speakers of a language; for instance, the [t] of *military* is retained when the productive affix *-istic* is added to form *militaristic*, and the [ɾ] of *capital* is retained in *capitalistic*, yielding a close minimal pair, even though [t] and [ɾ] do not normally contrast in English.

But missing from the aforementioned discussions is a recognition that not all lexically diffused changes behave the same. It is only acknowledged that some proceed more quickly than do others. But some lexically diffused changes affect the most frequent words first, whereas others affect the least frequent (Phillips 1984, 1994, 1998c). And this, too, has to be explained. A theory of the relationship between the lexicon and the phonology of a language must, in fact, account for even more. There are really at least six categories of change, some overlapping, which must be accounted for (the following list providing in parentheses one example of each type):

- Lexically diffused change affecting the most frequent words first (Modern English final *-t/-d* deletion, Bybee 1999, 2002b)
- Lexically diffused change affecting the least frequent words first (ME /ö(:)/ unrounding, Phillips 1984);
- Lexically diffused changes which eventually achieve neogrammarian regularity ($s > h > \emptyset$ in Gondi dialects, Krishnamurti 1998);
- Lexically diffused changes which do not achieve neogrammarian regularity (Philadelphia /æ/ tensing, Labov et al. 1972: 47–95, 1994: 436–7);
- Lexically diffused changes influenced by word class (Old English vowel lengthening before /ld/ clusters, Phillips 1983a);
- Lexically diffused changes which are also phonetically gradual (French [ɑ̃] > [ɔ̃], Hansen 2001).

The distinction between the varying subtypes of lexically diffused changes will be discussed in the following chapters. First, however, we need to clarify even further some misunderstandings about the nature of lexical diffusion.

1.1.1 Labov's complementary distribution of regular vs. lexically diffused changes

Labov (1994: 543) charts the "complementary distribution" of neogrammarian (or "regular") sound change and lexically diffused change. Under "Regular sound change" he lists "Vowel shifts in place of articulation," "Diphthongization of high vowels," "Consonant changes in manner of articulation," "Vocalization of liquids," and "Deletion of glides and schwa." Under "Lexical diffusion" he lists "Shortening and lengthening of segments," "Diphthongization of mid and low vowels," "Consonant changes in place of articulation," "Metathesis of liquids and stops," and "Deletion of obstruents." Yet even in this list, we can easily find counter-examples to the changes listed under "Regular sound change." Many of these will be discussed in the chapters to follow, but even a brief description of them here will substantiate why Labov's divisions do not always apply.

For example, Labov's evidence for regular sound change in vowel shifts involving place of articulation includes "raising, lowering, backing, and fronting" (p. 531). Yet a number of studies now show lexical diffusion either by word frequency or by word class affecting such changes. For instance, based on spellings from the Old English *Pastoral Care*, Phillips (1980) demonstrates how the raising of Old English [*a*] to [ɔ] before nasals affected the most frequent words first. And Labov himself cites Brink (1977) as reporting

> a wide variety of exceptions to sound changes.... [S]everal shortenings affect only a few words and are conditioned by frequency. But exceptions are also reported for simple lowerings and raisings. ... A raising of long [aː] does not affect Swedish and German loanwords. A lowering of [ø] before [n, m, f] ... is characterized as "very slow and affecting the vocabulary less systematically" than many other sound changes. On the whole, the findings of Brink and Lund [1975] indicate that analogy, frequency, and foreign status can influence the course of low-level output rules. (Labov 1994: 534)

Yet in the next sentence he adds, "At the same time, their overall findings support the principles presented above" (p. 534). But if, by his own definition, "regular sound change ... develops within a linguistic system, without lexical or grammatical conditioning or any degree of social awareness," then the changes Brink and Lund describe cannot be regular/neogrammarian changes. They describe changes in low-level

12 *Word Frequency and Lexical Diffusion*

output rules that are affected by lexical conditioning, i.e. that are lexically diffused.

Labov's second generalization, that the diphthongization of high vowels should follow a regular, neogrammarian path of no exceptions, while diphthongization of mid and low vowels should not, seems inherently implausible, and Labov offers no explanation for why these vowels should behave so differently. His attack (Labov 1992, 1994) of Ogura's (1987) evidence is refuted in Ogura (1995), who points out that lexical diffusion does not exclude simultaneous phonetic conditioning. In fact, she produces evidence that lexical diffusion operates within the narrow phonetic environments by calculating the number of sites in the *Linguistic Atlas of England* where phonetically similar pairs are pronounced differently. For the shift from Middle English /iː/, the vowels of words ending in [n] (*nine–mine*) differed in 70 sites, those of words ending in [f] (*wife–knife*) differed in 36 sites, those of words ending in [t] (*white–writing*) differed in 62 sites, and so forth for 8 phonetic environments. Only the pair *ice–icicle* was not significantly different within its narrow phonetic environment. A similar pattern was found for developments from Middle English /uː/, for which she documents lexical diffusion again within 8 phonetic environments: vowels in words ending in [s] (*house–mouse*) differed in 61 sites, those in words ending in [θ] (*south–mouth*) differed in 57 sites, those in words ending in [x] (*bough–plough*) differed in 91 sites, and so forth (Ogura 1995: 44–7).

As for changes in manner of articulation, Kerswill's (1983) investigation of the speech of young people in Durham, England, found that glottalization of [t] to [ʔ] occurred only in the word *time*. In addition, Barrack (1976) has found evidence of lexical diffusion in the devoicing stage of the High German Consonant Shift. He reasoned that since the shift originated in the south and proceeded northward, southern dialects should exhibit greater diffusion of the shift. Table 1.2 exhibits his data based on spellings in 17 Old High German documents.

I am unfamiliar with any work documenting lexical diffusion in the vocalization of liquids, but Labov's last category of "regular" changes, deletion of schwa, is contradicted by Bybee's (2000b: 68) documentation of lexical diffusion at work in the deletion of schwa in words such as *every* and *memory*. She notes that the "high frequency *memory*, *salary*, *summary* and *nursery* have a more reduced penultimate syllable than low frequency *mammary*, *artillery*, *summery* and *cursory*." Most likely of all to be pronounced with no schwa are the most frequent words, *every* and *evening*. (See Chapter 3 for further discussion.)

Table 1.2 Lexical diffusion of OHG consonant devoicing (based on Barrack 1976: 163)

Dialects, south to north	Percentages of words affected		
	b > p	***d > t***	***g > k***
Bavarian	98	100	52
Alemannic	43	88	73
East Franconian	01	98	02
South Rhenish Franconian	00	84	00
Rhenish Franconian	04	48	04
Central Franconian	00	31	00

In summary, Labov's division of sound changes does not work. In addition, the specific sound changes that he reports as exhibiting no evidence of lexical diffusion may well be influenced by some other factor. There are several possibilities. Sometimes, for instance, so few words meet the phonetic conditions of a change that all the pertinent words quickly adhere to it. Or perhaps the change in question has followed a path of lexical diffusion, but the synchronic state investigated represents a late stage, where all the words have been affected. And of course there is the possibility that all changes are lexically diffused but some diffuse so quickly that it is next to impossible to catch them in progress. In addition, it is possible that some lexical exceptions that Labov allows within his neogrammarian model are simply the last hold-outs in a change that has managed to affect all the other words. In fact, the next section will reveal that Labov himself acknowledges lexical exceptions to a change that he considers central to the neogrammarian puzzle.

1.1.2 A central puzzle: Æ-tensing in Northern cities

Labov identifies as a key to the resolution of the impasse between the neogrammarian and lexical diffusionist positions the behavior of æ-tensing in American English dialects. According to him (1994: 534–9), the puzzle rests in "the contrast between the Northern Cities short **a** system and that of the Middle Atlantic states." Lexical diffusion clearly occurs in the latter – as in Philadelphia /kæn/ "able to" contrasting with /kÆn/ "tin" – but Labov says that he has not found it in the former, that is, in the Northern Cities Chain Shift. He concludes that

14 *Word Frequency and Lexical Diffusion*

> the Philadelphia short a split is the continuation of a long-standing pattern of lengthening of English /a/, which proceeds by changes in lexical rules at a high level of abstraction. ... The Northern Cities tensing of short **a** appears to be an independent phenomenon: a postlexical shift of height at a low level of abstraction. (pp. 538–9)

This explanation, in fact, seems to be what led Labov to posit regular sound change as affecting "Vowel shifts in place of articulation" and lexical diffusion as affecting "Shortening and lengthening of segments" (p. 543), as discussed above. [4]

The history of each shift has been well documented, and Labov's stance seems strongly influenced by Trager's (1940) reconstruction of the development of æ-raising and subsequent tensing in cities like Philadelphia. His reconstruction of the events that led to the present-day evidence of "lexical diffusion" (a term unknown in 1940) in this dialect has clearly influenced Labov's thinking and that of other linguists, such as Janda and Joseph (2003a: 115), who believe lexical diffusion can be explained through analogy and borrowing. (For a larger discussion of analogy and borrowing, see Chapter 5.)

Trager claims that the original change was one of lengthening, that there was one phoneme originally, but its length became dependent on its position in the word. "The next step," he says, "was for the longer variety to assume a higher and tenser quality in some or all of its occurrences (but apparently never before [ŋ] and [l]) in closed syllables, and especially before [m], [n], and the voiceless spirants" (pp. 256–7). At that point the two sounds are still in complementary distribution. He reasons that this distribution is disturbed as follows:

> But with speakers of such a dialect, and in the recent history, one can assume, of speakers of the dialect first described, the situation may be disturbed by **analogical** factors at many points. One says *pad* with [æ·]. What more easy than to say *padding* with the same sound, if the two are in close proximity? *Can* the noun has [æ·]; *can* the auxiliary, when unstressed, has [æ]; an occasion arises to stress it, and it appears not with the "correct" positional variant [æ·], but with the analogically transferred [æ]. As soon as such cases have arisen, the speaker has two phonemic entities instead of one, and his phonemic system has been disturbed. But as yet the morphophonemic relations are quite clear and remain undisturbed. On the other hand, how can one explain *bade, adze* with [æ], *Abby* with [æ·], and the like? Here the two entities appear apparently without reason, and there

are two morphophonemes as well. The explanation seems to be this: the newer phonemic entity [æ·] is still the more limited in position; when a word is to be pronounced which is normally weak-stressed, or which is known only from the spelling, the freer of the two sounds, [æ], the one that can appear before all consonants, is chosen, and we get *can*, *adze*, *bade*, with [æ]; on the other hand, a popular name like *Abby*, tied up by **some obscure analogy** with frequently heard words ending in *b*, say *nab*, *grab*, *gab*, etc., which have [æ·], comes out with [æ·] instead of [æ]. . . . Another factor is the constant **contact** with speakers of other dialects. Words are heard with either [æ] or [æ·], and adopted as heard, since the two sounds are distinct phonemically to the hearer, and, with a few exceptions, he can use either in any position. (p. 257 – my bold)

Trager typifies the neogrammarian stance in his summation: "In the consideration of historical phonology, comparative linguists ought never to forget possibilities of the type here presented. They may appear to interfere with Lautgesetze. But when examined they are seen merely to supplement the usual rules and not supplant them" (p. 258).

Labov (1992: 69) echoes Trager:

These results add further evidence to the idea that low level sound changes – backing, fronting, raising, and lowering of vowels – are governed primarily by the phonetic environment of the segment affected, in a manner more regular than the Neogrammarians themselves might have imagined. Lexical diffusion does occur: but it is confined to changes of word class assignment. We can never rule out the possibility that lexical diffusion occurs in the major word classes in a manner more subtle than we can observe. If so, it must be confined to very short periods of time and space, and is far overshadowed by phonetic conditioning. There is no evidence here for lexical diffusion as the fundamental mechanism of sound change. Though some words may have their own history, each word does not have its own history.

With the appearance of his 1994 book, Labov seemed to have softened his position somewhat:

[T]here appear to be far more substantially documented cases of Neogrammarian sound change than of lexical diffusion. The upshot of this discussion is not, however, a victory for the Neogrammarians.

16 *Word Frequency and Lexical Diffusion*

> There are more than enough solid examples of sounds changing one word at a time to support the view that lexical diffusion is deeply rooted in the process of change. But where it is rooted, and where it flourishes, is more difficult to decide. (p. 471)

And he articulates the neogrammarian paradox, that is,

> if Wang and his associates are right about lexical diffusion, and the Neogrammarians were more right than they knew about sound change, how can both be right? ... One group has asserted that "Phonemes change," the other that "Words change." Neither formulation is very useful as it stands; they are abstract slogans that have lost their connection with what is actually happening. (p. 541)

In order to describe what might indeed be happening, it is first necessary to look more closely at the Northern Cities Shift, Labov's prime example of a neogrammarian shift, the "most extreme forms [of which] are to be found in the largest cities: Rochester, Syracuse, Buffalo, Cleveland, Detroit, and Chicago" (Labov 1991: 20). The tensing of /æ/ is described as follows: "*Short a* is tensed as a whole, and rises along the front peripheral track as the phoneme /aeh/ with a wide range of phonetic conditioning." Labov describes the "fine-grained phonetic conditioning of a single phoneme /aeh/" in the vowel system of an informant from Buffalo:

> As usual, vowels before nasal consonants are most peripheral and are furthest advanced in the raising process. Vowels before voiceless fricatives are next most peripheral, followed by voiced stops; least peripheral are voiceless stops. Cross-cutting the dimension of manner, the features of place show the highest vowels before palatals, the apicals, and the lowest vowels before labials and velars. Following syllables and consonant clusters give lower F2; initial liquids give lower F2 and F1. Initial liquid clusters have the strongest effect in retarding the process, so that the word *black* is regularly found at the lower right of the distribution, overlapping other word classes. (p. 14)

Unfortunately, Labov does not specify how many or which words were used as evidence of the fine-grained phonetic conditioning of the raising of /æ/. The problem with this is that lexical diffusion is always found inside of phonetic conditioning. So the fact that fine-grained phonetic conditioning is found does not exclude the possibility of lexical diffusion. In fact, in the earlier work by Labov et al. (1972), some hint of lexical conditioning was found for the raising of /æ/. Specifically, they state first that "all of this discussion has a strong bearing on the problem of studying lexical diffusion. We find no strong evidence for lexical diffusion in the (æh) patterns of Detroit and Buffalo and Chicago." However, they then add,

> Despite some initial oscillations the (æh) word class seems to move upward as a whole, with fine phonetic conditioning in the process. There is some indication that **the word _mad_ is lower than its phonetic class would justify** for several speakers .... It also appears as low and peripheral in the reading passage for Vinney M., an 11 year-old Syracuse boy. Since in other dialects we find that initial _m-_ does have a raising effect, **the low position of _mad_ as compared to _bad_, _ads_, etc., seems to be lexically determined**. But we would hesitate to come to grips with an issue of this size without a much larger scale study of many lexical items in each category. (p. 93 – my bold)

Labov (1991: 16) also singles out specific words in the chain shifting of /a/ into the [æ] position for a "relatively advanced speaker from Rochester": "The words _not_ and _got_ are as usual among the most advanced; vowels before velars and labials are further back" (p. 16). Of course the words _not_ and _got_ are extremely frequent words, and since frequency, as well as word class (which is probably tied to sentence stress), often play a part in the lexical diffusion of a change, it would be useful to know what the quality of the vowel is for this speaker in words like _cot, dot, knot, pot, sot,_ and _tot_ before ruling out lexical diffusion.

Before the "neogrammarian paradox" can be resolved, it is crucial to reemphasize that phonetic conditioning does **not** rule out lexical conditioning. Lexical diffusion acts always within phonetic environments, as will be amply demonstrated in Chapters 2 and 3. This makes it distinct, for example, from sporadic cultural borrowing of individual lexical items from other dialects or languages, where often the pronunciation of an individual lexical item is borrowed (_tomato_ /tometo/ vs. _tomato_ /tomato/, _either_ [iðɚ] vs. _either_ [aɪðɚ] in the most simplistic of examples). In addition, the connection between phonology and lexicon must be reexamined. Labov's attempt to distinguish between regular/neogrammarian sound change and lexically diffused sound change assumes a clear boundary between phonology and lexicon. Yet the empirical evidence does not support clear divisions, phonetically regular vs. lexically

18 *Word Frequency and Lexical Diffusion*

diffused. Indeed, a number of studies have now documented phonetically gradual changes that are also lexically diffused. (See Chapter 2 and the references therein.) In fact, very often phonetic and lexical conditioning interact, sometimes in surprising ways. Boberg and Strassel (2000), for example, find that in Cincinnati the tensing of short-*a* was once lexically diffused but is currently phonetically conditioned, with the lax vowel occurring now everywhere except before nasals (p. 120). That is, "Both the non-segmental factors and the lexical exceptions that make the Mid-Atlantic patterns so complex were dropped in favor of a set of exceptionless phonological environments, forming natural classes, that condition tense or lax vowels" (p. 119).

Therefore, it seems reasonable to look for a model that can incorporate both lexical and phonological conditioning, a model where phonology and lexicon truly interact. A usage-based model incorporating exemplar theory is clearly the best current model for accounting for the behavior of lexically diffused changes. Such a model allows for phonetic detail embedded in lexical items, but also includes extrapolation of phonological patterns, enabling sound change to affect particular sounds in particular environments, but always also within particular words. Optimality Theory has also attempted to incorporate word frequency effects into its model, however. Therefore, the next section reviews those efforts.

1.2 Optimality Theory and word frequency

As a model that was originally aimed at modeling competence, it is not surprising that Optimality Theory (OT) has had difficulties in incorporating performance differences and diachronic developments beyond those which involve reanalysis on the part of the learner (with the changes which prompt the reanalysis often being left to performance factors outside of the theory). Although recent attempts have been made within OT to account for gradient phenomena (most notably Boersma and Hayes 2001) and diachrony (see papers in Holt 2003a), no consensus has yet emerged about how to handle word frequency effects, despite Hammond's (1998) call for a model that incorporates frequency and makes the goal of its description "the most frequent forms, as opposed to the most 'regular'" (p. 165). For example, in describing the Rhythm Rule in English, Hammond (1999b: 334) notes that "high-frequency modifiers like *àntíque* undergo the shift more readily than infrequent modifiers like *àrcáne*." (See Chapter 2 for further discussion.) But within OT there is no a priori way of indicating this fact. Pater (2000: 258) suggests using lexically specific constraints for such variation, which he exemplifies using the nonuniformity of stress preservation in English. In discussing the difference between words like *còndensátion*, which do not maintain the stress of their stems (*condénse*), and words like *imàginátion*, which do maintain the stress of their stems (*imágine*), he states, "The basic idea is that constraints can be multiply instantiated in a constraint hierarchy: in a general and a lexically specific version." Lexical items then must be marked as belonging to a special set, a set which might vary from speaker to speaker. Pater (2000: 260) proposes that perhaps a third constraint might be needed to reflect the fact that some speakers accept either of two pronunciations. But Pater's proposal is clearly an ad hoc method of labeling lexical exceptions without accounting for them in any systematic, explanatory fashion. Myers (2003), in fact, argues that a key claim of OT, namely, "that markedness is explicitly referenced by the grammar[,] ... makes false predictions about the effects of lexical frequency on phonological patterns," and that Hammond's (1999a) analysis "gives no explanation for why the ranking here should run exactly opposite to the well-motivated ranking necessary for negative frequency effects."

Gess (2003) addresses frequency problems in OT by suggesting a "register-dependent phonology ranking" as part of the "postlexical constraints," which are "production-oriented," compared to "lexical constraints" which "simply reflect phonological generalizations that hold over the lexicon" (p. 76). He proposes that

> [a]s a change spreads, some speakers will begin to store some of the output forms (i.e., the most frequent ones) as lexical representations, through lexicon optimization (according to which underlying representations directly reflect output forms, unless alternations dictate otherwise...). At this point there will also be two rankings in the lexical phonology. The dominant ranking will reflect the phonological properties of individually less frequent, but numerically greater...forms. A less common ranking will reflect the lexicalization of the change in some of the most common words. (p. 77)

Once the ranking corresponding to innovative forms applies to over half of the relevant lexical items, the register-dependent ranking reverses itself, and the conservative outputs become associated with only formal and careful speech (pp. 77–8). Again, the necessity of handling changes which affect the frequent forms first is addressed, but not sound changes which affect the least frequent words first. And it is clear that the

20 Word Frequency and Lexical Diffusion

grammar is not expected to explain why some changes have affected the most frequent words first, but only to record changes that have already happened. By incorporating a postlexical component to the grammar separate from the lexical one, it has adopted the same problems inherent in a Lexical Phonology model, when it comes to word frequency. Indeed, Labov's (1981, 1994) resolution of the "neogrammarian controversy" is all too often accepted uncritically, as by Holt (2003b: 9) in his introduction to the collection of essays on *Optimality Theory and Language Change*. As shown above, regular, neogrammarian change is difficult to find even in low-level phonetic rules such as the Northern Cities Vowel Shift, and Chapters 2 and 3 will provide further evidence that the most frequent words can be affected first in both "lexical" and "postlexical" innovations, as can those that affect the least frequent words first.[5]

The most notable attempt to incorporate variation into OT has been the GLA (Gradual Learning Algorithm) model, developed by Boersma (1998) and Boersma and Hayes (2001). Pierrehumbert (2003: 225) notes, however, that the GLA model "does not distinguish effects related to type frequency from effects relating to surface, or token, frequency. It also provides no way to downweight the grammatical impact of extremely frequent words, as Bybee (2001) and Bailey and Hahn (2001) show to be necessary." One example of the use of the GLA model is Zuraw's (2003) account for language change, which handles frequency by incorporating the notion, borrowed from usage-based grammar (Bybee 2001: 6–7), of lexical strength: "the strength of a lexical entry grows gradually as instances of the word are encountered, and ... a lexical entry with strength of 0.5, for example, is available for use only half the time" (p. 165). He gives the example of the application of the constraint USE-LISTED, "which ensures that if a lexical entry exists, it is used as the basis for evaluating faithfulness" (p. 164): "Thus, in 50% of utterances, USE-LISTED and the faithfulness constraints will enforce the memorized pronunciation of such a half-strength word, but in the other 50% of utterances, the lower-ranked constraints will decide, because the lexical entry has not been accessed" (p. 165). Zuraw's suggestion noticeably only handles variation resulting from a sound change affecting the most frequent words first. And it does not mirror the truly gradient character of production; for example, in the loss of the /j/ glide after initial /t, d, n/, Phillips (1994: 125) found the less frequent word was, the less "glideful" it was judged by independent listeners. Nor does it account for the impact of discourse, that is, that the second appearance of a word in discourse is shorter than its first appearance (Fowler and Housum 1987), or for string frequency effects such as those shown by Bybee and Scheibman (1999) and Scheibman (2000), namely that the reduction of the word *don't* ranges from /do-/ to /ɾo/ to /ɾə/ to /ə/ depending on the frequency of the phrases in which it appears.

Even within OT, the attempt to incorporate frequency has its detractors. Keller and Asudeh (2002: 240), for instance, argue that modeling frequency is modeling a performance phenomenon, whereas the purpose of OT is to model linguistic competence. Indeed, they argue, since the underlying form or input into GEN in OT is, according to Prince and Smolensky (1993), the "most harmonic across grammatical contexts," if performance factors such as frequency were modeled, "there would not only be performance-related outputs, there would also be performance-related inputs, stored lexically" (p. 241). In fact, stratal versions of OT can be seen as an attempt to do precisely this, but suffer from the same shortcomings noted above for strata in Lexical Phonology when it comes to modeling word frequency effects. A usage-based model of language, on the other hand, is designed to incorporate performance directly into input.

As for the relationship between diachrony and OT, Holt (2003b) points out a number of ways in which OT has succeeded in incorporating insights from historical linguistics but also notes the following as areas that call for future research:

> the systematic study of possible and impossible changes (based on extensive crosslinguistic examination) and of the role of phonetics in sound change, attempts to study change at the level of the individual (instead of at the level of idealization or of the grammar of a language), the incorporation of sociolinguistic and discourse-oriented factors, as others. (p. 21)

In addition, the constraints that OT inputs are subjected to and which are supposedly universal also form a distinct contrast to the search for universals in a usage-based phonology. Bybee (1999: 234–5) argues that a diachronic dimension must be part of any theory of universals, that "the source of these universals is the architecture of the production and perception systems through which our cognitive structures are constantly funneled." Making a list of universals so as to rank them in different orders in different languages, as OT does, does not further our understanding of the basis of universals, some of which "come from phonetic factors, others arise because of the external context in which

22 Word Frequency and Lexical Diffusion

language is used, others from cognitive or perceptual factors that are independent of language" (p. 235). In the search for an understanding of how word frequency influences the direction of sound change, all of these factors must be considered.

1.3 Usage-based phonology and word frequency

In contrast to the aforementioned theories of phonological structure, Bybee's (2001) usage-based model easily incorporates effects of word frequency on sound change. In particular, this theory posits that speakers/listeners have stronger representations for items they have heard frequently than for items they have encountered infrequently. Among other examples of sound changes supporting this principle, Bybee (2000b: 70) offers evidence from 2000 tokens from 41 speakers of word-final t/d in American English. She found that high-frequency words were significantly more likely to delete the stop than were low-frequency words: 54.4 percent of the 1650 tokens of high-frequency words underwent deletion, versus 34.4 percent of the 399 tokens of low-frequency words.

To account for this frequency effect, Bybee first notes, based on Fowler and Housum (1987), that words repeated in a discourse "are shorter than in their first mention." She reasons that since the most likely words to be repeated are high-frequency words, it is understandable that they would undergo reductive sound change at a faster rate. As speakers produce and listeners hear more and more instantiations of the reduced pronunciation, it becomes part of the lexical entry. In this way, the effect of word frequency on the spread of sound change within the lexicon is explained (2000b: 71–2). But the only model of the lexicon that accommodates such changes is

> a lexicon in which considerable phonetic detail and ranges of phonetic variation are represented with each word or phrase. Not only do lexical representations have to be fully specified and represented in concrete phonetic units, these units cannot be an idealized systematic phonetic set of units, but rather must represent in some realistic way the range of variation occurring in the individual pronunciations that are constantly being mapped onto the existing representations. (Bybee 1999: 221)

In fact, as early as 1981, Bybee (under the name of Hooper), argued that lexical representations must contain a significant amount of phonetic material. Since then, evidence for such detail has been accumulating in psycholinguistic studies such as Pisoni (1997), which show that listeners encode even such specific information as speakers' voices and their speaking rate. Lachs et . (2003) evidence for DETAILED ENCODING of the word form:

- Remez et al. (1997) found that "listeners could explicitly identify specific familiar talkers from sinewave replicas of their utterances," sinewaves "preserv[ing] none of the traditional 'speech cues' that were thought to support the perception of vocal identity, such as fundamental frequency" (p. 222).
- Goldinger (1992) "found that subjects were faster and more accurate in repeating words spoken by old talkers who were used at the time of the initial presentation than new talkers" (pp. 223–4).
- Nygaard and Pisoni (1998) found that "words spoken by familiar voices were recognized in noise more accurately than words spoken by unfamiliar voices" (p. 226).
- "Lively et al. (1992) found that the English /l/ and /r/ contrast was better retained by Japanese listeners when they were exposed to a large corpus of stimuli spoken by many different talkers during training" (p. 226).

This detailed encoding becomes part of IMPLICIT MEMORY, that is, memory which "facilitates performance on a task which does not require conscious or intentional recollection of those experiences" (Schachter 1987: 501 as quoted by Lachs et al. 2003: 223).

Bybee (2002a: 69) summarizes the encoding of such detailed information into exemplars:

[T]he cognitive representation of a word can be made up of the set of exemplars of that word that has been experienced by the speaker/hearer. Thus all phonetic variants of a word are stored in memory and organized into a cluster in which exemplars that are more similar are closer to one another than ones that are dissimilar, and moreover, exemplars that are frequently-occurring are stronger than less frequent ones (Johnson 1997; Bybee 2000[b], 2001; Pierrehumbert 2001). In this model, the exemplar "cloud" or cluster continues to change as language is used and new tokens of words are experienced. Thus the range of phonetic variation of a word can gradually change over time, allowing a phonetically gradual sound change to affect different words at different rates.

24 Word Frequency and Lexical Diffusion

She explains how this model especially works well for reductive changes, which affect the more frequent words (which are also the more predictable words) first, but this model can work with other types of change as well. Bybee (2001: 6–8) enumerates basic principles that allow generalizations to emerge from such forms, saying that "generalizations over forms are not separate from the stored representation of forms but emerge directly from them" and "lexical organization provides generalizations and segmentation at various degrees of abstraction and generality. Units such as morpheme, segment, or syllable are emergent in the sense that they arise from the relations of identity and similarity that organize representations."

Having lexical entries contain such detail does not, therefore, preclude abstract categories being derived from them. As Booij (2004: 227) notes, having detailed phonetic representations of words, with the best exemplar being the most frequently attested one, "cannot be the full story: there must be a more abstract speaker-independent phonetic representation, which abstracts away from the experienced individual realisations of a word, for the purpose of perception: the hearer is able to recognize a word uttered by an unknown speaker." Pierrehumbert (2003: 179–81) also shows how the detail in lexical entries provides just one part of an overall stochastic model of phonology. She identifies as minimally necessary to such a model the following levels along "a ladder of abstraction, each level having its own representational apparatus":

- *Parametric phonetics* constitutes "a quantitative map of the acoustic and articulatory space. In speech perception, it describes the perceptual encoding of the speech signal on each individual occasion. In speech production, it describes the articulatory gestures as they unfold in time and space."
- *Phonetic encoding* "abstracts over the parametric phonetic space, defining the inventory available in the language for encoding word forms (phonological representations of words)." This inventory is not traditional, minimal-pair-distinguishing phonemes, however. Phonetic categories are much less abstract than such phonemes, and "can be viewed as peaks in the total phonetic distribution of the language (e.g., areas of the parametric space that the language exploits preferentially) or as positional allophones." Also encoded at this level are those "aspects of prosody and intonation that are defined with respect to the speech signal."
- *Word forms in the lexicon* contain representations which allow each word "to be recognized despite variation in its phonetic form

resulting from speaker differences and context. The same representation presumably mediates between perception and production.... [W]ord-forms are also abstractions over phonetic space. A given word is learned through repeated exposure to that word in speech.... [and] a word's frequency of occurrence affects the long-term representation of that word."

- *The phonological grammar* "encompassing both the prosodic structure and phonotactics, describes the set of possible words in a language. ...The grammar is revealed by well-formedness judgments as well as neologisms and borrowings."
- *Morphophonological correspondences* describe how "a given stem or affix can assume phonologically different forms in different, related words."

Beyond the phonology, there is another level, the LEMMA, which bears the meaning and syntactic information about the WORD FORM or LEXEME. (I will follow the practice of using word form interchangeably with lexeme, since we will not be discussing such cases as English *a~an*, which can be considered one lexeme comprised of two word forms.)

The following chapters will draw upon this model in describing the effects of word frequency on different types of sound changes. Of particular interest will be how these levels are accessed in production, for psycholinguists have found no word frequency effect on perception, but the effect is robust in production (Laubstein 1999; Jescheniak and Levelt 1994).

Since production involves going from meaning to form, within the lexical representation, speakers must first access the lemma, which bears the meaning and the syntactic information of a word. Next to be accessed is the lexeme or word form. Even at this level, speakers do not access the memory traces of every phonetic instantiation of each word. The memory traces have helped to create the phonological shape of the word form, but what it contains and what speakers access is phonological information that has been abstracted from those traces. Only then does the speaker reach the final step of PHONETIC ENCODING. That influence from each of the levels bleeds into the others, supporting a connectionist view of the lexicon, is shown for example by the existence of malapropisms, speech errors whereby an intended word is replaced by a phonologically similar word, thus choosing an incorrect lexeme on the basis of phonological information (Dell and O'Seaghdha 1991: 604). Also, findings on speech errors and the so-called neighborhood density effect that phonetically similar words have on the speed of

26 Word Frequency and Lexical Diffusion

lexical access in both perception and production imply that connections persist between words (Stemberger 2004: 421). But even in a connectionist model, production must proceed in this general direction from meaning to sound; and Dell and O'Seaghdha (1991: 612) "acknowledge the strength of the case for modularity in the system." They contend, however, that although "[t]he tendency of activation to diminish sharply over distance entails a natural limitation on the availability of distant information,... in contrast to a strictly modular two-stage account, the limitation is not categorical; rather, it arises from the structure of the network and the extent to which activation applies." Stemberger (2004: 414) summarizes a connectionist model that incorporates spreading activation as follows:

> In the interactive activation model of Dell (1985), activation spreads from meaning units to lexical units (morphemes). Lexical units compete with each other. Many lexical units are activated at once, as a function of the degree of connectedness to the set of activated meaning units. Activation spreads from lexical units to phonological units. Unlike in symbolic models in which processing is strictly serial, activation spreads from activated phonological units back up to lexical units, reinforcing the activation of the target lexical item, but secondarily spreading activation to nontarget lexical units, as a function of the degree of phonological relatedness. Activation then spreads from the secondarily activated lexical units back to the phonological units, reinforcing phonemes that are shared by nontarget words, or by words that are nearby in the sentence.

More specifically, Frisch (2004: 353) describes how frequency effects are incorporated into a spreading activation model

> by giving units different thresholds of activation for encoding. High-frequency units require less activation to fire than low-frequency units, so high-frequency units are more reliably encoded. Also, high-frequency neighbours to a word will provide more competition than low-frequency neighbours to a word as high-frequency neighbours will be more likely to fire when only partially activated.

1.4 Actuation versus implementation

Also indispensable to an understanding of lexical diffusion is a theory of diachrony: how changes begin, how they impact the phonology of speakers and hearers, and how they diffuse through the population, through the lexicon, and through time. In contradistinction to some formal theories of phonology and change, the stance taken here is that expressed by Milroy (1993), who argues that linguistic change originates with **speakers**, not with linguistic **systems**: "Innovation and change are not conceptually the same thing: an innovation is an act of the speaker, whereas a change is manifested within the language system. It is *speakers*, and not *languages*, that innovate" (p. 221). He also makes an important distinction between innovators and early adopters of a change, claiming that Labov's (1980: 261) ideal speaker/innovator is really in the latter group, that is, an early adopter (p. 226), and quantitative data typically displayed in variable rules are seen to portray the linguistic system and pattern of social variation that has developed in the community (p. 223). This is not unlike Janda and Joseph's (2003b) "Big Bang" theory of sound change, which posits the origin of sound change in a "very 'small', highly localized context over a relatively short temporal span" (p. 206). Thus, the implementation of a change, how it spreads from this very narrow context to a larger group of speakers, becomes the center of interest – or at least as crucial to the study of sound change as its actuation.

The social and areal spread of a sound change requires its further adoption by speakers, usually, as demonstrated by Milroy and Milroy (1985), through networks of associations. The lexical diffusion of a shift is concomitant with that spread, and reaching an understanding of how word frequency affects the spread of a change through the lexicon is integral to our understanding of the change's overall implementation. As Cavalli-Sforza (1994: 21) observes, the spread of a sound change is like the course of an epidemic or infectious disease proceeding in two dimensions, one by words and the other by individual speakers. Lexical diffusion is "caused by a brain mechanism which tends to homogenise the pronunciation for phonetically similar parts of different words ... allowing economy of the memory process. ... It seems likely that the spread among words (within individuals) is faster than that among individuals" (p. 22). That is, it would be a very slow process indeed if the pronunciation of every word had to be borrowed from other speakers. Instead, each speaker for which the change is productive must be generalizing the innovative pronunciation through phonetic analogy with similar phonetic sequences in other words. The question becomes which other words the change is generalized to first, and why does word frequency make a difference. A major part of the answer, it will be shown, hinges on the degree of analysis that the implementation

28 *Word Frequency and Lexical Diffusion*

of a change requires in consulting the phonetic encoding, the word forms in the speaker's grammar, the phonological grammar, and the morphophonological correspondences.

1.5 Conclusion and preview

In this chapter, evidence has been presented to show that Labov's (1994) characterization of lexical diffusion fails to account for the growing data on lexically diffused sound changes and that nonusage-based theories require ad hoc solutions to reflect lexical diffusion. Bybee's (2001) usage-based phonology within a stochastic grammar provides a far better framework for accommodating word frequency effects.

The following chapters demonstrate the evidence for the lexical diffusion of sound change and how that evidence may be accounted for within a usage-based theory of the lexicon. Along the way, the following misrepresentations about lexical diffusion will also be dispelled:

- *That lexical diffusion is sporadic:* Although changes that affect some words and not others are often referred to as "sporadic" (as in Hinskens 1998: 169; Aski 2001a: 43), a word which implies unusualness and irregularity, we will find that the diffusion of a sound change through the lexicon is very systematic. While the word "sporadic" seems appropriate for isolated cases that have not attained any degree of productivity, as in many Americans' pronunciation of the word *either* with an initial diphthong /aɪ/ rather than usual /i/, lexical diffusion as a process of implementation is quite systematic, hence not sporadic.
- *That lexical diffusion affects only phonetically abrupt changes:* Chapter 3 is devoted to examples of phonetically gradual changes that have been demonstrated to be lexically diffused.
- *That lexically diffused changes show no clear phonetic conditioning:* Not only may lexically diffused changes show phonetic conditioning, they typically occur within narrow phonetic environments. (See Chapter 3.)
- *That lexically diffused changes always affect the most frequent words first.* Although this was Schuchardt's original formulation of the lexical influence on sound change, Phillips (1981, 1984, 1994) has demonstrated that sometimes the least frequent words change first in the diffusion of a sound change. (See Chapters 2 and 3.)
- *That lexical diffusion is associated with lexical rather than postlexical rules.* Evidence exists for lexical diffusion among all types of sound

Word Frequency and the Neogrammarian Controversy 29

change, including "postlexical" phonetically conditioned changes such as assimilations and reductions. (See Chapter 3.)

- *That phonetically regular changes are productive, whereas lexically diffused changes are not* (Bakken 2001: 67). Since lexical diffusion is part of the implementation of a change, it occurs while a change is still productive, as the changes discussed in Chapters 2 and 3 demonstrate. The lexical diffusion of sound changes should not be confused with the sporadic borrowing of individual lexical items, as discussed in Chapter 5.

- *That analogy and borrowing suffice to account for lexical diffusion.* Chapter 5 is devoted to dispelling this notion. Since analogy, that is, generalizations drawn from connections between lexical items, is inherent in language, and the implementation of a change through a population of speakers must of necessity proceed via borrowing, ascribing the effects of lexical diffusion to either category is meaningless and does not constitute an explanation.

In particular, Bybee's (1985: 118) notion of lexical analysis will prove central to understanding the systematicity behind the influence of word frequency on the progression of a sound change through the lexicon: "High-frequency words form more distant lexical connections than low-frequency words. In the case of morphologically complex words...high-frequency words undergo less analysis, and are less dependent on their related base words than low-frequency words." Bybee formulated this theory primarily to explain semantic and morphological change, but this book will develop a notion first suggested in Phillips (1998c), that the degree of lexical analysis a change entails can help explain word frequency patterns of sound change as well. Because its application is clearest in the diffusion of stress shifts, Chapter 2 addresses "The lexical diffusion of phonetically abrupt changes." Chapter 3 deals with "The lexical diffusion of phonetically gradual changes," showing how such sound changes affecting more frequent words first may also be said to undergo less analysis than those which affect less frequent words first. Chapter 4, "Lexical diffusion and word class," explains how grammatical categories affect the diffusion of change and why lexical frequency effects are most clearly found within word classes. Chapter 5 clarifies the relationship between "Analogy, borrowing and linguistic diffusion"; and Chapter 6, "Applications of lexical diffusion," demonstrates how lexical diffusion can help in analyzing scribal variation and in deciding between competing explanations of particular changes. The concluding chapter, Chapter 7, provides a summation and synthesis of issues raised in the preceding chapters, as well as a discussion of related issues. Throughout, my primary assumption is that Kiparsky (1968: 174) was right when he called linguistic change "a window on the form of linguistic competence," and my goal will be to demonstrate that the diachronic evidence for word frequency reveals an integral part of that competence.

2
The Lexical Diffusion of Phonetically Abrupt Changes

2.0 Introduction

Chapter 1 demonstrated that a usage-based grammar incorporating exemplar theory is currently the most appropriate model for accommodating the lexical diffusion of sound change. In particular, it was shown that some lexically diffused changes are also phonetically gradual, which contradicts Labov's (1994: 541–2) hypothesis that lexically diffused changes are confined to the Lexical Phonology and phonetically gradual changes to the postlexical phonology. This chapter demonstrates that even among changes such as stress shifts, which are by their very nature not phonetically gradual (and which are always treated within the lexical component of Lexical Phonology), different types of lexical diffusion present themselves. Some affect the least frequent words first, while others affect the most frequent words first. Such distinctions are not predicted by Lexical Phonology or Optimality Theory, but are consistent with a usage-based phonology into which word frequency, reflected by lexical strength, and the notion of lexical analysis have been incorporated.

Wang (1969: 14) outlines four types of sound changes:

1. phonetically abrupt and lexically abrupt;
2. phonetically abrupt and lexically gradual;
3. phonetically gradual and lexically abrupt;
4. phonetically gradual and lexically gradual.

The first type (1) at first glance seems impossible, unless one adopts a "quantum theory" of sound change, whereby phonetically gradual changes are seen as a series of small steps. It is hard, in fact, to imagine

32 *Word Frequency and Lexical Diffusion*

a scenario by which all the words fitting a phonetic description would one day suddenly be pronounced quite differently. This would be tantamount to saying that, for instance, in a dialect undergoing a merger of the vowels /a/ and /æ/, one day speakers would wake up producing with /a/ all the words that the day before had been pronounced with /æ/. Janson (1983), however, has suggested that phonetically abrupt changes (or, as he prefers to call them, "phonetically discrete" changes) might also be lexically abrupt, if the innovative pronunciation is restricted to a particular register, after which it is accepted into another register. He gives the example of the switch from apical [r] or flapped [ɹ] to uvular [R] or flapped [ʁ] in most of Western Europe, for which studies have not found lexical conditioning. Thus, he suggests, speakers can incorporate into their everyday speech the pronunciation once reserved for a special register, without regard for the lexical item involved. Such a path of implementation will be discussed in Chapter 5, where it will be shown that such a path of implementation is not typically lexically abrupt.

The second type of change (2) listed by Wang refers to sound changes such as metathesis, tone shifts, or stress shifts and is the type discussed in this chapter. Type (3), phonetically gradual and lexically abrupt, is the traditional neogrammarian approach to sound change and, along with type (4) phonetically gradual and lexically gradual, will be investigated further in Chapter 3. Suffice it to say here that it has long been acknowledged that many sound changes must be phonetically abrupt. Wang and Cheng (1977: 148–9), for instance, list "metathesis, epenthesis, and deletion, as well as certain discontinuous shifts in position of articulation, such as Middle Chinese labials becoming dentals in Sino-Vietnamese in which altogether different articulators are used."

The focus of this chapter will be, then, on the effect of word frequency on phonetically abrupt yet lexically gradual changes. We will see an interplay of type frequency effects (which drive productivity)[1] and token frequency effects (which influence lexical diffusion). For some phonetically abrupt changes not enough data exists or not enough research has been devoted to the question of word frequency to be certain of token frequency effects. For instance, metathesis is a clear example of a phonetically abrupt change that never seems to affect all the words of a language at the same time (although it appears as a regular synchronic process in some languages, according to Hume 2004) and Kiparsky (1995: 658–9) points out that the results of metathesis can be regular: "Dissimilation is regular where it serves to implement constraints such as Grassmann's Law, and the same is true of metathesis (Hock 1985;

The Lexical Diffusion of Phonetically Abrupt Changes   33

Ultan 1978): e.g., the Slavic liquid metathesis is part of the phonological apparatus that implements the ... syllable structure constraints." Blevins and Garrett (2004: 139) claim that in the late West Saxon dialect of Old English "*sk* clusters regularly inverted their linear order and became *ks* clusters." But a look at their sources reveals that there is no compelling evidence for its regularity. Campbell (1959: 177–8) says that, instead of undergoing assibilation to [ʃ], "internally before back vowels (if the preceding vowel had not undergone umlaut) and finally after back vowels [sk] remained, and **frequently** underwent metathesis to [ks] in lW-S" [my bold]. Similarly, Hogg (1992a: 304) states that before back vowels, "LWS texts show **a great many** metathesized forms with ≪x≫ representing /ks/...." [my bold]. That is to say, there is no evidence that this metathesis was regular. In fact, Hogg (1992a: 304) notes that *betwix* "between" is a metathesized form that occurs in other dialects as well and that occurs early: "The form occurs as early as 888 in ChHead 1204 1.1 and at CP 423.4, also CP *betwēox* (5×)."

Unfortunately, I know of no study documenting such changes in progress, so the lexical diffusion of dissimilations and metatheses remains to be researched. Blevins and Garrett (1998, 2004) see perceptual ease/phonetic optimization as the basis of metathesis, which may provide the impetus behind it, but they do not consider word frequency effects. Type frequency, however, is very influential on the output of metathesis, the end result apparently always being a sequence that is more frequent in the language (Hume 2004: 210). Fay's explanation (1966: 88) still holds true: "When listeners hear speech that is expected to be in the native language, their perceptual identifications are directed by their knowledge of sequential probabilities in the language as well as by the acoustic stimulus" (as quoted by Hume 2004: 210). This observation is fully in line with current stochastic models of language, which acknowledge speakers' awareness of common versus rare sequences. Metathesis, therefore, reflects a type frequency effect.

Cheng and Wang (1977), Wang and Cheng (1977), and Wang and Lien (1993) all investigate phonetically abrupt–lexically gradual tone shifts in the historical development of Chinese, shifts which acted on homophones to create splits which were clearly not phonetically conditioned. For instance, in the Chao-zhou dialect's development of Middle Chinese tone III in syllables beginning with voiced segments, Cheng and Wang (1977: 89) found that almost equal numbers developed into tones 2b and 3b, 127 versus 107, respectively. And, as they point out, influence from other dialects cannot explain the pattern since no other dialect shares a large number of the tone 2b in these forms (p. 92). The role

34 *Word Frequency and Lexical Diffusion*

of word frequency in the Chao-zhou tone shift was not investigated, however, and since English is not a tone language, the most similar kind of abrupt phonetic shift that it has undergone is shifts in stress. In particular, two different stress shifts in English will be highlighted, beginning with the shift of stress in English diatones.

2.1 Diatonic pairs in English: the least frequent words changing first

Diatones are noun–verb pairs, such as *cónvict* (noun) ~ *convíct* (verb), which differ only in the placement of stress. Earlier in their history, many such pairs in English were given final stress for both noun and verb, for example, *convíct* (noun/verb). Only two diatonic pairs existed, in fact, before 1570: *rebel* and *record* (Minkova 1997: 160); in 1570, the word *outlaw* was added (Sherman 1975: 52, in reference to Levins 1570). Sherman (1975: 54) found that the number of diatones in English has "steadily been increasing since the onset of the era of modern English," from just 8 in 1582 to 33 in the seventeenth century, plus 35 new diatones in the eighteenth century, culminating in 90 new diatones added between 1880 and 1934. Of these, final-stressed pairs such as *prefíx* (originally noun or verb) were more likely to become diatonic than were words with initial stress, such as *óutlaw*. Most do, however, remain homophones: "of 1,315 disyllabic N–V pairs, only 150 were diatonic (11 %); of 442 trisyllabic or greater pairs, only 70 were diatonic (16 %); out of a total of 1,757 polysyllabic pairs, only 220 (13 %) showed stress alternation for the noun and verb forms" (p. 51). Sherman based his list upon the computer-generated *English Word Speculum* (Dolby and Resnikoff 1964), and pronunciations given in *The Oxford Universal Dictionary on Historical Principles* (Onions 1944) and *Webster's Seventh Collegiate Dictionary* (Gove 1963).

In an appendix, Sherman (1975: 68–9) provided a list of the oxytonic homographs which he predicted would eventually become diatones. Table 2.1 lists the diatonic pairs that Sherman identified as having developed from oxytonic (i.e. final-stressed) pairs, as well as the oxytonic pairs that he predicted would become diatonic. Frequency counts are given, based on the *American Heritage Word Frequency List* (Carroll et al. 1971), as reported by Phillips (1984: 333). This database was generated from written texts such as "textbooks, workbooks, kits, novels, poetry, general nonfiction, encyclopedias, and magazines" designed to represent reading required and recommended to students between grades 3 and 9 in public schools in the United States (p. xiii). Only

35

Table 2.1 Diatonic/shifted vs. oxytonic/unshifted stress in English noun–verb homophones (modified from Phillips 1984: 333)

		Average frequency	
		Shifted	Unshifted
a-			
N ' -, V - '	address, affect, affix, alloy, ally, annex, assay	7.4	
N - ', V - '	abuse, accord, account, advance, affront, alarm, amount, appeal, approach, array, arrest, assault, assent, assign, attack, attaint, attempt, attire, award		15.8
con-/com			
N ' -, V - '	compress, concert, concrete, conserve, content, contract, contrast, convict	10.6	
N - ', V - '	command, compare, conceit, concern, consent, control		37.1
de-			
N ' -, V - '	decoy, decrease, defect, defile, detail	5.2	
N - ', V - '	debate, debauch, decay, decease, decline, decree, default, defeat, delay, delight, demand, demean, demise, demur, derout, design, desire, despair, devise		8.0
dis-			
N ' -, V - '	discharge, discount, discourse	1.6	
N - ', V - '	disdain, disease, disgrace, disguise, disgust, dislike, dismay, dismount, dispatch, display, dispraise, dispute, disquiet, dissent, dissolve, distress, distrust, disuse		4.9
es-			
N ' -, V - '	escort, essay	3.1	
N - ', V - '	escape, escheat, essoin, estate, esteem		10.6
ex-			
N ' -, V - '	excise, exploit, export, extract	2.5	
N - ', V - '	exchange, excuse, exempt, exhaust, express		22.0
pre-			
N ' -, V - '	prefix, prelude, presage	3.7	
N - ', V - '	preserve		8.1
re-			
N ' -, V - '	rebate, rebound, recall, recess, recoil, redress, refuse, relapse, relay, research	8.0	
N - ', V - '	rebuff, rebuke, rebus, receipt, recruit, reform, refrain, regale, regard, regret,		11.1

36 Word Frequency and Lexical Diffusion

Table 2.1 (Continued)

	Average frequency	
	Shifted	**Unshifted**
release, remand, remark, remove, repair, repeal, replay, reply, report, repose, reprieve, reproach, repulse, repute, request, reserve, resist, resolve, resort, respect, respond, result, retard, retort, retouch, retreat, retrieve, return, reveal, revenge, reverse, revert, review, revise, revoke, revolt, revolve, reward		

stem words were counted, not suffixed forms, whether inflectional or derivational. A note of caution should be given here: it is difficult to know how best to sample frequencies since the more frequent a suffixed word is, the more likely it has its own representation in the lexicon, compared with lower-frequency words, which are more likely to be decomposed (Meunier and Segui 1999). As Bybee (2001: 109) expresses it, "What determines the forms that are actually in memory is usage: verb forms that are used frequently are stored in memory. Those that have not been used and those of very low frequency do not actually exist in memory, but if they are regular, they can easily be derived by using the associations in the network." In the data used in this book, I will therefore always make clear which forms have been sampled.

Figure 2.1 shows how the pairs that have undergone the shift to diatones (Series 1) compare graphically with their unchanged counterparts (Series 2). The Y-axis gives the average frequencies of each prefix group, revealing that the average frequencies of the unchanged pairs are quite varied, yet the average frequencies of the changed, diatonic pairs form a steady cline from 1.6 to 10.6, depending on the word's prefix. That the prefix should be a conditioning factor in these words is not so surprising when one considers that in the left-to-right processing of speech forms, prefixes trigger connections to all other words with that prefix (Cole et al. 1989). (See further discussion below.)

That this stress shift should affect the least frequent words first does not at first glance seem unusual. It very much resembles analogical changes, which affect the least frequent words first as a result of "imperfect learning" (Hooper 1976: 101). For instance, Hooper (1976: 100) points out that the verbs *keep, leave, sleep* (which have frequency ratings of 531, 792, and 132, respectively, according to the *American Heritage*

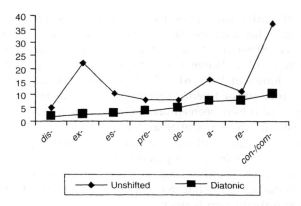

Figure 2.1   Development of noun–verb homographs

Word Frequency Book) resist changes to their past tense forms *kept, left, slept*, whereas less frequent *creep, leap, weep* (frequencies of 37, 42, and 31, respectively) have developed regular past forms: *creeped, leaped, weeped*. That is, unlike word forms such as *kept* and *slept* that are used frequently and hence are stored in memory, word forms like *crept* and *wept* are not used very frequently, are difficult to remember, and are therefore more likely to develop new forms based on the "regular" pattern, one which has a high type frequency (see also Bybee 2001: 181).

Therefore, in the diatonic stress shift, speakers regularize infrequent nouns and verbs to follow the more regular pattern. This explanation has also been bolstered by the behavior of diatonic noun/verb pairs of Romance origin. Minkova (1997: 158) agrees with Jespersen 1909: 175) that the preservation of verbal stress on the final syllable of such pairs may be due to analogy with native prefixed verbs, which since Old English times received stress on the root rather than on the prefix. For example, Jespersen gives the Old English examples of 'andgiet (n. 'understanding') vs. on'gietan (vb. 'understand'), æfþunca (n. 'insult') vs. of'þyncan (vb. 'insult'), and 'orþanc (n. 'intelligence') vs. ā'þencan (vb. 'to think out') and the Modern English examples of an 'offset vs. to off'set and an 'upset vs. to up'set (pp. 174–5). Minkova points out that the shift of stress in two-syllable Latinate nouns is also a process of nativization, since the noun generally in English most frequently begins with a stressed syllable. For example, Sereno (1986, as reported by Sereno and Jongman 1995: 59) found that "93% of the 1,425 bisyllabic nouns [in English] were forestressed while 76% of the 523 bisyllabic verbs were backstressed." That this shift in stress must be based on

38 Word Frequency and Lexical Diffusion

analogy with native stress patterns of nouns versus verbs rather than analogy with other Latinate pairs is also revealed by the fact of "the vast majority (90 %) of categorically ambiguous bisyllabic words... do not shift stress with a change in grammatical class (e.g., *answer, design*)" (Sereno and Jongman 1995: 61). The type frequency of initial-stressed nouns and final-stressed verbs, therefore, is high in English, and the homographic pairs have been emulating these frequent types when they become diatonic. In fact, Cutler and Butterfield (1992) have shown the psychological reality of this pattern for Modern English speakers through experiments in speech perception. Thus type frequency is of utmost importance in motivating this change and no doubt helps in its implementation. But what determines which lexical items will be affected first is their token frequency.

Effects of type and token frequency may meet in the explanation provided by Kelly and Bock (1988). They found that in the production of English sentences, speakers tend toward rhythmic alternations of stress. In particular, they confirm their hypothesis that

> the stress patterns of nouns and verbs are related to the typical rhythmic contexts in which they occur. For example, if disyllabic nouns are often preceded by unstressed syllables but followed by stressed syllables, as in *The —— sléeps* or *A —— rán*, the pressure for rhythmic alternation would predispose a strong beat in the first syllable. For verbs, on the other hand, the occurrence of contexts such as *The bóy —— the girl* or *A gírl —— a bóy* would predispose a weak beat in the first syllable. Over time, a word that consistently occupied a particular rhythmic context might come to reflect the pressures imposed by that context in its citation stress pattern. (p. 391)

Thus disyllabic nouns come to be associated with initial stress and disyllabic verbs with final stress, a type frequency effect. In the case of individual lexical items, token frequency becomes involved, with a frequent word more entrenched and thus more capable of resisting the general tendency for its word class. An infrequent word, on the other hand, adapts itself more readily to the dominant stress pattern of its word class.

It seems appropriate here also to note that stress may be gradient. That is, Sereno and Jongman (1995) found varying degrees of indicators of stress dependent on word category. They show that speakers of English recognize the two stress patterns as inherent to the respective grammatical word classes by analyzing the results of five speakers reading 16 bisyllabic words which were orthographically all ambiguously noun or

The Lexical Diffusion of Phonetically Abrupt Changes   39

verb, although not diatonic. Half of the 16 words were noun-dominant, meaning that they were most frequently used as nouns; the other half were verb-dominant, or most frequently used as verbs. Four of the words were more frequently used as forestressed nouns (*favor, poison, practice, struggle*), four as backstressed nouns (*control, debate, dispute, report*), four as forestressed verbs (*handle, notice, rescue, welcome*) and four as backstressed verbs (*embrace, escape, neglect, reply*). The speakers were recorded twice, first reading a list of 75 pure verbs which included the 16 ambiguous word forms, then reading a list of 75 pure nouns which again included the 16 ambiguous forms. Sereno and Jongman (1995: 68) found a significant dominance effect: "For all speakers, stimuli that were more frequent as nouns in English (e.g., *poison, debate*) showed significantly different amplitude ratios than word stimuli that were more frequent as verbs (e.g., *notice, escape*)." That is, forestressed verb-dominant nouns had less amplitude on the first syllable than did noun-dominant nouns; and backstressed noun-dominant nouns had less amplitude on the last syllable than did verb-dominant nouns, independent of whether the words were read as nouns among other nouns or as verbs among other verbs. For example, a noun-dominant word like *poison* received greater amplitude on its initial syllable than a verb-dominant word like *notice* in both lists. Sereno and Jongman conclude that "The significant Dominance effects suggest that speakers maximized the difference between noun- and verb-dominant words in conformity with the lexical distribution of English in which the majority of bisyllabic nouns are stressed on the first syllable and the majority of bisyllabic verbs on the second syllable" (p. 69). So the evidence is clear that the generalization that bisyllabic nouns typically receive initial stress and bisyllabic verbs final stress has psychological reality for speakers. But no one has suggested that the diatonic stress shift has been phonetically gradual. There are no instances, for example, where each syllable receives equal stress. Rather, at some point in the history of each of the affected words, the main stress of the affected nouns has been reassigned to the initial syllable.

2.2   Other product-oriented schemas

Schemas are generalizations over lexical material that may serve as the basis for further innovation. They contrast with rule-driven innovations in other theories of phonology by not requiring specific rules acting on underlying forms to guide how new forms are generated. Rather, they serve as templates that the speaker may use to form innovations. For example, among other evidence cited by Bybee (2001) are studies of

40   *Word Frequency and Lexical Diffusion*

verb forms in Modern English. For instance, among the strong verbs, historically the base form of one set contained lax [ɪ], which became [ʌ] in the past tense form, as in *spin/spun*, *win/won*, *cling/clung*, etc. This group has become semi-productive in English, so that new past tense forms such as *struck*, *snuck*, and *drug* have entered it – despite not having a lax [ɪ] in their base forms (*strike*, *sneak*, and *drag*). Thus, the development of these new past tense forms relies solely on the model of the surface forms with [ʌ] (pp. 126–7). Similarly, she points to evidence provided by Menn and MacWhinney (1984) and by Stemberger (1981) that past tense forms with zero allomorphs, such as *cut* and *rid*, are not subject to regularization by children, probably because they already exhibit final /t/ or /d/. For the same reason, English does not add progressive *-ing* to words like *lightning* or adverbial *-ly* to words like *friendly* (p. 128). The "product" that speakers are seeking is a word ending in *-ing* or *-ly*, so the fact that *lightning* and *friendly* already exhibit that appropriate ending suffices, and no extra morphological marker is required.

Although arguing for a rule-based approach incorporating multiple stochastic rules, Albright and Hayes's (2003) experiments also support many of Bybee's observations. Their elicitations of novel productions and acceptability ratings of both regular and irregular past tense forms for nonce words, such as *spling* and *blafe*, provide additional evidence that speakers have an awareness of the gradient acceptability of certain past tense forms based on the forms of actual English past tenses. In analyzing the results of their "wug test" – so-called from Berko's (1958) experiment on the generation of past tense forms – they find they share with connectionist researchers "the view that inductive learning of detailed generalizations plays a major role in language. In particular, although learners of English could get by with only a single default rule for regulars, it appears they go beyond this: they learn a set of specific environments that differentiate the degrees of confidence for the regular outcome" (p. 154). That is, in addition to findings similar to those reported by Bybee (2001) for irregular forms, they also find "island of reliability" effects for both irregular **and** regular forms. ISLANDS OF RELIABILITY are "phonological contexts in which a particular morphological change works especially well in the existing lexicon," as in the fact that "every verb of English that ends in a voiceless fricative ([f, θ, s, ʃ]) is regular" (p. 127). Specifically, Albright and Hayes found that "wug pasts were rated higher, and were volunteered more often, when they occupied an island of reliability" (p. 141) and, more surprisingly, that "island of reliability effects were also observed for *regular* pasts" (p. 142), which

The Lexical Diffusion of Phonetically Abrupt Changes   41

is incompatible with a model that derives regular past tense forms by a single default rule (p. 144).

The same tendency toward product-oriented schemas most likely also explains Pierrehumbert's (2003: 224) finding that the /k/ to /s/ shift in English before the *-ity* suffix is still fully productive for noun formation in English, despite its phonetic unnaturalness. Six experimental subjects who were led to create 18 novel words, such as *crioticity* or *crioticness* from the prompt *criotic*, invariably produced the softened /s/ in the *-ity* form rather than retaining the /k/ of the provided adjective. Indeed, my own search of the CELEX database, which she also used in her study, found all of the words with /k/ plus the same final sounds, whether spelled *-ity* or *-ety*, were adjectives: *finickity, pernickety, persnickety,* and *rickety.* Hence, surface forms such as *criotickity* would most likely be interpreted as adjectives, not as nouns.

The concept of lexical strength helps to explain why product-oriented schemas tend to affect low-frequency words first. The more frequent a word is, that is, the more tokens the speaker encounters or produces, the more entrenched the word becomes in the speaker's mental lexicon, the more autonomy it develops, and hence the less likely it is to participate in a change based on a product-oriented schema (Bybee 2001: 136). The bases of such schemas, on the other hand, are patterns with high type frequency (e.g. the regular *-ed* past tense ending in English that is extremely productive and applies to almost all newly created words in English) (Bybee 2001: 136).

Since the diatonic shift in stress affects the least frequent words first and seems to be a typical product-oriented change, one might think that all stress shifts would follow this path. Indeed, Phillips (1984) implies that this should be true when she ties the lexical diffusion of a shift to its actuation. But subsequent evidence has shown that not all shifts in stress do affect the least frequent words first. Some do just the opposite.

2.3   Stress shift in *-ate* verbs: a case of the most frequent words changing first

In contrast to the stress shift creating diatonic noun/verb pairs in English, the shift in stress assignment in verbs ending in *-ate* is affecting the **most frequent** words first. This stress shift has been in progress for over a century, according to the *New English Dictionary on Historical Principles* (Murray et al. 1888–1928): "[W]here the penult has two or three consonants giving positional length, the stress has historically been on the penult, and its shift to the ante-penult is recent or still in progress, as

42　*Word Frequency and Lexical Diffusion*

in *acervate, adumbrate,...*; all familiar with penult stress to middle-aged men" (as quoted by Danielsson 1948: 93). Bisyllables in *-ate* are also clearly shifting, and both shifts are clearly affecting the most frequent words first. For instance, as displayed in Table 2.2, in the most recent British dictionary in Phillips's (1998c) sample, Ramsaran's 1991 revision of Gimson's 1988 *English Pronouncing Dictionary*, the three most frequent disyllabic verbs (*frustrate, dictate, prostrate*) are listed with only ultimate stress, the next four most frequent (*pulsate, stagnate, truncate, mandate*) are listed with variable pronunciations, and the four least frequent (*lactate, palpate, filtrate, gestate*) are listed with only initial stress.[2]

The full findings for two-syllable verbs whose first syllable is closed by a consonant (the largest identifiable subgroup) are tabulated in Table 2.3 for British dictionaries ranging in date from 1955 to 2003. The data are taken from Phillips (1998c: 226), plus the most recent *English Pronouncing Dictionary* (2003), which, however, is no longer based on Received Pronunciation but on BBC English. The dictionaries were chosen on the basis of coverage of the time period selected and relative ease of finding all – or nearly all – of the words under question. Dictionaries of course have an advantage over poetic evidence because one does not have to worry about whether the poet is exercising poetic license or utilizing a rare or archaic form to make the line scan. Landau's (1984 [1989]) *Dictionaries: the Art and Craft of Lexicography* and Bronstein's "The History of Pronunciation in English-Language Dictionaries" (1986) were used in determining which dictionaries to use. British English is represented by Samuel Johnson's (1755) *Dictionary of the English Language,* Henry John Todd's 1824 revision of Johnson, *Chamber's English Dictionary* (1872), the four editions of Daniel Jones's *An English Pronouncing Dictionary* (1917, 1937; Gimson 1988; Roach et al. 2003), and Brown's *The New Shorter Oxford English Dictionary on Historical Principles* (1993).[3]

Table 2.2　Stress patterns for C$C(C)-*ate* disyllables (Gimson 1988 [1991])

Frequency group	Conservative ' -	Variable	Innovative - '
0–7 (filtrate, gestate, palpate, lactate)	×		
9–36 (mandate, truncate, stagnate, pulsate)		×	
39–666 (prostrate, dictate, frustrate)			×

The Lexical Diffusion of Phonetically Abrupt Changes 43

Table 2.3 British English, disyllables in C$C(C)-*ate* (Phillips 1998c: 226, amended and enlarged)

Verb	Frequency	1755	1780	1824	1872	1917	1937	1988	2003
frustrate	666	−	−	−	+	+	+	+	+
dictate	233	−	−	−	−	+	+	+	+
prostrate	39	−	−	−		+	+	+	+
pulsate	36				−	+/−	+/−	+/−	+
stagnate	29	−	−	−	−	−/+	−/+	+/−	+/−
fixate	20								+
truncate	15	−	−	−	−	−/+	−/+	+/−	+/−
mandate	09						−/+	−/+	+/−
lactate	07					−	−	−	+
palpate	05					−	−	−	+
filtrate	00	−	−	−	−	−	−	−	+
formate	00								
gestate	00							−	+/−
lustrate	00		−						
testate	00		−						

+ = ultimate stress (*dictáte*); − = initial stress (*díctate*).
1755: Johnson, *Dictionary of the English Language*.
1780: Sheridan, *A General Dictionary of the English Language*.
1824: Todd, revision of Johnson's *Dictionary of the English Language*.
1872: Chambers, *Chamber's English Dictionary*.
1917: Jones, *An English Pronouncing Dictionary*.
1937: Jones, *An English Pronouncing Dictionary*, 4th edn.
1988 [1991]: Gimson, *English Pronouncing Dictionary*, 14th edn.
2003: Roach et al., *English Pronouncing Dictionary*, 16th edn.

Table 2.4 presents comparable data from American English, represented by Noah Webster's *A Compendious Dictionary of the English Language* (1806) and his enlarged *An American Dictionary of the English Language* (1828), *Webster's New International Dictionary* (Porter 1909), Kenyon and Knott's *Pronouncing Dictionary of American English* (1953), *Webster's Third New International Dictionary* (Gove 1961), and the latest edition of *Merriam Webster's Collegiate Dictionary* (Mish 2004).[4] Of course the individual characteristics of each of these dictionaries will have to be taken into consideration when looking at the data drawn from them.

The word frequencies cited are taken from the CELEX Lexical Database (Center for Lexical Information 1993), whose frequency numbers are based on the COBUILD corpus of about 17.9 million words, taken mainly from written sources, with 1.3 million words coming from spoken texts (Burnage 1990: 4-102, 4-108). This corpus has the advantage of not only being exceptionally large but also of separating verbs from identically

44 Word Frequency and Lexical Diffusion

Table 2.4 American English, disyllables in C$C(C)-*ate* (Phillips 1998c: 227, enlarged)

Verb	Frequency	1806/1828	1909	1953	1961	1993	2004
frustrate	666	–	–	–	–	–	–
dictate	233	–	–	–/+	–/+	–/+	–/+
prostrate	39	–	–	–	–	–	–
pulsate	36	–	–	–	–	–/+	–/+
stagnate	29	–	–	–	–	–	–
fixate	20		–	–	–	–	–
truncate	15	–	–	–	–	–	–
mandate	09			–	–/+	–	–
lactate	07			–	–	–	
palpate	05	–	–	–	–	–	–
filtrate	00	–	–	–	–	–	
formate	00			–			
gestate	00			–	–	–	–
lustrate	00	–		–	–	–	–
testate	00			–			

+ = ultimate stress (*dictáte*); − = initial stress (*díctate*).
1806: Webster, *Compendious Dictionary of the English Language*.
1828: Webster, *An American Dictionary of the English Language*.
1909: Porter, *New International Dictionary*.
1953: Kenyon and Knott, *Pronouncing Dictionary of American English*.
1961: Gove, *Webster's Third New International Dictionary*.
1993: Mish, *Merriam-Webster's Collegiate Dictionary*, 10th edn.
2004: Mish, *Merriam-Webster's Collegiate Dictionary*, 11th edn.

spelled nouns or adjectives. The words' frequencies are based on modern English, but the general pattern of relative frequencies probably holds for earlier English as well. For example, it would be very surprising if the three-syllable verbs with CELEX frequencies over 100 – *concentrate, demonstrate, illustrate, contemplate, compensate, designate,* and *alternate* – were not also much more common in 1755 than those with frequencies of 0 – *altercate, auscultate, condensate, defalcate, eructate, exculpate, expurgate, extirpate, fecundate,* etc.

The question, of course, is how this change is different from the stress shift toward diatonic noun–verb pairs. Is the shift of the verb's pronunciation from *díctate* to *dictáte* not following the pattern of other bisyllabic verbs in the same way that the shift of the noun *decréase* to *décrease* follows the patterns of other disyllabic nouns? Yet the different paths of diffusion tell us there must be a difference. And the concomitant change of stress in three-syllable verbs also indicates that the shift from *díctate* to *dictáte* is more closely tied to the stress shift in trisyllabic words (for example, from *demónstrate* to *démonstráte*) than to the diatonic stress shift.

The Lexical Diffusion of Phonetically Abrupt Changes 45

Table 2.5 British English trisyllabic verbs in -*ate* (Phillips 1998c)

Frequency	Year							
	1755	1780	1824	1872	1917	1937	1988	2003
Over 100	0	0	14	36	100	100	100	100
11–100	0	0	0	27	79	75	83	81
0–10	0	0	0	13	83	84	83	84

Table 2.6 American English trisyllabic verbs in -*ate* (Phillips 1998c)

Frequency	Year						
	1806	1828	1909	1953	1961	1993	2004
Over 100	67	71	50	79	86	93	93
11–100	25	36	27	46	73	77	77
0–10	25	31	25	50	67	71	71

Tables 2.5 and 2.6, taken from Phillips (1998c), summarize the data on trisyllabic verbs, the details of which are included in Appendix A. Based on the CELEX database for English (Center for Lexical Information 1993), 7 verbs exhibit a frequency over 100 (*alternate, compensate, concentrate, contemplate, demonstrate, designate, illustrate*), 13 a frequency between 11 and 100 (*confiscate, devastate, elongate, enervate, hibernate, impregnate, inculcate, infiltrate, inundate, masturbate, orchestrate, promulgate, remonstrate*), and 23 a frequency between 0 and 10 (*adumbrate, altercate, auscultate, bifurcate, commentate, condensate, consternate, coruscate, defalcate, demarcate, eructate, exculpage, expurgate, extirpate, fecundate, fenestrate, incarnate, inculpate, incurvate, obfuscate, objurgate, prolongate, sequestrate*). The numbers in the cells represent the percentage of innovative pronunciations in that frequency group in the dictionary published in the year indicated. In every dictionary, words with a frequency over 100 are leaders in the change. Again, the most frequent words are changing first.

A likely explanation for the stress shift among -*ate* verbs has been provided by Gąsiorowski (1997). Following similar suggestions by Hogg and McCully (1987: 122–3), he suggests that the -*ate* was originally treated as an extrametrical suffix:

In the passage from late Middle to Early Modern English the final foot of a noun or adjective became destressed if it dominated a monosyllabic suffix. As a result, a large number of adjectival suffixes became extrametrical – that is to say, they were ignored in stress assignment. Such, no doubt, was the fate of -*ate*, which was basically an adjective-forming suffix at the time.... When some of the -*ate* words began to be used as verbs, the same stress pattern was assigned at first. In the course of time, however, verbs and adjectives began to develop along divergent paths.... There was a gain in doing away with the extrametrical labelling of -*ate*$_V$: first, its secondary stress could now be generated by the English stress Rule rather than a special word-level rule; secondly, the -*ate* verbs would be stressed like all normal English verbs. (pp. 175–7)

In sum, in words where the suffix has lost its extrametrical status, the stress pattern follows the default rules for stress placement in English. Recall, for instance, that Sereno (1986) found that over three-fourths of the bisyllabic verbs in English received final stress. Whether one accepts Gasiorowski's analysis of this suffix as extrametrical or supports another analysis, the verbs so encompassed must be marked in some way to keep them from behaving like other verbs in English.

In producing the innovatively stressed -*ate* forms, in other words, speakers are accessing the full form from their lexicons, without analysis of the -*ate* suffix as extrametrical. Recall that according to Pierrehumbert (2003: 179), a word form's representation "mediates between perception and production," "is learned through repeated exposure to that word in speech," and is influenced by its word frequency. One would expect frequent -*ate* verbs to become entrenched with their antepenultimate stress pattern, but they have undergone change first. How the most frequent words came to change first is the subject of the next section.

2.4   The role of lexical analysis

The different patterns of diffusion of the two different stress shifts must be linked to the different levels of LEXICAL ANALYSIS required by each, as proposed in Phillips (1998c). The term "lexical analysis" comes from Bybee's (1985) description of how "[h]igh-frequency words form more distant lexical connections than low-frequency words. In the case of morphologically complex words ... high-frequency words undergo less analysis, and are less dependent on their related base words than low-frequency words" (p. 118). For instance, a high-frequency word such as *dictator* is less dependent on the base word *dictate*, as seen by its semantic freedom, than is a low-frequency word such as *gyrator* on its base, *gyrate*. Being a *dictator* implies more than *dictating* to someone

The Lexical Diffusion of Phonetically Abrupt Changes 47

taking *dictation*. But a *gyrator* does *gyrate*, and its movement is called *gyration*. The higher-frequency word *dictator*, therefore, undergoes less analysis, the low-frequency *gyrator* undergoes more analysis.

Of course, the *dictator/gyrator* example involves semantic analysis, but lexical analysis also has phonological consequences. Obscured compounds such as *hussy* from original *housewife*, *gossip* from *God's sibb*, *daisy* < *day's eye*, are often given as examples of the semantic shift, but they have also undergone radical phonetic change – surely due at least in part because of their high frequency.[5] Thus, in the implementation of sound change, *lexical analysis* becomes an important factor. Low-frequency words undergo more analysis during production, more detailed access of information in the lexical entry, including generalizations drawn from associative networks with other words in the lexicon. For the diatonic stress shift, information necessary to implement the change includes grammatical class – only if the word is a noun will it undergo change to initial stress. This means that an infrequent word such as the noun *concert* will undergo the shift to initial stress more readily than will a more frequent word such as the noun *concern* – that is, through more detailed lexical analysis, the statistical advantage of nouns starting with stressed syllables is revealed and the infrequent word is more likely to follow that pattern – very much like traditional analogy.

Note that in most modular approaches to phonology, the procedure for stress assignment should be the same for words like *dictáte* (verb) and *cóncert* (noun): the underlying form undergoes stress assignment – in both cases the default stress pattern for nouns and verbs – before progressing to the postlexical component. There is no way, therefore, of explaining why the default stress is assigned to very frequent verbs in one case but to infrequent nouns in the other. As Berg (1999: 138) found in his study of variant lexical stress in British and American English,

> Since the stress-divergent words defy a straightforward analysis in terms of general rules, any rule-based account of stress (e.g. Chomsky and Halle, 1968) loses in credibility. If rules exist, they [stress-divergent words] would have to change, i.e. all words which meet the structural description of the rule must behave alike. This is certainly not the case. It is much more probable therefore that word stress is stored with each lexical item (as proposed by, e.g., Cutler, 1984) rather than assigned by rule.

Within a usage-based model of language, on the other hand, the difference in stress assignment reflects how words are stored and processed.

48   *Word Frequency and Lexical Diffusion*

"Generalizations over forms are not separate from the stored representation of forms but emerge directly from them. In Langacker's [1987] terms, there is no 'rule/list separation'" (Bybee 2001: 7).

Recall that, although the phonological representation in a usage-based model is based on the detailed memory traces, the phonological representation itself is an abstraction. Also recall that while the innovation behind both stress shifts may have been motivated by reshaping toward a desired schema, it is not the **innovation** that determines a change's pattern of lexical diffusion, but its **implementation** in speakers' production. And the psycholinguistic evidence on production makes clear that segmental shape and stress pattern are not stored together, but, rather, during production, stress is imposed on the segmental representation (Levelt 1999, 2002; Dogil and Möbius 2001; Booij 2004). For instance, speech errors typically disrupt the sequence of segments but leave the stress pattern in place.[6] Stress assignment for verbs such as *díctate* must contain some indication that the stress pattern is exceptional (as in the analysis of the *-ate* suffix being extrametrical), compared to other verbs ending in heavy syllables. It is in ignoring that exceptionality that the innovative pronunciation, *dictáte*, is produced. Thus, *-ate* words shifting their stress are undergoing minimal analysis, and thus affect the most frequent words first. An infrequent verb like *mandate* will undergo a higher degree of lexical analysis, accessing the morphophonological information that its *-ate* suffix is extrametrical, an exception to the stress pattern of most verbs.

Indeed it may be that the high-frequency verbs have not even been identified as having a suffix, as suggested by such experimental research as Meunier and Segui (1999). They experimented to see if priming effects of stems (e.g. *travail* "work") for derived words (e.g. *travailleur* "worker") and of derived words for their stems were equal, and if those priming effects varied depending on the word's frequency. In one experiment they found that "low surface frequency suffixed words prime their stem as much as stems prime themselves, but this is not the case for high frequency words" (p. 57) and in another that not only were high-frequency words identified more quickly than low-frequency words, but "a stem primes a high frequency suffixed word more than a low one. The priming effect is smaller (37ms) when the target is a high frequency suffixed word than when the target is a low frequency suffixed word (71ms)" (p. 58). These findings lead them to the conclusion that "on the one hand,... members of a given morphological family share a common decomposed morphological representation, and, on the other hand, that some members of the family (i.e., free

The Lexical Diffusion of Phonetically Abrupt Changes   49

stems and high surface frequency affixed members) are also represented in a whole word form" (p. 59).

The case of the stress shift in diatones (i.e. nouns like *convict* shifting from final to initial stress), follows a very different path in production however, which led it to affect the least frequent words first. Since such stress patterns are determined by syntactic information, noun rather than verb, information from the lemma is required before stress assignment in phonological encoding can proceed. It must be this deeper level of ANALYSIS that leads to the least frequent words being affected first. That is, both stress shifts examined above were apparently motivated by the same product-oriented schema, but they have followed very different paths of lexical implementation because of the different depths of analysis required in their production.

In sum, it is important to remember that it is not the original impetus behind the change that determines its lexical diffusion. Its implementation is what is crucial. The word frequency effect for *-ate* verbs is different from that for the noun–verb pairs such as *cónvict* (n.)/*convíct* (v.) because the stress pattern that has to be superimposed on the segmental form during production is being treated differently in each case during production. In the case of *-ate* verbs becoming stressed on the final syllable, like most verbs in English, for words with strong memory traces the speaker is ignoring any special indicators on the word form and allowing the default stress pattern to apply; in the case of earlier *convíct* (n.) shifting stress to *cónvict* (n.), for words with weak memory traces, the speaker is accessing grammatical information [+noun] that leads to the imposition of the stress pattern associated with nouns in English.

2.5   Word frequency and the Rhythm Rule

The Rhythm Rule in English refers to the shift in stress of words like *thirtéen* when they occur in phrases before initially stressed words, as in *thírteen mén*. Hammond (1999a) reports on an experiment wherein 14 native speakers reported their intuitions about whether the stress sounded better on the first or last syllable of each modifier in 15 phrases, randomized and embedded among 15 complex forms and 9 distractors. The 15 phrases were evenly divided among those that began with high-frequency words, medium-frequency words, and low-frequency words, based on "phondic.english," an online dictionary of 20,000 English words. Those beginning with high-frequency words were *concrete type, naïve friend, antique book, compact range,* and *ideal road*. Phrases beginning with medium-frequency words were *concave step, mundane play,*

50 *Word Frequency and Lexical Diffusion*

transverse stage, austere word, and *humane act.* And phrases beginning with low-frequency words were *arcane sort, blasé care, obese child, oblique view,* and *urbane world.* Fifteen similarly stratified complex phrases were also included, that is, phrases which began with a morphologically complex word such as *unreal, farfetched,* and *postpaid,* as were nine distractors. The results of the experiment revealed that the frequency of the modifier affected the subjects' judgments of well-formedness. That is, phrases containing high-frequency modifiers like *antíque* that had undergone the Rhythm Rule to create the stress pattern *ántique book* were judged more well-formed than phrases containing infrequent modifiers like *arcane* (p. 340).

Hammond (1999a: 352–4) suggests an Optimality Theoretic (OT) account for handling such phrases, using parochial constraints. Thus in order to rank words differently with respect to *CLASH (defined as "avoid adjacent main stresses") depending upon their lexical frequency, he proposes "constraints that require prosodic identity in isolation and context forms for particular lexical items" and posits a rule called "Isolation-Context Correspondence [c(X)]," which reads: "The stress of context forms for some form X must mirror that of the isolation form of X." The ranking of Isolation-Context Correspondence constraints with respect to *CLASH then reflects the frequency of the lexical items: ">>low frequency words >> *CLASH >> high frequency words" (p. 354). Thus words like *arcane* would rank above *CLASH and those like *antique* below it. Hammond boasts that "this approach can capture the difference between modifiers like *arcane* and *antique* without appealing to arbitrary diacritics" (p. 354), yet every lexical item has to be marked as either high frequency or low frequency. Hammond explains why parochial constraints should be ranked according to frequency in terms very familiar to usage-based phonology: "The more frequent an item is, the more ingrained it is in the phonology of the language. In terms of the model here, the constraints corresponding to that item become lower-ranked and hence susceptible to more of the phonological generalizations of the language in question." But the OT account, although perhaps in this instance descriptively adequate for the phrases in question, fails in explanatory adequacy. That is, the reason for the ordering can be built into the model, but the model itself does not provide an explanation for why these words should behave as they do. Most compellingly, Myers (2003) has pointed out that

the real problem with this [Hammond's (1999a)] analysis is the frequency-ranked hierarchy itself, since it is the exact inverse of

The Lexical Diffusion of Phonetically Abrupt Changes 51

the well-motivated ranking necessary for negative frequency effects. First, it seems counterintuitive to suppose that faithfulness to lower frequency words like *arcane* actively overrides *CLASH, since lower frequency words have weaker memory traces. Second, this inverse ranking does not allow for a one-to-one mapping between constraints and lexical items, since the highest-ranked constraint is associated with the lowest-frequency lexical item, not a well-defined concept given the fuzzy borders of the lexicon. Finally, this inverse ranking cannot be made to follow from the simpler assumption that faithfulness constraints are parochial with respect to tokens rather than types. (p. 355)

In a usage-based model, different patterning of high- versus low-frequency words is to be expected. Just as losing the extrametrical marking on -*ate* verbs takes place in verbs which have not been fully analyzed during their access, high-frequency modifiers like *antíque* can be accessed without their stress patterns being so closely analyzed that the Rhythm Rule cannot override the stress pattern given in lexical storage. The extra analysis that low-frequency words require is apparently what interferes with the application of the Rhythm Rule.

An interesting second finding in Hammond (1999a) is that morphologically complex words – *unreal, worthwhile, postwar, insane, unknown* (high frequency); *preflight, farfetched, innate, malformed, unclean* (medium frequency); *impure, postpaid, unsought, nonskid, inlaid* (low frequency) – undergo the Rhythm Rule (like frequent simple adjectives) no matter what the frequency. The explanation may be that proposed by Cole et al. (1989), whose study, using written stimuli, found that response times for suffixed words correlated not just with a word's frequency but even more so with its cumulative root frequency, that is, with the sum of the root plus all affixed forms that shared the same root. Prefixed words, on the other hand, showed no such frequency effects. They suggest that "affixed words (prefixed and suffixed) are stored in the lexicon as whole word forms while their morphological structure is reflected by the organization of the family" (p. 10). Left-to-right processing causes access to a whole morphological family when the root is at the beginning of the word (p. 10). With prefixed words, this same left-to-right processing causes access to a family of words with that prefix, but not access to the root and the family associated with that root. In the same vein, Melinger (2003) finds no difference in forced speech errors between words formed from prefix + bound root or + free stem, as in *reject* (*re* + bound root) versus *recharge* (*re* + free stem). Therefore, it seems that in accessing

52 *Word Frequency and Lexical Diffusion*

a prefixed word, the whole word family, e.g. all the *re-* words, are activated. For this reason, their joint family frequency seems to account for their uniform behavior in undergoing the Rhythm Rule. The Rhythm Rule does not require any closer analysis of the morphological structure or semantics of the modifiers and thus applies equally to all prefixed words, which benefit from the combined frequency of words in their morphological family, say of words with the *un-* prefix.

Compare the frequency effects of the stress shift in diatones discussed above, which takes place inside subcategories of that lexical class, identifiable by prefix. In other words, disyllables beginning with *con-* behave separately from those beginning with *re-*, which are separate from those beginning with *a-*, etc. And frequency effects for that change **are** found within each prefix family. The fact that the least frequent words within each family are affected first was attributed to the deeper level of lexical analysis that was needed to produce these forms; that is, in order to implement the change, for infrequent words whose pronunciation is not firmly entrenched, the speaker defaults to the general pattern for nouns or verbs, which requires information on grammatical category.

The connections between prefixed forms that allow them to be treated uniformly as a family are easily mapped in a connectionist or network grammar, where words freely relate to each other and generalizations can emerge on the basis of phonological similarities. In contrast, they are inexplicable in those modular phonologies in which a word's input form consists of a stem which then has prefixes and suffixes attached to it during a derivation. The following section presents further evidence of the independence of variously suffixed forms.

2.6 Forms in *-ate* versus *-ator*

The existence of affixes that affect word stress has been a particular problem for the traditional theory of Lexical Phonology because that model recognizes one underlying stem for related words such as *édit*, *edítion*, and *éditor*. This stem is then modified through lexical rules to produce related words, with different strata assigning stress patterns to words depending on the type of affix. A suffix like *-(t)ion*, which shifts the stress to a different syllable, as it does in *edition*, must be added at the Level 1 stratum. A suffix like *-or*, on the other hand, must be added at the Level 2 stratum, since it does not change the stress, that is, *editor* maintains the initial stress of the base word *edit*. (For a visual representation of the levels, see Kiparsky (1982 [1999].) Even in Kiparsky's (2000) modifications to the theory, these basic levels seem to remain intact. In this

The Lexical Diffusion of Phonetically Abrupt Changes 53

section the history of a number of related forms involving the suffixes -*ate* and -*ator* is investigated, a history which shows how independent each form is from the other – both in its historical development and its stress pattern – which supports the theory that they are independently listed in the lexicon.

In British English, except for the word *orator*, words in -*ator* overwhelming stress the penultimate syllable. American English, however, has been shifting the stress in almost all these words to the antepenult: *díctator, tránslator, équator, nárrator, cúrator*, and so forth (Phillips 1998a). If the nouns are created from underlying verb forms plus -*ator*, one would expect two things: (1) any change in stress should affect both words simultaneously; and (2) -*ator* forms should not exist without a base verb form. As for (1), it is true that often the verbs and their corresponding nouns have changed simultaneously, but not always. When they have not, again with the sole exception of *orator*, the -*ator* form of the word has changed first: *dictátor, rotátor* and *narrátor* in British English; *dictátor, donátor, pulsátor, narrátor, gyrátor, mandátor*, and *curátor* in American English. This pattern exists despite the -*ator* being the "derived" form and despite its being usually less frequent than its verbal counterpart. As for the second expectation (2), for many pairs, the -*ator* form appears in dictionaries well before the verb form, as it does for *rotator, equator, pulsator, mandator, curator*, and *testator*. Singh (1996: 34) is wrong, then, to call back-formation "rare indeed," but he is right when he says that "neither Marchand (1969) nor Kiparsky (1982) do justice to linguistic competence by treating it only as exceptional. What it shows must be built into a potential-oriented grammar."

Proponents of Lexical Phonology have recognized the problem of affixes that trigger varying stress patterns. Katamba (1993: 135) notes, "For the principle of recognizing strata on the basis of affixes to work reliably, it should be the case that each affix belongs to just one stratum. If affixes belonged simultaneously to several strata, that principle would be subverted."

In a comment on Goldsmith's (1990: 262) observation of a similar situation involving the -*ize* suffix, Katamba suggests

> that the standard lexical morphology can be defended in most cases of this kind ... that (normally) affixes belong to just one stratum. If the same affix appears to belong to two strata, we can attribute this to an ongoing language change. The affix morpheme may be splitting in two. So, what we have are closely related homophonous forms, with different characteristics, occurring at different strata. (pp. 135–6)

54 *Word Frequency and Lexical Diffusion*

Katamba's answer – to create homophonous forms on different strata – is clearly an ad hoc solution that reacts to diachronic change rather than accounting for it. Such a solution is not necessary in a usage-based grammar that provides connections between lexical items.

Giegerich (1999) offers a different solution to the problem of the same affix belonging to two strata. He redefines the strata of Lexical Phonology so that they are not determined by which affixes they take, and he notes that "the outputs of the stratum-1 morphology in any case have to be individually listed for semantic and other reasons" (p. 59). He explains,

> Stratum-1 suffixation is in principle stress-shifting, but stress shifts do not show up in every stratum-1 form. Nor do stratum-1-specific phonological rules or the application of stratum-1-specific phonotactic constraints. And so forth. Such partial indeterminacies may well have constituted the diachronic cause for what is something of a synchronic mess. (p. 52)

His goal is not to develop a grammar that explains diachrony further, however, but "[a]n adequate model of the lexicon [that] will at the very least be able to accommodate such facts in a descriptively adequate synchronic account" (p. 52). As for diachronic changes in stress assignment, they still seem to require the reassignment of a lexical form from one stratum to another since

> the two strata of English are distinguished by a syndrome of interrelated properties. Phonological properties of stratum-1 suffixation include stress alternations (*átom–atómic*), syllabicity alternations (*rhythm–rhythmic*) and the application of stratally restricted phonological rules such as Trisyllabic Shortening (*serene–serenity*). Stratum-2 forms are characterised by the absence of those phonological features. The semantic diagnostic of stratum-1 processes is the non-compositionality of their products; the morphological diagnostic is the non-productivity of the processes involved. (Both are expressed through the listing of all stratum-1 formations, as we have seen.) (p. 97)

Thus the suffix *-or* is still assigned during derivation; only it is no longer confined to Stratum 2. It may be assigned in Stratum 1, as required if the speaker has *díctator* derived from *dictáte* or *tránslator* from *transláte*; or it may be assigned in Stratum 2, as required if the speaker shifts their pronunciation to *dictátor* or *translátor*. Generally, Giegerich's model seems to assume the opposite direction of change; that is, "a form may establish

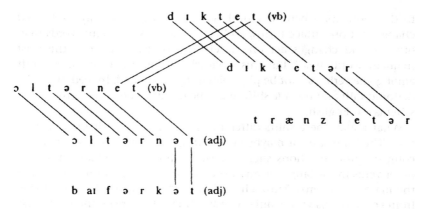

Figure 2.2 Connectionist links in the mental lexicon (Phillips 1998c: 175)

itself on stratum 1 purely through the phonological structure simplification caused by frequent use," as in "the case of *smuggler*, which shows no signs of non-compositionality but is clearly so well-established that it is listed (unlike *waddler*, for example, which is trisyllabic) even in pocket-size dictionaries" (p. 34). In any case, there seems to be no mechanism by which variant word frequencies are recorded (as they are in a stochastic grammar), so that in his model the **orderly** progression of a change by word frequency cannot be accommodated, much less a means by which some stress changes could affect the most frequent words first and others the least frequent words first.

In a stochastic usage-based grammar, in contrast, generalizations over lexical forms can become the basis for change in stress, with the most frequent words being changed first when the change involves shallow access to the form, but with the less frequent words being changed first when deeper lexical analysis is required to implement the change. Figure 2.2, taken from Phillips (1998a: 175), displays in a simple fashion (dictated by the two dimensions of the printed page) the sets of lexical connections that would allow words sharing morphological matter to be related to each other without being derived from one another.

2.7 Motivation, actuation, implementation

Perhaps it will help at this point to clarify the distinctions between the motivation, the actuation, and the implementation of sound change. Phillips (1984: 337) suggests that word frequency effects are connected

56 *Word Frequency and Lexical Diffusion*

to the motivation behind sound changes: "Physiologically motivated changes act on surface forms, and affect the most frequent words first; other sound changes act on underlying forms, and affect the least frequent words first." But this is clearly wrong, since the stress shift among -*ate* verbs cannot be physiologically motivated. Indeed, both the diatonic shift and the -*ate* shift might be motivated by productive stress schemas in English.

What makes these shifts different, then, must be their implementation. The innovator or maybe even multiple innovators unconsciously compare pronunciations such as *díctate* (vb.) or *concéntrate* (vb.) with other verbs in the language and note that the stress pattern differs from the majority of verbs. Through analogy – that is, generalizations made from connections with similar words – then, they create the new stress pattern. There must therefore be some way of marking verbs like *díctate* (vb.) as different from most other verbs, as "irregular", equivalent to an [+extrametrical] marking on the suffix. As with the *convict* example, the innovative pronunciation is based upon the statistical weight of the majority of verbs ending in a stressed syllable. When speakers copy that pronunciation in the propagation of the sound change, they must ignore the extrametrical marking on that lexeme, thus performing less lexical analysis. Since more frequent words are more strongly entrenched and less likely to undergo lexical analysis, then the more frequent words change first. For that reason, Phillips (2001: 134) proposed that "Changes which require analysis ... during their implementation affect the least frequent words first; others affect the most frequent words first."

3
The Lexical Diffusion of Phonetically Gradual Changes

3.0 Introduction

Phonetically gradual changes, also known as gradient changes, are those whose direct observation Bloomfield (1933: 347) would have called "inconceivable," but which modern techniques have shown not only can be captured in synchronic variation but also are often salient to speakers. That is, not only can the degree of reduction, the degree of rounding, the degree of raising, the degree of affrication, etc. be measured, but speakers actually encode such information in memory (Pisoni 1997: 10; Lachs et al. 2003). Because these types of change appear as "low-level output rules" operating below the level of speakers' conscious awareness, Labov (1994: 78) and Kiparsky (1995: 659) have identified them as typical of neogrammarian changes. Studies such as Hansen's (2001) investigation of vowel nasalization in French have shown that such changes may also be lexically gradual, however; that is, even "low-level," phonetically gradual changes can be lexically diffused. For instance, she found that, in the vowel shifts currently affecting nasal vowels in French, "there are significant differences between the percentages of [ɑ̃-ɔ̃]/[ɔ̃] from one word to the next, lexical differences remain when prosodic/phonetic factors are kept constant, and homonyms such as *en* (pronoun) and *an(s)* do not behave identically" (p. 248).

Of course, as Milroy (2003a: 149) reminds us, even though we can measure fine phonetic detail, perhaps Bloomfield was right that we still

> cannot "observe" language change in progress (even though it is sometimes claimed that we can). This is because we cannot observe dynamic processes directly in abstract objects: we can observe the products of change, as historical linguists always have. The claim can

58 *Word Frequency and Lexical Diffusion*

therefore be rephrased as a claim that we can *detect* change in progress in synchronic states by comparing outputs or products of variation in present-day states of language.

So when we look below at data about phonetically gradual changes, we will actually be looking at the outputs of synchronic variation. And we will find that determining the phonetic environments which impact the change does not solve the actuation problem of why this change occurred when it did nor does it fully explain the implementation problem – what drives this change to be diffused through similar phonetic environments, through the population of speakers, and through the lexicon. But it should shed some light on the paths through which a sound change is implemented in the lexicon.

This chapter, then, looks closely at the lexical diffusion patterns of phonetically gradual changes and examines their implications for a usage-based theory of language. The chapter first considers phonetically gradual changes that have affected the most frequent words first, starting with vowel and consonant reduction and deletion, since those processes have been most heavily investigated in this regard, and proceeding to assimilations and vowel shifts. The second half of the chapter reviews phonetically gradual sound changes that have affected the least frequent words first: /j/-deletion in Southern American English, the twelfth-century unrounding of English /ø(:)/, and the late Old English lengthening of vowels before homorganic consonant clusters.

3.1 Gradual changes affecting the most frequent words first

Gradual changes which affect the most frequent words first include vowel and consonant reductions and deletions, assimilations, and vowel shifts. Each type is exemplified below.

3.1.1 Vowel reductions and deletions

Jespersen (1909–49, Part I: 256) was perhaps the first to note that word frequency could affect the reduction of vowels in unstressed syllables in words like *career, tradition, grammarian*: "Before consonant groups, [æ] may also be heard: *ambition. campaign*, etc., though [ə] is very frequent indeed, at any rate in the interior of a sentence. The less colloquial a word is, the oftener the full vowel is retained, as in *campestral. sanguineous. spasmodic*." Fidelholz (1975) later examined the reduction of vowels in

The Lexical Diffusion of Phonetically Gradual Changes 59

the initial syllable of words stressed on the second syllable, observing, for example, that frequent words such as *astronomy, mistake, abstain,* and *thermometer* are more likely to exhibit a reduced vowel than are relatively infrequent *gastronomy, mistook, abstemious,* and *tercentenary* (p. 200). A further study of vowel reduction involving adjectives ending in *-ate* was undertaken by Phillips (1998a), who found that the twentieth-century British and American dictionaries consulted – Jones (1917), Gimson (1988 [1991]), Brown (1993), Barnhart (1947), Kenyon and Knott (1953), and Mish (1993) – all listed the frequent adjective *alternate* with syllable-final schwa [-ət], as compared to the full vowel [-et], which appeared as the more common pronunciation in infrequent adjectives such as *bidentate, incarnate,* and *insensate.* Hooper (1976) provided a more detailed investigation into the relationship between vowel reduction and word frequency. Using frequency counts from Francis and Kučera (1982), she found that words with very high frequency had no schwa (*every* 492, *evening* (n.) 149), words with intermediate frequency had syllabic [r̩] (*memory* 91, *salary* 51, *summary* 21, *nursery* 14), and words with low frequency retained schwa + [r] (*mammary* 0, *artillery* 11, *summery* 0, *cursory* 4, *evening* (v.) 0). Similar results have been found for vowel reduction in other languages, such as Russian (Barinova 1971), which Fenk-Oczlon (2001: 437) summarizes:

> Barinova's (1971) examples for deletion of vowels, consonants or even syllables show that although reduction processes occur first in casual speech, not all items are deletion-prone to the same extent. Again, the most frequent words reduce first. For example, *tebja* [t'ia] you (Acc.), *chodit* [choit] he, she walks, *vidit* [v'iit] he, she sees, *nič ego* [n'čo] nothing, *segodnja* [s'odn] today. All these words belong to the 204 most frequent words in Russian (Josselson 1953).

Stress relationships within a word can also lead to vowel reduction. As Minkova and Stockwell (2005) show, stress clash led to vowel reduction in English of the suffix *-dom,* which in Middle English occurred after a stressed syllable more often than did the comparable suffix *-hood,* which did not undergo reduction. Specifically, by 1330 the percentage of lexemes containing a strong syllable before the ending *-dom,* as in kingdom, was 68 percent (with, conversely, 32 percent containing a weak syllable in that position, as in *martirdom*). In comparison, only 27 percent of the lexemes with the suffix *-hood* contained a preceding strong syllable, as in *manhod* 'manhood', as opposed to *liklihod* 'likelihood' (p. 271). The difference in the token frequency of

60 *Word Frequency and Lexical Diffusion*

the lexemes is also striking. In the Old English Dictionary Corpus, on which Minkova and Stockwell based their data, the most frequent word containing a weak syllable before *-dom* was the word *Cristendom* 'Christendom,' whereas the most frequent word containing a strong syllable in that position was *wisdom*, with almost twice as many forms (p. 270).

A corpora analysis of the frequency of schwa deletion in conversational English is reported in Patterson et al. (2003), who studied its "lexical variables, lexical stress environment, word frequency, and morphological complexity using the Switchboard database, ... a collection of approximately 2,400 two-sided telephone conversations based on prompted topics among 543 speakers, from all areas of the United States" (p. 46). Patterson et al. separated the words amenable to schwa deletion into four groups. Two-syllable words stressed on the second syllable with a schwa in the first syllable formed one group. The other three groups were all three-syllable words: (1) those with the schwa in pre-stressed position and morphologically related to the two-syllable words; (2) those with the schwa in pre-stressed position but not morphologically related to the two-syllable words; and (3) those with schwa in a post-stressed position (p. 49). They found that neither the sex nor the regional accent of the speaker showed any reliable effect on schwa deletion (p. 49), nor did morphological complexity (p. 52). The greatest predictor of schwa loss was the position of lexical stress, with lexical frequency contributing to "a small increase in predictability beyond that given by stress environment for the potential schwa alone" when looking across the entire data set (p. 49). This is what one would expect from the other cases of lexical frequency examined above, namely lexical frequency effects operating within phonetic environments. It is true that Patterson et al. (2003) found that the frequency effect "was not sufficiently robust to hold when the data were analyzed by lexical stress pattern subgroups" (p. 53), but this finding does not necessarily negate the frequency effects that were observed in the larger environment. The subgroup environments may have been overly fine in defining the environment of schwa deletion or there may have been insufficient numbers of words within the subgroups to reflect a stronger word frequency effect. Patterson et al. also note that

> one notable aspect and perhaps limitation of the Switchboard database is that the speakers are strangers who are conversing on the telephone. A concern is that the relationship between speakers has been shown to influence both variation in word duration and the

The Lexical Diffusion of Phonetically Gradual Changes 61

application of phonological rules, with increased familiarity leading to less fully articulated speech. (p. 55)

This concern should only apply to the overall frequency of schwa deletion in their corpus, not to the relative effects of frequent words versus infrequent words. One important factor that Patterson et al. (2003) did not consider is word class, an issue which will be revisited in Chapter 4.

Bergen's (1995) study of vowel reduction in Dutch also confirms that word frequency plays an important role. His experiment testing the influence of sentence accent, word stress, and word class on the spectral characteristics and the duration of vowels led to the finding that although word class and word stress played a role in vowel reduction, frequency of occurrence seemed "of greater importance, because the frequency effect is also clearly present across word classes" (p. 56). The effect of sentence accent was deemed "of minor importance" (p. 56). Bergen distinguishes between "acoustic vowel reduction" and "lexical vowel reduction," the former being "the continuous counterpart" of the latter, based on the observation "that all vowels in a normal speech situation have to some extent a tendency to become a schwa." *Lexical vowel reduction* requires that schwa be a phoneme in the language, assignable by rule. Yet he finds that "exactly the same factors" affect each type of reduction: "For example, in a word that is very frequently used, either acoustic vowel reduction is likely to be strong, or the probability that lexical vowel reduction occurs is relatively high" (p. 93).

In a recent study on a different kind of vowel reduction, this time across word boundaries, Alba (2003) found that in hiatus resolution in New Mexican Spanish, high-frequency items favor reduction, while low-frequency items disfavor it. Alba analyzed sequences of the singular feminine articles *la* 'the' and *una* 'a' and following vowel-initial nouns, such as *iglesia* 'church' and *hija* 'daughter' in 20 hours of tape-recorded interviews with 20 native speakers of Spanish. Hiatus resolution could take any of four forms: deletion of the first vowel [leskwéla], deletion of the second vowel [laskwéla], diphthongization [laiskwéla], or coalescence [liskwéla, lɛskwéla, lɪskwéla, etc.]. Using the GoldVarb program, Alba was able to identify three significant factors in hiatus resolution: stress of the second vowel, quality of the second vowel, and the ratio frequency, determined "by dividing the token frequency of a string of words x + y, (or the string frequency of that string), by the token frequency of one of the two words (x or y) alone." Strings with high ratio frequency underwent hiatus resolution 87 percent of the time, compared to 48 percent

62 *Word Frequency and Lexical Diffusion*

for strings with low ratio frequency. That is, high string frequency positively impacted vowel reduction.

Two other studies of string frequency effects, Bybee and Scheibman (1999) and Scheibman (2000), have shown that phonetic reduction of the word *don't*, ranging in degree from initial /do-/ to /ɾo/ to /ɾə/ to /ə/, is dependent upon the frequency of the phrases in which it appears. In their study of 45 minutes of conversational English, Bybee and Scheibman (1999: 580) found that "not only do pronouns occur with *don't* more often in the data than do other subject noun phrases, but the pronoun that appears most often (*I*) also occurs with the most reduced forms of *don't*." In addition, vowel reduction occurred in their data more frequently before the most frequent verbs, namely, *know, think, have (to), want, like*, as it does before three other frequent verbs – *mean, feel*, and *care* – that happened not to occur very often in their limited corpus. Scheibman (2000: 123) finds the most frequent phrase which contains *don't* with a reduced vowel is *I don't know* and links this tendency toward reduction to grammaticization and the extended discourse functions of *I don't know*, which include "conveying epistemic senses, with both local scope (e.g. over a following proposition) and global (e.g. by making reference to an extended stretch of talk). There is also evidence that these more global uses, due to their important face-saving functions in interactive contexts, have become grammaticized as markers of turn exchange." Therefore, again, high string frequency incorporating highly frequent verbs positively impacts vowel reduction.

A possible explanation for why frequent words would allow more reduction may have beesn found by Wright (2003) in his study of the phonetic details of vowel reduction in hard words versus easy words, hard words being defined as low-frequency words with many phonetically similar "lexical neighbors" and easy words being the inverse (i.e. high-frequency words with few phonetically similar neighbors). He found that "vowels from 'hard' words are more hyperarticulated than vowels from 'easy' words. The expansion of the vowel space occurs in such a way that overall distances between vowels are maximised" (p. 84). Vowels from "easy" words, on the other hand, are produced with less peripheral qualities. Munson and Solomon (2004: 1049), whose own study found that more expanded vowel spaces were associated with lower-frequency words, note that Wright's findings are "consistent with Lindblom's (1990) hypospeech and hyperspeech theory of speech production, which argues that talkers actively modify their articulation in different tasks and speaking environments to maintain an adequate level of intelligibility."

3.1.2 Consonant reductions and deletions

Consonants, of course, can also be reduced. To quote an example given in Bybee (2001: 73), "the reduction of a consonant such as [p] along a path which is crosslinguistically common (namely, [p] > [ɸ]/[f] > [h] > Ø) can be characterized as a successive decrease and loss of muscular activity." Evidence supports the most frequent words changing first in these reductions. Krishnamurti (1998: 197), for instance, reports that as part of the development of $s > h > Ø$ in Gondi dialects "the dialects in the north and west show *s-* in most cases (*sowar* 'salt') but *h-* in the case of the high frequency verbs (*sūr* 'see', *son-* 'go', and *sille* 'not to be')."

More in-depth evidence on consonant reduction is reported in Bybee (2000b), who details several studies on t/d reduction and deletion in the regular past tense of English verbs. By concentrating on this one morphological category, she is able to focus on the effect of word frequency on the production of the *-ed* suffix. First, she cites Lociewicz's (1992) findings on the relative duration of the *-ed* suffix of native English speakers' readings of sentences containing regular past tense near homonyms such as "*called, mauled; covered, hovered; needed, kneaded; expected, inspected*... (For example, *The workers expected/inspected all the mail at noon every day.*). ... The results show that on average the *-ed* suffix on low frequency verbs is 7 msec. longer than on high frequency verbs" (p. 78). Bybee's own study of the correlation between word frequency in these verbs and the deletion of the final *-t* or *-d* found that the high-frequency verbs were more than twice as likely to undergo deletion as low-frequency ones; 39.6 percent compared with 18.9 percent of the lower-frequency tokens sampled (p. 78). She found the same pattern for double-marked past tense forms in verbs such as *kept, slept, sent*, and *meant*. Since she found some phonetic influence, especially of a labial stop preceding the /t/, I have rearranged her data by phonetic environment in Table 3.1 and have used the word frequency numbers given in the CELEX Lexical Database. CELEX distinguished between *felt* (n.) and *felt* (v.), but not between *left* (adj. or v.) or *lost* (adj. or v.). Nonetheless, it is clear that within every phonetic category, the more/most frequent word has undergone deletion more readily: *told* (1763) more than *held* (765), *felt* (1449) more than *built* (456), *sent* (551) more than *meant* (515) or *lent* (25), *kept* (750) more than *slept* (120), and *left* (1503) more than *lost* (759).

Evidence for word-final /t/-deletion has also been gathered for Dutch by Goeman and van Reenen (1985: 182). Table 3.2(a) presents their data for the deletion of /t/ in present and past tense forms in that language,

64 *Word Frequency and Lexical Diffusion*

Table 3.1 Deletion of /t/ in double-marked pasts (based on Bybee 2000b: 80)

Phonetic environment	Verb	% Deletion	*CELEX* – raw word form frequency	
			More susceptible to deletion	**Less susceptible to deletion**
-ld	told	68	1763	
	held	0		765
-lt	felt	55	1449	
	built	0		456
-nt	sent	25	551	
	meant	0		515
	lent	0		25
-pt	kept	66	750	
	slept	50		120
-ft/st	left	25	1503	
	lost	0		759

Table 3.2(a) Deletion of [t] in final [xt] and [st] clusters in Dutch, present and past tense forms (based on Goeman and van Reenan 1985: 182)

Words	Frequency UitdB	Average % deletion
Phonetic environment: [st]		
leest, blaast, vriest, kiest, dorst, danst, barst	0	12.14
wast	2	14.00
wist	22	34.00
moest	160	42.00
Phonetic environment: [xt]		
buigt, vraagt, weegt, jaagt, vocht, lacht, dreigt, zwijgt, draagt, vecht, zucht	0	13.36
bracht, krijgt, zocht, kocht, legt, ligt, vliegt, spuugt	1–5	20.75
mocht, dacht	18–36	42.50
zegt	122	27.00

divided into frequency groups and separated into the two phonetic environments, [st] and [xt]. Goeman and van Reenan used the Uit den Boogaart (UitdB) corpus (1975), which was at least partly collected in the dialect area they were investigating and which they found to be "more concordant with our data base of rural dialect speakers mostly" (p. 182).

If one uses frequencies from the much more extensive CELEX database, which was not available at the time Goeman and van Reenan

The Lexical Diffusion of Phonetically Gradual Changes 65

did their study but also which does not include data from the spoken language, the correlation between word frequency and /t/ deletion becomes even more striking, as demonstrated in Table 3.2(b). This correlation, in turn, reinforces Bybee's conclusion that "high frequency

Table 3.2(b) Deletion of [t] in final [xt] and [st] final clusters in Dutch, present and past tense forms (Goeman and van Reenan 1985: 182, plus CELEX frequencies)

Word	CELEX frequency	% Deletion	Average % for 0, 1–100, 101–1000, over 1000
Phonetic environment [st]			
dorst	0	10	**10.00**
vriest	22	15	
barst	66	3	
wast	71	14	**10.67**
blaast	104	16	
danst	105	9	
kiest	400	14	
leest	555	18	**14.25**
wist	19986	34	
moest	31941	42	**38.00**
Phonetic environment [xt]			
spuugt	24	8	
zucht	27	11	
vecht	63	11	**10.00**
jaagt	101	15	
weegt	144	16	
buigt	214	17	
zwijgt	235	12	
vliegt	243	16	
vocht	250	13	
dreigt	330	12	
lacht	678	13	
kocht	981	19	
legt	987	19	
draagt	991	11	**14.82**
vraagt	2840	16	
zocht	2955	24	
krijgt	3614	30	
ligt	5693	18	
bracht	7061	32	
mocht	7089	56	
zegt	9502	27	**29.00**
dacht	19358	29	**29.00**

66 Word Frequency and Lexical Diffusion

words are represented in the lexicon even if they are morphologically complex. The facts also support the hypothesis that sound change occurs in real time, with its effects being registered in the lexicon as small incremental changes, such that words that are used more often will undergo change at a faster rate" (p. 81).

The favorable effect of increased frequency on consonants is also found on reductive processes. Using the Switchboard corpus, Patterson and Connine (2001: 264) for instance, found that the most frequent morphologically simple words undergo flap production in English, with high-frequency words undergoing the process 95 percent of the time, compared to 76 percent for low-frequency words. They did not investigate word class, but the great majority of the words in their corpus were nouns (in bold): **battle, beauty, beetle**, better, bitter, **bottle, butter, cattle, city, cottage, data, duty**, fetish, **ghetto**, glitter, **gutter, Latin**, latter, **letter, lettuce, litter**, little, **lotus, matter, metal, motive**, notice, **party, pattern, photo, potty**, pretty, **quota**, rattle, settle, shuttle, stutter, **theater, title, total, turtle, tutor**, vital, **water** (pp. 270–1). They also discovered a difference between high- and low-frequency morphologically complex words – batter, batting, beating, booted, brutal, coated, fatal, footing, gritty, hater, heating, hitting, hotter, putting, rating, rotter, shooter, sitter, starter, voter, waiting, writer. In the less frequent words, medial /t/ was flapped 61 percent of the time in such words, compared to 66 percent for the more frequent words (p. 264). But since neither word class nor suffix group nor the frequency of the root word was controlled for, that figure seems less reliable.

In addition, Bybee (2001: 148–53) discusses the findings of D'Introno and Sosa (1986) on *t/d* deletion in Spanish past participles. She notes that, although deletion occurs more often in the first conjugation suffix, *-ado(s)/ -ada(s)*, than in the second conjugation suffix, *-ido(s)/-ida(s)*, the morphological ending by itself does not trigger higher rates of deletion, that the frequency of the whole word is a significant determiner of which words undergo deletion. Specifically, in the data under analysis, the 36 low-frequency words were evenly split between retention and loss of the medial /d/; the 55 high-frequency words, on the other hand, deleted the /d/ 64 percent of the time (p. 152).

Bybee (2001: 58–9) identifies three factors inherent in a usage-based grammar which influence the most frequent words to change first in reductive changes]:

(1) "These [reductive] changes occur in real time as language is used. Words and phrases that are used more often have more

The Lexical Diffusion of Phonetically Gradual Changes   67

opportunities to undergo these changes, just as other types of motor skills that are used more often become more compressed and efficient."

(2) Reduction "also occurs within discourse. Fowler and Housum (1987) have demonstrated that the second occurrence of the same word in the same discourse is shorter than the first occurrence. ... The result of this tendency is that words that occur more often in the same discourse may also be more frequent words and undergo more reduction."

(3) "D'Intono and Sosa (1986) argue that familiar, and thus high-frequency, words tend to be used in familiar social settings, where there are fewer restrictions on reduction."

Fenk-Oczlon (1989a: 93) connects reductive processes to information theory:

> Wo etwas auf Grund hoher Häufigkeit (in einem bestimmten Kontext) geläufig ist und auch beim Kommunikationspartner als geläufig vorausgesetzt werden kann, kann man – wenn die Zeit- (Ökonomie) Reduktion zweckmäßig erscheinen läßt – am ehesten reduzieren, ohne die Kommunikationsziele zu sehr zu gefährden...." [Where something is familiar on the basis of high frequency (in a particular context) and also can be assumed to be familiar to one's communication partner, one can – if the time (economy) reduction is practical – most easily reduce, without endangering one's communication goal too much.]

All of the above observations about reductive changes apply as well to assimilatory changes, not surprising since both types of change involve overlap of articulatory gestures (Browman and Goldstein 1991). The following section will reveal that, as expected, assimilatory sound changes also affect the most frequent words first.

3.1.3   Assimilations

Assimilations begin as articulatory coarticulations and thus are often described as low-level output rules, which one might expect to be regular. However, careful studies reveal that they are in actuality lexically diffused and affected by word frequency. An examination of an apparent assimilatory rule, that of vowel raising before nasals in Old English, will

68 Word Frequency and Lexical Diffusion

be investigated as part of the discussion of borrowing in Chapter 5, since manuscripts from the earliest stages of the shift are not long enough to yield evidence on word frequency effects, even though they do show that lexical diffusion must be operative (Toon 1983: 98–107). A better example for our purposes here is the development of new diphthongs in Early Middle English. Not only does our manuscript evidence reflect an early stage of this shift, which allows us to discount dialect borrowing as a factor in its implementation, but there is also no basis for an appeal to analogy.

During the transition from Old English to Middle English, all of the Old English diphthongs became monophthongs, and an assimilation of postvocalic glides led to the creation of a new set of diphthongs. As described in Phillips (1983c), on which the discussion below is based, sequences of vowel + /j/ and vowel + /w/ are clearly in transition in the c. AD 1180 manuscript of the *Ormulum*, as indicated by spellings in *aȝȝ* /ai/, *eȝȝ* /ei/, *aww* /au/, *oww*/ou/, *eoww* /öu/, and *eww* /eu/ versus *aȝ* /aj/, *eȝ* /ej/, *aw* /aw/, *ow* /ow/, *eow* /öw/, and *ew* /ew/.[1] The change occurred first before consonants, where all the Old English vowel + glide sequences appear as diphthongs, as detailed in Table 3.3. For the sake of simplicity, only one form of each lexeme is given. Forms for *eow* /öw/ and *ew* /ew/ have been combined because of the concomitant sound change of /ö/ merging with /e/.

Word-finally, diphthongization appears to have affected all words with Old English /aj/ and /ej/, but not /ew, öw/; hence, only the latter are indicated in the varying spellings in Table 3.4. Although only four such forms are attested, it is perhaps significant, especially in light of our findings below for intervocalic diphthongization, that the most frequent

Table 3.3 Preconsonantal diphthongization in the *Ormulum*, *c.* 1180

aȝȝ /ai/	*eȝȝ* /ei/	*aww* /au/	*oww* /ou/,	*e(o)ww* /eu/ (/öu/)
faȝȝre	eȝȝþerr	clawwstremann	fowwre	re(o)wwsenn
fraȝȝnenn	eȝȝlenn		owwþerr	re(o)wwsunng
maȝȝdenn	eȝȝwhær		nowwþerr	þe(o)wwtenn
maȝȝstre	fleȝȝl		trowwþe	
maȝȝþe	innseȝȝless			
naȝȝlenn	leȝȝd			
waȝȝn	reȝȝn			
	seȝȝd			

The Lexical Diffusion of Phonetically Gradual Changes 69

Table 3.4 Word-final *-e(o)ww* in the *Ormulum*

Diphthongized	Unchanged	
þe(o)ww 'servant' 55×	hew 'form'	2×
	ne(o)w 'new'	2×
	cne(o)w 'knew'	23×

one, *þe(o)ww* 'servant,' is the one that exhibits diphthongization, indicated by the final *-ww*.

Intervocalically, the lexical path of diphthongization is much clearer, as is its phonetic path. Old English sequences that resulted in Middle English /ai/ and /au/ had affected all the eligible words attested in the *Ormulum*: *daȝȝes* and its related forms (henceforth indicated by 'etc.') [15×], *faȝȝerr* etc. [4×], *tawwenn* [2×], *clawwess* [1×], *strawwenn* [1×]. The Old English sequence of long [o:w], however, had not yet undergone diphthongization in any words intervocalically: *towarrd* [38×] (morphologically probably *to + warrd*), *floweþþ* and its related forms [3×], *glowennde* [2×], and *þrowinnge* [1×]. Diphthongization in the remaining vowel + glide sequences vary by lexeme, as shown in Table 3.5. Word class seems to have some impact on this change, as in *cnewe* 'knew' (5×) versus *cnewwe* 'knee' (5×), but the effect on frequent verbs over infrequent ones is still evident, especially in forms that have developed from /e:ow/, where frequent nouns – *þe(o)wess* (56×), *tre(o)wwess* (11×), and *cnewwe* 'knee' (5×) – have the diphthongal spelling, and infrequent nouns – *he(o)we* (7×), *hewenn* (2), *larewess* (1) – do not. Thus, it is fair to conclude that the change, assimilating the glide to the syllabicity of the surrounding vowels, affected the more frequent words first.

The frequency effects in assimilation, therefore, mirror those of deletion, lenition, and reduction, which effects are attributed to gestural overlap in casual speech, as discussed by Browman and Goldstein (1991: 324). Such overlap may also cross word boundaries, resulting for example in the palatalization of /d/ + /j/ in more frequent phrases such as "did you," "don't you," and "would you," than in less frequent phrases such as "good you", "meet you," and "not yet," as shown in Bush (2001), where 65 such phrases from the Carterette and Jones (1974)/MacWhinney (1995) corpus were analyzed. The increased overlap of gestures, Browman and Goldstein believe, may even lead to regular phonological alternations and lexical simplifications as a result of speaker/hearer interpretations of the output. Gestural overlap

70 *Word Frequency and Lexical Diffusion*

Table 3.5 Lexical diffusion of intervocalic voicing in the *Ormulum*

OE > ME	Diphthongized	Frequency	Unchanged	Frequency
/ej/ > /ei/				
Nouns	eȝȝe 'fear'	10	forrleȝerrnesse 'adultery'	3
	weȝȝe 'way'	58		
Verbs/participles	leȝȝeþþ 'lay'	2*	forrleȝenn 'having committed adultery'	3
Other	aweȝȝe 'away'	1**		
/eːj/ > /ei/				
Verbs/participles			feȝedd 'joined'	4
			wreȝenn 'accused'	8
Other	beȝȝenn 'both'	1		
	tweȝȝenn 'twice'	70		
/eːow/ > /eu/***				
Nouns	þe(o)wwess 'servants'	56	he(o)we 'form'	7
	tre(o)wwess 'trees'	11	hewenn 'family'	2
	cnewwe 'knee'	5	larewess 'teachers'	1
Verbs/participles	chewwenn 'chew'	4	cnewe 'knew'	5
Other			newenn 'newly'	43

* Compare *leȝȝ(d)(e)* [14×].
** Compare *aweȝȝ* [17×].
*** Five words which contained OE /eːow/ shifted the stress within the diphthong to the second element, resulting in Orm's *fowwerr/fowwre* 'four' (106×), *fowwerrtiȝ* 'forty' (35×), *trowwe* 'true' (5×), *trowwenn* 'trust' (94×), *trowwþe* 'truth' (68×). See Phillips (1983c) for discussion.

may also be the source of insertions, such as Old English *þymel/þymle*-becoming modern *thimble* (327) or Old English *þunor/þunr* becoming modern *thunder*. Both of these would have been very frequent words in earlier stages of English. It would be instructive if rigorous studies were conducted on the effect of word frequency on the progress of modern articulatorily based epentheses, whether on epenthetic vowels, as in *ath-ə-lete*, or epenthetic consonants, as in *prince* /prɪnts/. For

The Lexical Diffusion of Phonetically Gradual Changes 71

now, we will turn our attention to a sound change not attributable to gestural overlap but which nonetheless affects the most frequent words first.

3.1.4 Vowel shifts

Taking her data from the *Survey of English Dialects* compiled by Orton and his associates, Ogura (1987) presents a thorough study of the diphthongization of the high vowels in that part of what is known as the Great Vowel Shift, as reflected in Modern English dialects, including the influence of word frequency. She concludes that Labov's (1981: 300) statement that the diphthongization of the high vowels /iː/ and /uː/, which apparently initiated the shift, was regular "is not factually correct" (p. 45). For the diphthongization of Middle English /iː/, Ogura found 17 different reflexes of that vowel in the present-day dialects of England, dependent upon location and phonetic environment, but also upon lexical item. Ogura (1995: 44) details the number of sites where each of the following pairs of words contains a different reflex of the vowel, even within fine phonetic environments:

Words ending in [d]; hide–spider 70, hide–slide 54, spider–slide 67.
Words ending in [v]; five–hive 62, five–ivy 56, hive–ivy 39.
Words ending in [n]; nine–mine 70.
Words beginning with liquid clusters; dry–Friday 90.
Words ending in [t]; white–writing 61.
Words ending in [f]; wife–knife 36.
Words ending in [s]; ice–icicle 23, mice–slice 85, mice–lice 57, slice–lice 76.
Words ending in [r]; fire–iron 79.

Evidence of the influence of word frequency is shown in Table 3.6, which displays her findings for *ice, mice, slice,* and *lice* in the order in which she argues the diphthongized forms have developed (Ogura 1987: 64).[2] The frequency counts are based on the *American Heritage Word Frequency Book* (Carroll et al. 1971). From these data alone, it is clear that lexical diffusion must be taking place, since such phonetically similar words do not pattern identically. Ogura did not claim word frequency effects for this portion of the shift, but there is some indication word frequency may play a role in any case. In Table 3.6, I have divided the reflexes into two groups: the earlier stages ([iː] through [æː]) and the later stages ([ai] through [ɔ̈i]). Under each lexeme, the

72 Word Frequency and Lexical Diffusion

Table 3.6 Development of Middle English /iː/ (based on Ogura 1987: 64)

	ice	mice	slice	lice
Frequency	176.94	33.83	13.44	1.96
iː		5		7
ïi		8		2
ei		1	1	1
əi	31	33	34	35
ɛi	5	11	9	14
ɛ̈i	8	7	8	8
æi	15	13	15	14
æː	4	3		2
Total earlier stages	**63**	**81**	**67**	**83**
ai	85	79	91	78
aː	1	1		1
ɑi	59	53	51	45
ɑː	2	5	4	6
ɒi	34	37	34	37
ʌi	23	19	19	21
ɔi	33	25	30	27
ʌ̈i		1		1
ɔ̈i	11	10	15	12
Total later stages	**248**	**230**	**244**	**228**
% Sites with later stages	**79.7**	**74.0**	**78.5**	**73.3**

subtotal for each group was calculated, and the percentage of forms which have advanced to the later stages is given in the last row. Certainly the most frequent word in this group, *ice*, has the highest percentage of the advanced forms, 79.7 percent; and *lice*, the least frequent word, has the lowest percentage, 73.3 percent. And the two word pairs that are most similar phonetically, *ice/mice* and *slice/lice*, also evidence that the more frequent word is more advanced in more dialects: *ice* in 79.7 percent versus *mice* in 74 percent, and *slice* in 78.5 percent versus *lice* in 73.3 percent.

As for Middle English /uː/, Ogura (1987) says that "it seems that word frequency plays a role within a narrow phonetic class. When we look at the vowel in final position, before [s], [θ], [z], and [x], [more] words with high frequency show the later stages than those with low frequency" (p. 44), and that some "dialects of Northern English...show a diphthong [əu] or [ɛu] in *house* but [uː] in *mouse* and *louse*" (p. 110). Labov (1992, 1994) attributes the differences in some dialects between the pronunciations of *mouse* and *louse* to dialect borrowing, which Ogura

The Lexical Diffusion of Phonetically Gradual Changes 73

(1995: 49) refutes, giving the example of [aː] for *mouse* just south of Westmorland as an example of a pronunciation which does not occur in any neighboring region. Table 3.7 displays the percentage for the later stages from the data given by Ogura (1987: 64) for the development of Middle English /uː/ before /s, θ, z, x/. Before the voiced fricative /z/, there were no two phonetically similar words from the same word class to compare. Before each of the voiceless fricatives, however, the more or most frequent word – *house, south,* or *bough* – is, indeed, more likely to contain the more developed form: *house* at 58.6 percent versus the much less frequent *mouse* and *louse* at 53.8 and 55.1 percent, respectively; *south* at 58.2 percent versus the less frequent *mouth* at 55.8 percent; and *bough* at 51.6 percent versus the less frequent *plough* at 48.6 percent.[3]

The question becomes what connects this shift with the other changes that affect the most frequent words first. Stockwell and Minkova (1988: 376) suggest that the earliest stage was a result of assimilation:

Table 3.7 Development of Middle English /uː/ by phonetic environment and dialect (based on Ogura 1987: 90)

	__s#			__θ#		__x#	
	house	mouse	louse	south	mouth	bough	plough
Frequency	533.18	37.18	0.11	255.61	129.21	2.18	0.28
uː	33	33	33	33	32	33	40
ʊu	5	4	5	7	7	8	10
ou	1	1				5	1
əu	28	35	35	32	34	31	31
ɔu	1	2	2	1	1	5	1
ʌu	8	6	7	5	8	9	6
ɒu	1	2	2	1	2	2	2
ɒː		1					
Subtotal, earlier stages	77	84	84	79	84	93	91
au	52	45	52	46	51	52	34
aə	5	3				1	
aː	10	5	6	20	8	3	1
æu	42	44	45	44	47	43	51
æa		1					
Subtotal, later stages	109	98	103	110	106	99	86
% Sites with later stages	58.6	53.8	55.1	58.2	55.8	51.6	48.6

74 *Word Frequency and Lexical Diffusion*

Loss of friction in the post-vocalic fricative glides of Old English words like *twiges, tigel, nigon*; and *fugol, sugu, bugan*, generated [ii] and [uu], or more likely [ɪi] and [ʊu], which remained in the system at first as free variant forms of [iː] and [uː]. The former were gradually favored at the expense of the latter; by Chaucer's time, it is likely that all instances of putative long high vowels were already diphthongal and that, in advanced dialects, glide optimization had begun.

Perhaps significantly, this diphthongization and its later developments did not involve a merger. Only a new phonetic realization of the phoneme has been involved at each stage of the shift. Unlike the earliest stage, [iː] > [ɪi], for the later stages Stockwell (2002: 269) suggests a perceptual basis, namely

that the center drift through the sequence [ij] to [əj] to [ɔj] (Cockney) or [aː] (Southern American] – and similarly for the corresponding back diphthong – is plausibly motivated in the dissimilatory stages (i.e., as it gets further from [ij] and closer to [ɔj]) by perceptual optimization of the diphthong followed at the assimilatory stage by articulatory optimization.... [I]t is a phonetically conditioned low-level drift, not in principle different from the development of intervocalic flapping of /t/ or /d/ in *latter–ladder*, or of nasalization in *can't* and *don't*.

He bases his explanation on Boersma's (1998: 413) observation that

If a language has a single diphthong, its primary perceptual feature may well be its **diphthongal character** (e.g., the presence of an unspecified F_1 fall), by which it is contrasted with all the other vowels. Lowering of the first part of the diphthong amounts to enhancing the contrast with the other vowels: the more the two parts of the diphthong differ from one another, the more they will contribute to the diphthongal character.[4]

Minkova and Stockwell (2003) have translated their understanding of the phonetic underpinnings, both in perception and production, of vowel shifts into four Optimality Theoretic constraints:

"IDENT IO (Contrast): Preserve categorial contrasts" (p. 184) is a cover term for avoiding mergers.

The Lexical Diffusion of Phonetically Gradual Changes 75

"HEAR CLEAR: Maximize the auditory distance between the nuclear vowel and the following glide (measured in formant frequency)" (p. 173) is perceptually motivated.

"MINIMAL DISTANCE (MINDIST): Maximize the auditory distinctiveness of contrasts" (p. 182) is also perceptually motivated.

"EFFORT: An articulation which requires more effort is disfavored" (p. 179) accounts for economy of effort in production.

Nucleus–glide dissimilation, nucleus–glide assimilation, chain shifting, and merger are each seen as dependent upon different rankings of these constraints (p. 186).

Phillips (1984) suggested that all changes affecting the most frequent words first had their basis in the articulatory processes of the language – the kind of gestural overlap and reduction that leads to assimilation, reduction, and deletion. But when viewed from the perspective of implementation of a sound change within a usage-based model whose lexical entries contain phonetic detail and are connected to words with similar phonetic shape, from which connections larger phonological units emerge, processes of perceptual optimization logically are implemented in the same way. That is, there is no need to access more abstract units such as syllables or phonotactic generalizations in order to implement the change. The changes that affect the most frequent words all require very shallow access, just of the phonetic forms of the words. The network that associates the various words allows the change to spread to similar words, and the more frequently those words are encountered/produced the greater chance there is for the innovation to spread – whether that innovation has an articulatory or a perceptual basis.

3.1.5 Summary

In sum, phonetically gradual sound changes that affect the most frequent words first appear to be those whose basis lies in fine phonetic detail, including the overlap of articulatory gestures typical of assimilatory and reductive processes, as well as "perceptual optimization" of the type found in the further development of the diphthongal reflexes of [ɪi] and [ɔu]. These processes seem typical of what Labov (1994: 534) calls "low-level output rules" and Chambers (1995: 249) calls "primitive processes" – a term taken from Braine (1974: 285) with respect to language acquisition and natural phonology. Chambers identifies these "primitive processes" with regular sound changes, leaving lexical diffusion to affect "learned processes." But since these sound changes are lexically

76 *Word Frequency and Lexical Diffusion*

diffused, Chambers's hypothesis does not hold, nor does Labov's identification of neogrammarian change with low-level output rules (1994: 534).

3.2 Gradual changes affecting the least frequent words first

All of the changes examined thus far in this chapter have affected the most frequent words first, and for a century after Schuchardt made his claim that this was true of all sound changes, no examples were brought forward to dispel this notion. Evidence now exists, however, that the least frequent words change first in the progression of some sound changes. If changes which affect the most frequent words require no access to more sophisticated structures than surface phonetic forms, then one should expect changes which affect the least frequent words to require such access, that is, a deeper level of lexical analysis. That this is so will be shown in four sound changes: glide deletion in words such as *tune, duke*, and *news*; deletion of the initial aspirate in /hn, hr, hl, hw/ clusters; Middle English /ø(:)/ unrounding; and Old English vowel lengthening before homorganic consonant clusters.

3.2.1 Glide deletion in Southern American English

The first study to document a sound change affecting the least frequent words first was Phillips (1981), which investigated the deletion of /j/ between alveolar stops and a following /u/ in Southern American English (hereafter SAE). At that time, the deletion of this glide was well underway; Stephenson (1970), in fact, reported on the differences between his 20 undergraduates (average age 21.3 years) and his 16 graduate students (averaging 40 years), all native white Southerners, mostly from Georgia, finding that the older speakers preserved [ju] 75 percent of the time – "12 instances of [tjun], 4 instances of [tun]; 11 instances of [djuk], 5 of [duk]; 13 instances of [njuz], 3 of [nuz]" – whereas the younger speakers preserved the [j] only 55 percent of the time – "12 instances of [tjun], 8 instances of [tun]; 10 instances of [djuk], 10 of [duk]; 11 instances of [njuz], 9 of [nuz]" (p. 299). Phillips (1981) taped 60 native Georgian students, aged 18–21, reading a list of 100 words, in which were embedded 30 words of varying frequencies which could potentially have the glide. In the final analysis, *tumult* was discarded, however, because of its unfamiliarity to most of the students, shown by only 21 responding with [tuməlt] or [tjuməlt], the rest responding with [tʌməlt]. Table 3.8(a) summarizes her results, based

The Lexical Diffusion of Phonetically Gradual Changes 77

Table 3.8(a) Southern American English glide deletion (based on Phillips 1981: 74)

Frequency group	Words	Average % glideless pronunciations
0–1	nude, Tudor, tuber, tunic, dues, neutron, duly, tuba, dude	74.4
1–10	nutrient, tutor, duel, duke, durable, tulip, dune, nuisance, neutral, nucleus	71.8
11–100	Tuesday, numerous, tune, duty, numeral, due, tube	60.1
101–500	knew, during	54.5
997	new	43.0

on frequencies per million tokens provided by the *American Heritage Word Frequency Book* (Carroll et al. 1971).

In order to demonstrate that SAE glide deletion was indeed a change in progress and not due to age-grading or the residue of an arrested sound change, Phillips (1994) replicated the experiment, using native speakers from one rural county in south Georgia (Telfair County), divided into two groups: 24 older speakers aged 66–88 and 26 younger speakers aged 13–19. Speakers who, in the postexperiment interview, expressed an awareness of the /ju/ versus /u/ distinction and a preference for one pronunciation over the other, were omitted from the study. The results are presented in Table 3.8(b), which makes it clear that this is indeed

Table 3.8(b) Southern English glide deletion in apparent time (based on Phillips 1994: 118–19)

Frequency group	Words	Average % glideless pronunciations	
		Older group, 66–88 years	Younger group, 13–19 years
0–1	nude, Tudor, tuber, tunic, dues, neutron, duly, tuba, dude	59.4	69.8
1–10	nutrient, tutor, duel, duke, durable, tulip, dune, nuisance, neutral, nucleus	39.3	73.3
11–100	Tuesday, numerous, tune, duty, numeral, due, tube	19.0	54.1
101–1000	knew, during, new	11.3	53.0

78 *Word Frequency and Lexical Diffusion*

a change in progress. In fact, the change seems to be progressing in a typical S-curve. That is, the loss of /j/ seems in its earlier stage to affect a smaller portion of words, especially the least frequent ones, first. As the change spreads across the lexicon, differences between the frequency groups narrow. One might expect a later stage of the change to reveal all of the words as having been affected, save a few very frequent ones.[5]

Bybee (2000b: 82) suggested that the least frequent words being affected in this change might be due to "dialect borrowing or accommodation to the standard dialect. Words learned at the mother's knee, so to speak, would be the most conservative, while the least frequent words would be affected first." It is true that the glideless pronunciation is characteristic of the North and North Midlands, whereas the glided pronunciation is typical of the South Midlands and South, both traceable to folk speech in different parts of England, the glideless variety from "some of the Home Counties and of East Anglia" and the glided variety from "the western counties, supported by Standard British usage," according to Kurath and McDavid (1961: 174), who also report a third pronunciation, with /iu/ "is largely confined to New England and the Yankee settlements to the west. It is especially common in folk speech, but is also used by some cultured speakers in New England (not in Upstate New York, it seems)." The prestige factor of the glideless pronunciation is unclear. Not only does Standard British English maintain the glide, but within the United States, Pitts (1986) finds that

> both the glided and glideless variants are prestigious, but each for a different group of speakers. Glidelessness is valued by speakers only now gaining a place in broadcasting – women, local Southern announcers, and perhaps blacks, all of whom still face linguistic discrimination in the media. In the meantime, the better-established white non-Southern male announcers . . . are adopting or maintaining the glide in a limited set of words, especially the item *news*, and sometimes the *consumer* subclass.

One way that Phillips (1994) responded to the suggestion of dialect borrowing was to exclude participants who, in a postexperiment interview, expressed a preference for one variant over the other. Surprisingly few participants did express such a preference. In fact, during this interview, most would ask which one was the "correct" form. Such an attitude seems to reflect Niedzielski and Preston's (2000: 95) finding that although Northern speakers are prejudiced against Southern speakers, "Southerners do not express rampant insecurity. ... [T]hey rate themselves very high for pleasantness and Northerners very low." Another sign that Southerners are not just borrowing the pronunciation from Northerners is that in other areas of the phonology, Southerners are clearly following their own distinct paths: the Southern Vowel Shift is very different from the Northern Cities Vowel Shift and Georgia Southerners do not partake of the *caught–cot* merger (Labov 1991). So borrowing from an outside, higher-prestige dialect in this case seems very unlikely, although as Milroy (1999: 22) points out, "A recurrent difficulty that empirical studies face is that... variation within a variety can never be absolutely conclusively shown to be wholly internally motivated and distributed, however probable such internal origin may be in some instances." Nevertheless, once the implementation stage of the change begins, in order for it to spread, it must of necessity disperse from speaker to speaker within the speech community. Speakers within the fairly homogeneous speech community of Telfair County, Georgia, are spreading the change in a clear pattern, beginning with the least frequent words and advancing to the more frequent words.

As another response to the suggestion that this change was dialect borrowing, Phillips (1994) incorporated a measure of phonetic gradualness, since as Holder (1990: 75) points out, "discreteness or phonetic abruptness has been proposed as the property which most typically distinguishes borrowed variants from sound change." Phillips (1994) therefore had each of three listeners indicate along a 5-centimeter line the extent to which a glide was noticeable, which lines were then divided into 10 segments. Not only were the more frequent words rated as more "glideful," but this result held even when the results were divided into narrower phonetic environments, as shown in Table 3.9. The only word that does not fit the pattern perfectly is *during*, which is the only preposition and the only word in its most frequent group after /d/. Chapter 4 will investigate more thoroughly the role of word class on sound changes. Here, perhaps it will suffice to note that all of the words in the first listed phonetic environment, namely after /t/, are nouns, and clearly show the least frequent words also being the least glideful. That is, the least frequent words are changing first in a phonetically gradual sound change.

It remains to explain why this sound change should affect the least frequent words first. It is a gradual deletion, as were the deletions of final t/d and of schwa recounted above. Yet those had a clear phonetic basis. That [j] deletion is not simply a complete assimilation to the stop may be seen in the behavior of a sound change acting counter to it in Southern US speech. That is, very frequent words, such as *Tuesday*, often

80 *Word Frequency and Lexical Diffusion*

Table 3.9 Phonetic gradualness of glide deletion by initial phoneme (based on Phillips 1994: 125)

Frequency	Words grouped by initial consonant	Average glidefulness
0–1	Tudor, tuber, tunic, tuba	7.69
1–10	tutor, tulip	6.94
11–100	Tuesday, tune, tube	4.75
0–1	dues, duly, dude	6.70
1–10	duel, duke, durable, dune	6.19
11–100	duty, due	4.99
361	during	5.23
0–1	nude, neutron	7.35
1–10	nutrient, nuisance, neutral, nucleus	6.38
11–100	numerous, numeral	5.01
101–1000	knew, new	3.95

are pronounced with an initial affricate, as in [tʃuzdi], a phonetic process of assibilation, which in most dialects of English affected alveolar-stop + [j] clusters word-internally, as in *Christian* and *creatures*. Clearly, then, some more abstract constraint must be affecting initial /tj, dj, nj/ clusters in the Southern US.

Cooley (1978: 127–30) argues that the deletion of /j/ is intricately tied to the phonotactic patterns of English. She sees the historical basis of this deletion as the disruption of surface phonetic constraints caused by the introduction of the glide in this position when earlier [iu] became [ju], a disruption of the sequences of consonants that were admissible prevocalically in sixteenth-century English: SPIRANTS + STOPS + NASALS/LIQUIDS/SEMIVOWELS. New clusters such as [knj], [rj], and [strj] violated these constraints, leading to two different results. One was the reassignment of nasals to the second position, with the other stops, which led to the dropping of [k] and [g] before nasals, as in *knight* and *gnaw*. The other "repair strategy" was to delete [j] after coronal nasals and liquids. Therefore [j] was lost earliest after [l] and [r], especially in clusters, as in *blew* and *grew*. The rule then spread to the other coronal consonants, [t, d, n] being the last affected. Of course, this same sequence of events could be accounted for without appealing to teleology. Psycholinguistic experiments have documented not just that speakers know the permissible phonotactic sequences of their language, but that they also know the probability of those sequences and apply these to acceptability judgments. Jusczyk et al. (1994), for instance, demonstrated that even nine-month-olds can discriminate frequent

The Lexical Diffusion of Phonetically Gradual Changes   81

from infrequent CVC sequences. In addition, Vitevitch et al. (1997) found that not only did speakers repeat nonsense words containing frequent phonotactic patterns more quickly than ones containing less frequent patterns, but also that the more frequently a phonotactic sequence occurred in English, the more likely English speakers were to deem nonsense words containing that sequence as more like English words. Vitevitch et al. (2004) followed up on this work to see if, in naming tasks, speakers would react more quickly to real words which contained high-probability phonotactic sequences. They found that "words with high phonotactic probability were produced more quickly than words with low phonotactic probability" (p. 524). Words with initial /d, n, t/ + vowel are without a doubt much more frequent than words beginning with /dj, nj, tj/ + vowel.[6] Significantly, these findings explain why this sound change behaves like analogical changes, say in morphology, where type frequency is a predictor of productivity and the least frequent words are the first to change (Baayen and Lieber 1991; Bybee 1985, 2001; Moder 1992; Wang and Derwing 1994).

The implementation of this change, then, proceeds as follows: With more familiar words, such as *Tuesday* or *during*, Southern speakers have the glided pronunciation more entrenched in memory. Unfamiliar words, such as *tumor* or *duel*, are not so entrenched (i.e. have less lexical strength) and thus undergo more analysis in production, which reveals a phonotactic constraint disfavoring coronal + /j/ clusters, an emergent generalization from the connections formed with phonetically similar words. The productivity of this sound change is encouraged by the type frequency of glideless onsets, and it affects the least frequent words first because, like analogical changes, it occurs "where memory fails" (Anttila 1972: 101).

In sum, the implementation of postalveolar /j/-loss in the English of south Georgia seems most likely related to the language's phonotactic constraints, which are abstractions drawn from the surface phonetics of the language. For them to affect, in turn, the surface phonetics requires a level of lexical analysis on the part of the speakers. Hence /j/-dropping behaves like analogical changes, affecting the least frequent words first.

3.2.2   Other consonant deletions/reductions

There is additional evidence that other consonant deletions based on phonotactic structure affect the least frequent words first. Toon (1976a), for instance, looks at the loss in early Old English of /h/ in the initial

82 *Word Frequency and Lexical Diffusion*

consonant clusters /hn, hr, hl, hw/. Tables 3.10 and 3.11 display his figures for the appearance of ≪h≫ in two tenth-century Old English manuscripts for words which etymologically contained /h/. The gospels referred to as *Rushworth 1*, reflecting the Mercian dialect (Coates 1997), and the glosses to the *Lindisfarne Gospels* reflect the Northumbrian dialect (Hogg 1992a: 5). The environments which contain enough data stretching over a range of frequencies indicate invariably that the least frequent words have lost the /h/ first. Specifically, in *Rushworth 1*, for /hr/ the average percentage of loss in word forms with frequencies 1–10 is 49 percent versus 10 percent for word forms with higher frequencies; for /hw/, the difference is 43.3 percent versus 16.3 percent. In the *Lindisfarne* glosses, /hw/ is never reduced, but the average for low-frequency words beginning with /hr/ is 46.7 percent versus high-frequency 6.5 percent; and for /hl/, it is 100 percent versus 8.3 percent.

Table 3.10 Rushworth 1 loss of /h/ (Toon 1976a: 616–17)

	Total	h-ful	h-less	Percentage h-less	Average h-less > 10, < 10
/hn/					
naescum	1	0	1	100	
genaged	1	0	1	100	
nett	1	0	1	100	
nutu	1	0	1	100	
gehynscet	1	1	0	0	80
/hr/					
ruxlende	1	0	1	100	
(h)reoweþ	3	2	1	33	
(h)read	6	5	1	17	**49**
(h)raþe	14	12	2	14	
(h)raegl	17	16	1	6	**10**
/hl/					
(h)laferd	10	8	2	80	80
/hw/					
welpas	1	0	1	100	
(h)waer	6	5	1	17	
(h)wile	8	7	1	13	**43.3**
(h)weorfan	14	8	6	43	
(h)wa	22	21	1	5	
(h)wilce	24	23	1	4	**16.3**

(h) = variable /h/.

The Lexical Diffusion of Phonetically Gradual Changes 83

Table 3.11 *Lindisfarne* loss of /h/ (Toon 1976a: 617)

	Total	h-ful	h-less	Percentage h-less	Average h-less 1–10, 10–89
/hn/					
(h)naese	4	3	1	25	25
/hr/					
rining	1	0	1	100	
(h)riofol	5	4	1	20	
(h)reaf	10	8	2	20	**46.7**
(h)raþe	20	18	2	10	
(h)reownisse	29	28	1	3	**6.5**
/hl/					
lutorlic	1	0	1	100	
lyding	1	0	1	100	
lutorlic	1	0	1	100	**100**
(h)lioniga	12	10	2	17	
(h)laferd	58	57	1	2	
(h)laf	89	84	5	6	**8.3**

(h) = etymological /h/.

Word class no doubt plays a role in this change, with function words resisting /hw/ > /w/, but even for them, the least frequent words had changed first in *Rushworth 1* – 15 percent versus 4.5 percent – as shown in Table 3.12.

Lutz (1991: 19–73; 1993: 289) describes the ways in which the loss of preconsonantal /h/ was phonotactically motivated, being influenced by factors such as syllable- and word-position, accent position, and neighboring consonants, as well as by pragmatic/prosodic conditions. Lutz (1988: 230) summarizes the historical relationship of /h + /C/ clusters with other word-initial clusters:

Table 3.12 *Rushworth 1* /hw/ > /w/ by word class (Toon 1976a: 616–17)

/hw/ Function words:	Total	h-ful	h-less	Percentage h-less	Average h-less 1–10, 10–24
(h)waer	6	5	1	17	
(h)wile	8	7	1	13	**15.0**
(h)wa	22	21	1	5	
(h)wilce	24	23	1	4	**4.5**

84 *Word Frequency and Lexical Diffusion*

The relative chronology of the simplification of word-initial clusters in English ... depends to a great extent on the strength relation between the two consonants of the clusters concerned. The further away this strength relation is from the preferred structure of initial clusters, the sooner these clusters become simplified. As regards the clusters beginning with /h/, which were simplified earliest, we can assume that the strength relation deteriorated as a result of a general weakening of /h/ over the centuries. In the case of the other consonants which were lost in word-initial clusters, namely /w/, /f/, /g/, and /k/, we cannot attribute their loss to such a general weakening process, but have to assume a general tendency towards erosion of initial clusers with an unfavourable strength relation in the history of English.

That the loss of /h/ in these clusters included gradient pronunciations is indicated in the *Lindisfarne Glosses* by the "frequent insertion of the sign for *spiritus asper* (|-) instead of ≪h-≫ before /-r-, -l-, -n-/," which Minkova (2003: 342) notes "can be seen as a reaction to different allophonic realizations before vowels and before sonorants." In fact, Lutz (1993: 286–7) identifies five ways in which it is clear that preconsonantal /h/ (< Gmc. /x/) was of interest to the scribe, Aldred: (1) noticeably frequent absence of ≪h≫ for etymological /h/; (2) frequent unetymological use of ≪h≫; (3) the use of "half h" (⊢), both in place of etymological and unetymological /h/; (4) the writing of ≪ ⊢≫ and ≪h≫ in especially small script above the line; (5) corrections, such as, for instance, the addition or erasure of ≪ ⊢≫ or ≪h≫. These practices make it clear that subphonemic differences were indeed salient to the scribe, salient enough for him to take care in his recording of them. It is unfortunate that Toon's study, based on Cook's (1894) edition, did not differentiate between the different types of *h* that appear in the manuscript. But it does nonetheless seem likely that this sound change is another example of a phonetically gradual change that has affected the least frequent words first.[7]

3.2.3 Middle English unrounding of /ø(:)/

Another type of sound change that has been documented as affecting the least frequent words first is the vowel change indicated by Early Middle English spellings in ≪e≫ for Old English ≪eo≫. In Old English, the digraph could represent either a short or a long diphthong Hogg (1992b: 87), phonemically /e:o/ or /eo/.[8] These diphthongs were

The Lexical Diffusion of Phonetically Gradual Changes 85

monophthongized "toward the end of the OE period" to /øː/ and /ø/, respectively, an interpretation "confirmed by the Anglo-Norman influenced spellings ≪ue, oe, o≫ in e[arly] M[iddle] E[nglish]" (Hogg 1992a: 215).[9] In the *Ormulum* manuscript, a series of homilies in rhymeless septenary verse comprising slightly more than 10,000 lines written in or near Lincolnshire around the year AD 1180, spellings in ≪eo≫ by the scribe Orm are considered to represent that /ø(ː)/.[10] Orm himself became aware at some point of the inconsistency of his spellings for OE ≪eo≫. Only one spelling in ≪eo≫ occurs after line 1384, nor does it occur in the "Dedication" and "Preface," which is taken as evidence that those portions of the manuscript were written last. In fact, Orm tried to go back and "correct" his earlier spellings in ≪eo≫, but a trace of the ≪o≫ remained, so the standard edition of the *Ormulum*, White and Holt's (1878), preserves Orm's original spellings.[11] In addition, several ≪eo≫ spellings which were overlooked by White and Holt have been identified by Holm (1922) and Burchfield (1956) and are included in the tabulations below, while inserted leaves which contain only ≪e≫ spellings have been omitted, as have all lines after line 13,000. The data are taken from Phillips (1984), and other limitations on the study are detailed there. The word classes that contained the most tokens are displayed in Tables 3.13 and 3.14.

In all three cases, the least frequent words have the higher percentage of spellings in ≪e≫. That this sound change was not based on

Table 3.13 Development in the *Ormulum* of /øː/ > /eː/ (Phillips 1984: 328)

Word class	Frequency	Words	Average % ≪e≫
Verbs	2–10	beodeþþ, forrbedeþþ, secnedd, nedenn, chesenn, fleʒhenn, cneolenn, wex, freollsenn, forrleosenn, (bi)reowenn, steorenn, dreʒhenn, forrseon	69
	11–47	leʒhenn, cneow, fell, fleon, heold, ʒede, streonenn	68
	69	seon 'see'	52
	355	beon 'be'	41
Nouns	1–8	breostlin, derrlinng, þeos, leo, fend, wheol, heowe, fe(hh), freond	49
	21–47	deor, leom, treo, stron, leod	6
	68–82	preost, þeod	4
	158	deofell	1

86 *Word Frequency and Lexical Diffusion*

Table 3.14 Development in the *Ormulum* of /ø/ > /e/ (Phillips 1984: 328)

Word class	Frequency	Words	Average % «e»
Nouns	1–2	berrhless, dorrf(like), barm, sede(full)	75
	26–90	weorrc, weorelld, heorrte	46
	154	heofenn	6

articulatory factors such as assimilation is shown by the fact that the incidence of «e» spellings is no greater in environments that might discourage unrounding of /ø(ː)/, such as a preceding or following /w/, than in those that might encourage it. For the short vowel, the percentage of forms with -we- is 65 percent versus 62 percent «e» overall. (There were no forms with -e(o)w-.) For the long vowel, even more vowels show unrounding in the environment of /w/: 73 percent with -we- and 56 percent with -ew-, versus 52 percent «e» overall (Phillips 1984: 330–1). Similarly, distance assimilation was ruled out by determining that an unrounded vowel in the following syllable showed no effect (p. 331). Also, Antonsen's suggestion (1961: 229) that the sound change involved not unrounding, but fronting, was considered, but the anteriority of the preceding or following consonant was also shown to exert no influence (p. 331, fn. 5). Therefore, some other motivation behind this shift must exist.

Phillips (1984) suggests that the motivation might be typological, namely, that as the only front rounded vowels in the phonological system of Orm's dialect – /y(ː)/ having already unrounded to /i(ː)/ – /øː/ and /ø/ were subjected to a constraint against rounded front vowels. Bybee (2001: 82), however, submits that the unrounding might be due to the perceptual difficulty in acquiring rounded front vowels:

In a discrimination learning task, Gilbert and Wyman (1975) found that five-, six-, and seven-year-old English-speaking and French-speaking children had more trouble discriminating [œ] than any of the other three vowels tested, which were [ɛ], [a], and [o]. The most frequent confusion for nonnasalized vowels was between [œ] and [ɛ]. These findings suggest that the vowel [œ] may be difficult to acquire for perceptual reasons. We could therefore reason that a word with a front rounded vowel must be highly available in the input to be acquired correctly. Thus, the Old English pattern of lexical diffusion described by Phillips could be explained as the correct acquisition of

/œ:/ and /œ/ in high-frequency nouns and verbs, but the failure to acquire the same vowels in words of low frequency.

Bybee's explanation accounts for the **innovation** stage of /ø(:)/ unrounding, why unrounding should begin in words of low frequency, and perhaps why there is such a common constraint against front mid rounded vowels. That this **innovation** led to a change is partly dependent upon the higher type frequency of the unrounded vowel, which would contribute to the productivity of the shift. The **implementation** of the shift, however, also required social embedding and propagation from speaker to speaker; that is, its implementation depended upon speakers' selection of the unrounded vowel when the phonetic word form was not well entrenched in memory, that is, when memory failed, as with analogical changes (Anttila 1972: 101). In other words, during speech production, the speaker could not easily access the phonetic shape of the word form and therefore relied on a deeper analysis requiring access to the segmental constraints of the language, revealing a stochastic constraint (based on the preponderance of unrounded front vowels) favoring the unrounded front mid vowel over the rounded one.

3.2.4 Old English lengthening before -*ld*, -*nd*, etc.

In Old English, at an indeterminate date, vowels lengthened before the consonant clusters -*ld*, -*nd*, -*ng*, -*mb*, -*rd*, -*rþ*, -*rn*, and -*rl*, a change that did not occur if a third consonant followed, resulting in different vowels for Modern English pairs such as *child* ~ *children* and *kind* ~ *kindred*. The lengthening was also not consistent for all the clusters listed above (compare modern *lamb* with a lax vowel versus *comb* with a tense vowel, and *wind* v. versus *wind* n.). Jones (1989: 30–1) notes accented spellings in the northern *Lindisfarne Gospels* (*c.* AD 975) that "appear to confirm the 'patchy' nature of the *homorganic lengthening* rule," captured more fully in the *Ormulum* manuscript (*c.* AD 1180). The scribe, Orm, devised his own spelling system and included lines admonishing anyone who copied his work to be careful to write the letters exactly as he had written them, earning him the epithet of the first spelling reformer in English. The main device he uses is to double consonants after short vowels, so the first vowel in *bocstaff* 'letter' is long and the second short, as they were in Old English. This device proves invaluable in indicating for us the progression of vowel lengthening before the above consonant clusters, and the *Ormulum* provides 225 such words appearing in 5419 tokens, excluding proper names, words not descended from Old

88 *Word Frequency and Lexical Diffusion*

English, words where the pertinent vowel is in unstressed syllables (-*inng* 'ing,' -*ennde* 'ing,' *weorelld* 'world'), and words subject to shortening processes (i.e. if the short vowel preceded either three consonants or two lesser stressed syllables).

Chapter 4 will provide evidence that this sound change was clearly influenced by word class, and in some phonetic environments – e.g. -*ld*, and two-syllable nouns ending in -*ell* or -*err(n)* – the sound change had already affected all the pertinent words in the *Ormulum*. But within other word classes and phonetic environments, especially -*nd* and -*ng*, word frequency effects are clear, as shown in Tables 3.15(a) and (b), where the average frequency of verbs, excluding auxiliaries, containing

Table 3.15(a) Average frequency in the *Ormulum* of nonauxiliary verbs containing changed (long) vs. unchanged (short) vowels before -*nd*

	Changed	Variable	Unchanged
-ind	24.0	–*	–
-e(o)nd	13.3	27.5	38.0
-ænd	–	–	–
-and	31.5	–	80.0
-ond	–	–	–
-und	28.7	–	–

* *finndenn* (1×) next to *findenn* (74×) is considered aberrant.

Table 3.15(b) Average frequency in the *Ormulum* of nonauxiliary verbs containing changed (long) vs. unchanged (short) vowels before -*ng*

	Changed	Variable	Unchanged
-ing	2.2	–	26
-e(o)ng	6.25*	4.0**	–
-æng	–	–	–
-ang	2.0	–	11.5***
-ong	–	–	–
-ung	2.6	–	–

* For calculating this number, *unnderrfengenn* and *onnfengenn* were counted as two separate word groups, contra Phillips (1983a).
** *heng* (1×), *henngedd* (3×).
*** *unnderrfangenn* (1×) is treated as aberrant, next to usual *unnderrfanngenn* (11×).

The Lexical Diffusion of Phonetically Gradual Changes 89

the lengthened vowels before *-nd* and *-ng* may be compared with the average frequency of verbs retaining the original short vowels, and similarly in Table 3.15(c) with nouns in *-nd* (the vowels in *-ng* nouns having all been lengthened). Word forms related by inflection, derivation, or compounding that did not affect the word class or the meaning of the base morpheme were considered as one word group. Also, if there was only one instance of a variant spelling against multiple instances of the usual spelling, the variant was considered aberrant and not counted, such exceptions being indicated below each table. Since ≪eo≫ also alternates with ≪e≫ in the *Ormulum*, reflecting a merger in progress at the time, as discussed above, words containing those alternate spellings are treated together. For instance, among the verbs containing postvocalic *-e(o)nd*, three indicate a long vowel (*blendeþþ, endenn, lendenn*), two vary in their vowel (*shendenn/shenndenn, wendenn/wenndenn*), and two indicate a short vowel (*brennd, senndenn*). Some differences are striking: *brinngenn* (51×) versus *ringenn* (5×), *senndenn* (68×) versus *endenn* (25×), *turrnenn* (119×) versus all other verbs in /rn/ (*eornenn* (17×), *ȝ(e)ornenn* (39×), *le(o)rnenn* (22×), *bærnenn* (7×)). At other times, individual lexical items fail to follow the expected pattern; for instance, of nouns in *-nd*, only the frequent *hand* (48×) has resisted the lengthening, reserving half its attestations with the unchanged short vowel, yet the even more frequent *land* (119×) never has a short vowel, a difference perhaps attributable to the fact that in daily conversation *hand* was no doubt more frequently used than *land*, as it is in Modern English, for which the CELEX database reports *hand* as having a lexeme frequency almost three times as great as that of *land* – 12,983 versus 4628.

Table 3.15(c) Average frequency in the *Ormulum* of nouns containing changed (long) vs. unchanged (short) vowels before *-nd*

	Changed	Variable	Unchanged
-ind	47.3		
-e(o)nd	58.0*		
-ænd	–	–	–
-and	19.4	48.0	
-ond	–	–	–
-und	5.6		

* *ennde* (1×) next to *ende* (112×) is considered aberrant.

90 *Word Frequency and Lexical Diffusion*

Why this sound change should have a stronger effect on the least frequent words is at first puzzling. It seems it might be a natural phonetic process. In fact, Ritt (1994: 111) goes so far as to claim,

> It seems to be a universal that duration of vowels depends on the sonority of the subsequent consonants. The effects of this tendency can be observed quite clearly in Modern English, but it also seems to hold – albeit not quite as obviously – for German (cf. Meyer 1903), Spanish (cf. Zimmermann and Sapon 1958), Norwegian (cf. Fintoft 1961), French, Russian or Korean (for all three cf. Chen 1970)....

Such studies led Phillips (1981, 1983a: 880–1) and Jones (1989: 32–3) to posit a phonetic basis for this lengthening.[12] Yet for other phonetically motivated changes, the most frequent words have been shown to change first. Therefore, it seems likely that some more abstract structural constraint is affecting the lexical diffusion of this shift, at least in its later stages for the environments detailed above.

Hogg (1992a: 211–14), who dates the lengthening as *c*. ninth century, sees this and other quantitative shifts in Old English as part of a tendency that has existed since the prehistory of English, namely the bimoric requirement of the rhyme constituent of stressed syllables, which is to say that the rhyme of such syllables "must be at least bimoric, that is, contain either a long vowel (or diphthong) or a short vowel (or diphthong) followed by a consonant in the same syllable" (p. 211). On this view, the motivation behind lengthening before liquid or nasal + homorganic voiced consonant clusters is "to equalize the lengths of stress feet, in this case by the lengthening of short stressed syllables."[13] For this theory to work, however, such consonant clusters must have had "a special status in syllable structure, in that their behaviour was more akin to that of a single consonant than that of a bimoric cluster," a position strengthened by later "M[iddle] E[nglish] changes such as the loss of certain voiced stops after a preceding resonant, such as in *lamb*, and also from the phonotactics of PDE syllables, see, for example, Hogg and McCully (1987: 45–7)."

Hogg's explanation for vowel lengthening before these clusters would, in fact, fit with the theory that sound changes more readily affecting the least frequent words include those which require lexical analysis beyond the surface phonetics of each word. The less frequent words would be affected when recourse to syllable structure was involved, as in the original lengthening, and the more frequent words would remain when those syllable structure constraints were ignored. That this sound

The Lexical Diffusion of Phonetically Gradual Changes   91

change in Old English does not represent an isolated phenomenon is suggested by the findings of Morin et al. (1990), who found that word-final [ɔ] is tensed to [o] based on a similar syllable structure constraint in French, whereby nouns and verbs must end in a tensed vowel. Having consulted pronunciations given in 14 dictionaries ranging in date from 1768 to 1973, Morin et al. (1990: 517) describe their results:

> In the last three dictionaries, the adverb *trop* is the only word with final [ɔ];. ... In the first four dictionaries, word-final O-tensing is almost non-existent. In the second (Gattel 1819 [1797]), tensing appears to have begun, but affects mainly learnèd words. The fourth (Rolland 1809) contains very few non-native words. ... In all other dictionaries, however, tensing in learnèd words always lags behind.

The crossover between originally affecting mainly learned words, which in later stages lag behind, is a curious characteristic of this change, but clearly the least frequent words have been affected first, since the only "relic" form untouched by the change is the extremely frequent adverb *trop*.

Another theory, one that specifically addresses Orm's spellings and not only lengthening of vowels in the data discussed above (i.e. homorganic cluster lengthening) but also other quantitative shifts in late Old English and into Middle English, is Murray's (2000) account based on syllable-cut theory, an expansion of Vennemann (2000). Murray argues that the Old English phonological structure that depended largely on quantitative differences was **reanalyzed** on the syllable level as dependent on syllable cut, similar to Modern German, in which "the contrast between *bitten* and *bieten* involves an opposition between close and loose contact, where the former is the marked member of the opposition" (p. 619), typologically plausible since most languages prefer long or tense vowels in open syllables. Murray suggests that syllable cut had become phonologized, and that syllable cut was what Orm was indicating with his method of doubling consonants. That is, Orm's double consonants indicate abrupt cut, as in both syllables of ≪hanndfull≫ 'handful'; a single consonant indicates smooth cut, as in both syllables of ≪childlæs≫ 'childless' (p. 642). "For Orm, it simply means that in the case of abrupt cut he apparently heard something 'extra'. Indeed he may have thought of the double graph as representing a long or strong consonant," an effect which Murray notes has been shown by von Essen (1962) for Modern German (Murray 2000: 642). The variation found in Orm's spellings is part of the transition to the syllable-cut system, one

92 *Word Frequency and Lexical Diffusion*

which does not involve lengthening per se, but rather reanalysis. As Murray explains:

> ... Vennemann 2000 argues that the lengthenings and shortenings in English (as well as similar developments in other Germanic languages) are an unambiguous indicator that quantity had already CEASED to be phonologically relevant. From this perspective, the original length contrasts were realigned in accordance with the prosody of syllable cut, with length manifesting itself as a possible redundant property of the particular syllable cut. Accordingly, these major changes were not quantity shifts at all, but evidence that English had become a syllable-cut language. Without the phonologization of syllable cut, such changes would not have occurred. (p. 648)

Murray, however, believes that his reconstruction of Orm's phonology "necessitates the assumption of an interim stage in the shift from quantity to syllable cut, a stage in which nuclear length and the syllable-cut prosody coexist" (p. 650) and as one justification for this view notes that "Since we are dealing with a kind of reanalysis, this situation is not surprising. As grammaticalization studies have aptly indicated, reanalysis is a tacit affair for which the evidence is often found only in subsequent (chronologically later) generalizations or analogical extensions (Hopper & Traugott 1993: 56)" (p. 650, fn. 37). Yet the concept of reanalysis alone does not explain the word frequency effects we have seen. Grammaticalization, for instance, typically affects frequent words and word sequences: "the more frequently a form occurs in texts, the more grammatical it is assumed to be" (Hopper and Traugott 1993: 103). Yet lengthening before -*nd* and -*ng* apparently affected the least frequent words first.

It makes more sense, given the evidence on lexical diffusion, to view lengthening of vowels before -*nd* and -*ng* as an adjustment to a new syllable template. Murray suggests as much when he describes the phonologization of syllable cut in late Old English as

> the introduction of a timing or quantity template [which] has the potential advantage of providing a general framework within which the various kinds of quantity changes can be treated in a unitary manner. Given that phonological units (word, foot, syllable) are governed by some form of a timing template, diachronic lengthenings and shortenings can occur to bring individual forms into greater conformance with a particular or "ideal" quantity. (p. 624)

The Lexical Diffusion of Phonetically Gradual Changes 93

Taking into consideration our other examples of sound changes that affect the least frequent words first, such a change originating in syllable constraints – whether defined by syllable cut or by phonotactic structure – understandably would affect the least frequent words first.

A change originating in syllable constraints or a syllable template must have some basis in the psychological reality of that constraint or template, however. Since the evidence from Orm shows that the lengthening had already been completed before *-ld*, it is possible that Minkova and Stockwell (1992) are correct in positing lengthening before /ld/ as a separate change. They attribute it to diphthongization of the vowel, or "late-breaking."[14] If so, this change would have affected the most frequent words first, and it does seem to have affected most, if not all, candidate words. Lengthening before some other clusters, especially *-rd*, which is phonetically most similar, may have resulted from phonetic analogy. At some point, however, there were enough words of the new type for the new syllable template to be generated, the evidence from Orm indicating that by the time vowels before *-nd* and *-ng* clusters were affected, speakers had developed such a new template, so that vowel lengthening in those environments affected the least frequent words first.

3.3 Conclusion

As with the phonetically abrupt changes investigated in Chapter 2, this chapter has documented phonetically gradual changes that affect the most frequent words first and others that affect the least frequent words first. The fact that any of these phonetically gradual changes are lexically diffused disproves Kiparsky's (1995: 659) characterization of gradient changes (labeled "major changes") as necessarily exceptionless. Phonetically gradual changes can be quite diverse, it turns out, depending upon the degree of lexical analysis required in their production.

Phonetically gradual changes that affect the **most frequent** words first seem in many cases to share one characteristic with Kiparsky's major changes; that is, they often have their basis in the articulatory limitations of the vocal tract – overlapping gestures and tendencies of vowels and consonants under certain situations to reduce. But they can also include changes with acoustic/perceptual bases, such as glide optimization, as long as those changes do not require for their implementation/production access to other components of the phonological

94 *Word Frequency and Lexical Diffusion*

system. That is, gradient sound changes that affect the most frequent words first have the following characteristics:

1. In perception, speakers add the innovative pronunciation to the lexical representation of the word form. Repeated exposure to the new pronunciation reinforces its memory trace and eventually leads to its becoming the default pronunciation.
2. In production, speakers access the lexical representations they have stored, choosing the one more ingrained in memory from more frequent use. Speakers also are accessing the most frequent words more easily, as Jurafsky (2003: 88) points out: "[M]odern models of lexical production such as those developed by Levelt, Roelofs, and Meyer (1999), Dell (1986a), and Dell et al. (1997) – indeed most models, back to Morton's (1969) seminal *lologen* model – are based on some idea of activation that is tied in some way to frequency. In a logogen-style model, a high-frequency word has a lower activation threshold and hence is quicker to access."
3. Because lexical representations contain rich phonetic detail, the connections they form with similar words create an easy path for innovations to spread along. Thus sound changes which change only fine-grained encodings of phonetic categories often spread quickly, seeming to be exceptionless (especially if one is viewing the change after its completion). In a homogeneous speech community, they may also be free of noticeable social marking, such cases leading Labov (1994: 78) to characterize them as changes from below the level of consciousness, but this characterization is misleading, since speakers are aware of and encode many fine nuances of the speech they hear, including social indicators (Lachs et al. 2003).

Phonetically gradual changes that affect the **least frequent** words first all seem to require a deeper level of analysis during their production. They may be characterized as follows:

1. In perception, as with changes involving more frequent words, speakers add the innovative pronunciation to the lexical representation of the word form. The innovative pronunciation is not reinforced as well, however, because, being infrequent, exposure to the new pronunciation is less.
2. In production, infrequent forms are accessed more slowly and memory traces are weaker. These properties give speakers the time and motivation to access other levels/components – the

prosodic and phonotactic structures of the language, segmental constraints/probabilities, the morphological attributes of the word form, and so forth – when producing these forms.

Production is particularly important, because the only way to explain how sound changes spread through the lexicon is to assume that each speaker is going through the same process, building toward a unified *langue*. Hence, studies of individuals tend to reflect the same lexical diffusion patterns that are found in larger databases, but the effect is often clearer over larger corpora than in individuals – as is true of most fields of study. Individuals do imitate the speech of others, but there has to be a path for the sound change to progress along, that is, connections with other word forms, through which generalizations across the lexicon are implemented – some affecting the most frequent words and others affecting the least frequent words, even for gradual phonetic changes.

4
Lexical Diffusion and Word Class

4.0 Introduction

The preceding chapters concentrated on the effect of word frequency on the lexical diffusion of various types of sound change, sometimes breaking the data down by phonetic environment and/or by word class. Not all writers who have appealed to lexical diffusion have kept these three influences – word frequency, phonetic environment, and word class – separate and thus have appealed to lexical diffusion when they found lexical exceptions of any kind or dismissed it when they found phonetic or grammatical conditioning, even if there were lexical exceptions. This confusion about the role of lexical diffusion is typified by Morin et al.'s (1990: 517) comment that if a rule they posited "had resulted from a regular sound change in which word-final [ɔ] becomes [o], all words would have been affected simultaneously, or – in the case of lexical diffusion – without regard to grammatical categories." Yet studies on lexical diffusion have never claimed that the spread of changes through the lexicon disregards grammatical categories. And many examples of lexical diffusion operating within the confines of narrow phonetic environment were presented in Chapter 3. The purpose of this chapter is to answer two questions: Why do some word classes undergo a sound change before others? Why do word frequency effects occur within word classes?

The importance of considering word class when investigating the lexical diffusion of a change may be demonstrated by the example of a study which failed to take word class into account when looking for frequency effects. Patterson et al. (2003) discounted the influence of frequency on vowel deletion because of their finding that it was "not sufficiently robust to hold when the data were analyzed by lexical

Lexical Diffusion and Word Class 97

stress pattern subgroups" (p. 53). Yet they did not analyze the data by word class. Table 4.1 shows how the data provided in their Appendices pattern within the word class for which they reported the most data, i.e. nouns. The Switchboard Corpus they used was that of Godfrey et al. (1992), which they describe as a collection of "approximately 2,400 two-sided telephone conversations based on prompted topics among 543 speakers, from all areas of the United States" (p. 46). The Narrative Corpus was their own data, based on conversations involving the retelling of a story by 54 subjects to their friends face to face (p. 56). Frequencies are based on those given in the CELEX database (Center for Lexical Information 1993), rather than the more limited frequencies of Francis and Kučera (1982) used by Patterson et al. If a word could belong to more than one class, I used the CELEX lemma information (EFL "English Frequency Lemma") and its syntactic

Table 4.1(a) Switchboard Corpus nouns (based on Patterson et al. 2003)

Nouns	Frequency	% Deleted	Average % deleted
Two-syllable			
tureen	14	0	
parole	20	6.7	**3.35**
balloon	112	11.1	
saloon	212	0	
parade	255	20	**10.37**
career	1187	13.4	
police	3694	18	**15.70**
Three-syllable			
broccoli	16	75	
gasoline	70	30.4	**52.70**
grocery	102	96.3	
buffalo	133	14.1	
surgery	224	34.8	
chocolate	274	93.9	
envelope	439	0	
criminal	445	82.8	
opera	456	85	
salary	510	82.6	
camera	651	82.9	
cabinet	835	50	**62.24**
memory	1584	72.2	
history	3414	80.5	**76.35**

* Excluding *violence* (frequency 1178, % deleted 23), whose phonetic conditioning, with the deletable vowel following another vowel, is markedly different from that of the other nouns.

98 *Word Frequency and Lexical Diffusion*

Table 4.1(b) Narrative Corpus nouns (based on Patterson et al. 2003)

Nouns	Frequency	% Deleted	Average % deleted
Two-syllable			
tureen	14	0	
parole	20	13.3	**6.65**
saloon	212	9.7	
parade	255	30.6	**20.15**
career	1187	36	
supply	1283	0	
support	2397	3	
police	3694	49.3	**22.08**
Three-syllable			
broccoli	16	63.1	
avalanche	51	28.6	
gasoline*	70	48.6	**46.77**
grocery	102	43.2	
buffalo	133	45.1	
ivory	201	92	
calorie	213	28.6	
surgery	224	46.7	
mineral	273	3.7	
chocolate	274	100	
criminal	445	17.9	
opera	456	95.7	
avenue	466	0	
salary	510	7.7	
camera	651	95.7	
gallery	666	4.2	
cabinet	835	42.9	**44.53**
factory	1064	57.1	
memory	1584	64.7	
history	3414	73.5	
family	7528	94.9	**72.55**

*In CELEX database, spelled *gasolene*.

information (ESL "English Syntax Lemma") to determine which part of speech was more frequent and assigned it to that class. In addition, I limited the data to word class groups for which at least three of the following frequency groups could be identified, 1–10, 11–100, 101–1000, over 1000. Tables 4.1(a) and (b), then, contain data on two- and three-syllable nouns taken from the Switchboard speech database. On average, schwa deletion has clearly affected the most frequent words first.

Similarly, writers confuse the effects of high word frequency and of function words, which are typically also high in frequency. For instance, Rusch's (1992: 87) discussion of variation between conservative ≪æ≫ spellings versus innovative ≪e≫ spellings in the Early Middle English *Peterborough Chronicle* attributes to high frequency effects which are limited to function words:

> [I]t may be more prudent ... to assume that ≪æ≫–≪e≫ variation in PC reflects a lexical diffusion of the sound change.... Relevant evidence from the high-frequency words, not yet discussed, dramatically support this hypothesis. In the 3rd pers. pret. sing. of OE "wesan," for instance, ≪æ≫ is overwhelmingly more frequent.... In the complementizer and relative pronoun "that," however, the spelling is invariably with ≪e≫. In the preterite system (including past participle) of OE "habban," ≪æ≫, ,e≫, and ≪a≫ all occur at roughly equal rates. The regularity of ≪e≫ in "þet" is especially germane, indicating that the authentically Mercian reflex became attached to one commonly used word. The meager spellings of (totally unexpected) ≪ea≫ in "weas" (for "wæs") and other words surely reflect the transitional status of this dialect in regard to *æ/e.*

An example of a study that looks for frequency effects but overlooks phonetic environments and word class is Goeman et al. (1993: 81), which investigates the development of West Germanic /î/ in Modern Dutch dialects. They claim that they

> do not find a relationship between token frequency and diphthongization. For instance, highly frequent items such as *krijgen, tijd* (> 200) do not behave differently as far as diphthongization is concerned from items such as *vijg* (0) and *vijl* (2). And among the items showing diphthongs rather often, such as *vrijdag, vrijen, vrij, fijn* and *vijf,* both low and high frequencies occur.

Yet several morphological classes are contained in their examples: *krijgen* 'to get' and *vrijen* 'to make love' are verbs; *tijd* 'time,' *vijg* 'fig,' *vijl* 'file,' and *vrijdag* 'Friday' are nouns; *vjig* 'free' and *fijn* 'fine' are adjectives. And the phonetic environments vary considerably: included are both one- and two-syllable words, as well as vowels in both open and closed syllables (*vrij* versus *vijg,* for instance). They do exclude *piepen* 'to squeak, creak' from their data, explaining that it is a relic form which "still has î in all dialects, except 10 in the eastern part

100 *Word Frequency and Lexical Diffusion*

of North-Brabant" (p. 77, fn. 3), but they do not connect this aberrant behavior with the word's clear onomatopoetic force. As for the data they do include, a closer look reveals that morphological category and phonetic shape are extremely important for this sound change. Table 4.2 displays the words which Goeman et al. investigated, divided

Table 4.2 Diphthongization of West German î in Dutch based on Goeman et al. (1993) and CELEX word frequency ( ) for Dutch

% Diphthongs	Nouns	Verbs	Adjectives	Numerals	Function words
66–77	vrijdag (723)	vrijen (272)	vrij (9214)		bij (160,583)
		vrijt (37)	vrije (1406)		mij (67,877)
53–60		rijden (1485)	blij (4277)/ blijde (225) fijn (2200)	vijf (7667)	
43–51	**One syllable** dijk (195)	bijten (276)	grijs (197)	vijftig (2362)	
	krijt (234)	blijven (8782)	rijk (1378)		
	lijk (993)	kijken (6305)	rijp (636)		
	pijp (810)	krijgen (7750)	rijpe (338)		
	prijs (3194)	schrijven (621)	rijpst (0)		
	schijf (331)	slijpen (36)	stijf (1040)		
	slijm (216)	wrijven (225)	wijd (1091)		
	tijd (40,615)	zwijgen (510)			
	vijg (14) vijl (22) wijf (381) wijn (5955)				
	First of two syllables ijzer (712) lijster (39) twijfel (2750)				
	Second of two syllables konijn (429)				

Lexical Diffusion and Word Class 101

by word class. Their percentages of innovative diphthongized pronunciations are given within three ranges, namely, 66–77, 53–60, and 43–51 percent, with the higher percentages being the more advanced. The words' frequencies are given as reported in the more recently compiled CELEX database (Center for Lexical Information 1993), rather than the Uit den Boogaart (1975) and de Jong (1979) frequency counts used by Goeman et al. but for which they did not give details in their article. For nouns, it is clear that the most innovative form is *vrijdag* 'Friday,' whose reported frequency (723) is surprisingly small, and which is closest in phonological structure to the less frequently diphthongized two-syllable words *ijzer, lijster,* and *twijfel*. The most innovative verb, *vrijen/vrijt* 'to make love/(s)he makes love' is the only verb with the diphthong in morpheme-final position, making the infinitival form the only verb whose diphthong is in an open syllable followed by a vowel. The most innovative adjective, *vrij/vrije* 'free' similarly is the only adjective whose diphthong is not followed by a consonant (aside from the word *blij*, which Goeman et al. conflate with the form *blijde*). The numeral *vijf* is more often diphthongized than the numeral *vijftig*, but the latter contains two syllables, and the development of the parallel words in English, *five* and *fifty*, demonstrate how the vowels may easily behave differently. The function words contain two very frequent words, *bij* 'by/near' and *mij* 'me,' both of which are in the highest category of diphthongization. Therefore, it appears that vowels in an open syllable are more likely to exhibit the diphthongized vowel. It is unfortunate that there are no minimal pairs within their word classes for the other leaders in this sound change – *vrijdag* 'Friday,' *rijden* 'ride,' and *fijn* 'fine' – so that word frequency effects might be more finely assessed, but the data available suggest that the most frequent words may be changing first within phonological environments within each word class: before alveolars, the verb *rijden* (1485) is diphthongized more often than *bijten* (276); *fijn* (2200) is diphthongized more often than any other closed-syllable adjective, including those where the vowel is followed by an alveolar consonant, including *wijd* (1091) and *grijs* (197). Also, note that for the more frequent words to change first in this sound change is not surprising given the parallel development in the diphthongization of Middle English /iː/, discussed in Chapter 3. The fact that two of the most innovative words, *bij* and *mij*, are function words may be significant but may also be due to their open syllable.

As for the advanced status of diphthongization in the function words *bij* and *mij*, one way to determine whether they have a special status in the diffusion of this and other sound changes is to look at how other

102 *Word Frequency and Lexical Diffusion*

changes have affected them and other word classes. The rest of this chapter will attempt to clarify the relationship between lexical diffusion, phonological environments, and morphological classes in the progression of a sound change. However, because function words and high-frequency words are so often conflated, the first section will start by looking at the relationship between word frequency and function words.

4.1 Function words

Function words often operate independently in the progression of a sound change, probably because of their low sentence stress.[1] This is the conclusion reached by Phillips (1983b), who found that sound changes that affected function words first were typically vowel or consonant weakenings. This finding has been substantiated by Lavoie's (2002) close study of the difference in pronunciation between the number *four* and the preposition *for*:

> Realizations of the number *four* always seem to have more segmental material, even in cases where the number is highly predictable, such as in the sequence *three, four, five*. The highly predictable contexts are where words usually show the greatest reduction. The number *four* never reduces to just its onset /f/, as the preposition *for* may do, nor does the number ever completely lack evidence of a coda /r/. (p. 197)

Similarly, function words resisted vowel lengthening in High German, Luther until 1533 writing writing *odder* (NHG *oder* 'or'), *wedder* (NHG weder 'neither'), *nidder* (NHG *nieder* 'down, low') and *widder* (NHG *wieder* 'again') (Becker 2002: 51).

Function words also usually occur more frequently than words in other classes, however, so the effects of word frequency versus those of word class are often difficult to detect and for that reason often confused. The discussion below, based largely on Phillips (1983b), is organized around four types of sound changes: changes which affect function words first and the most frequent words first; changes which affect function words first but the most frequent words last; changes which affect function words last but the most frequent words first; and changes which affect function words last and the most frequent words last. Since the category of function words conflates a number of word classes, the working definition used below is that provided by Bolinger (1975: 121–2): the linking verb *to be*, the prepositions; the determiners; the quantifiers; the coordinating conjunctions; the relative pronouns; the adverbial conjunctions; the intensifiers; the auxiliary verbs; the pronouns, proadverbs, and other prowords. It is widely recognized that function words are more closely tied to grammatical functions than are content words and thus are processed differently in perception and production (Aitchison 2003: 110–12; Alario and Cohen 2004). But the most important common element in the examples given below seems to be their low sentence stress, for weakening sound changes tend to affect function words first, whereas strengthening sound changes affect them last.

The sections below are organized so as to highlight the differences between word class effects and word frequency effects on the progress of a sound change. That is, there are four sections covering all combinatorial possibilities: (1) function words changing first and most frequent words first, (2) function words changing first but most frequent words last, (3) function words changing last but most frequent words first, and (4) function words changing last and most frequent words last.

4.1.1 Function words changing first and most frequent words first

It is not unusual for function words and the most frequent words to both be affected first in a sound change. For instance, in investigating the deletion of /t, d/ in final consonant clusters in English, Neu (1980) elicited approximately 10 minutes of natural speech from 15 informants (eight men and seven women of varying ages and places of residence) and analyzed the data using a number of variables, including the grammatical function of /t, d/, whether a vowel or a consonant followed the /t, d/, the manner of articulation of the following consonant, and the place and manner of articulation of the preceding consonant (p. 42). In addition to such constraints, she found that "High frequency lexical items (such as the word *and*) are more likely to undergo deletion than are most other items, that is, there is a high correlation between frequency of word occurrence and frequency of rule application. This correlation is most striking when the high-frequency items are function words whose only vowel is reducible to schwa" (p. 53). Her conclusion is particularly interesting in light of her observation that Labov (1975) decided to treat the word *just* as a special case and exclude it from his study. Neu's choice to include *just* led her to the finding that "A deletion rate of 49% was observed for /t/ in the word *just* as compared to a rate of 36% in other /st/ clusters. While the confidence intervals overlap, the difference in deletion rates is significant at the .025 level" (p. 45). More recent studies

104 *Word Frequency and Lexical Diffusion*

of /t, d/ deletion confirm its effect not only on function words first, but also on the most frequent words in other word classes first (Bybee 2000b; Goeman and van Reenan 1985), as discussed in Chapter 3.

An even clearer example of function words and high-frequency words within other word classes being favored in a sound change is Phillips's (1978, 1983b) study of spellings in conservative «an/am» versus innovative «on/om» in the Old English manuscript Hatton 20, which contains Alfred's late ninth-century translation of Gregory's *Pastoral Care*. Table 4.3 presents the average percentage of innovative spellings first by word frequency irrespective of word class and then by word class. Detailed tables are given in Appendix B. Not only do the number of «on, om» spellings increase as word frequency increases, but also adverbs and function words are clearly much more likely to contain the innovative spellings. (The latter two classes have been combined because of the difficulty of separating their forms in Old English. For instance, the form *ðonne* occurs 1400 times in the manuscript, sometimes as an adverb and sometimes as a conjunction.)

4.1.2 Function words changing first but most frequent words last

Sound changes, however, do not always affect the most frequent words and function words identically. In the case of Middle English unrounding of /ø(:)/ to /e(:)/, evidence from the *Ormulum* manuscript

Table 4.3 Percentages of innovative «on, om» spellings in the *Pastoral Care* (OE, late ninth century) (Phillips 1983b: 489)

By word frequency	Number of headwords	Average % of «on, om»
1–10	61	39
11–20	12	49
21–60	10	53
61–400	6	80
Over 400	4	98

By word class	Number of headwords	Average % of «on, om»
Verbs	33	32
Nouns	33	44
Adjectives	10	44
Adverbs and function words	17	84

Lexical Diffusion and Word Class 105

(*c.* 1180) indicates that, within word classes, the least frequent words have changed first, but function words as a class have changed last. The discussion in Chapter 3 looked at some of the data and it was argued that this change had its basis in segmental constraints, since there were no other front rounded vowels in the language at that time. The complete list of forms is given in Appendix C, but for our purposes here, Tables 4.4(a) and (b) (reproduced from Phillips 1983b: 490) suffice to summarize the data and to provide a comparison of the effect of the unrounding on words by word class and by frequency. From these tables, it is clear that for both the long and the short vowels, function words consistently occurred with the innovative unrounded vowel /e(:)/. (The only exception is the aberrant *he(o)re* 'their,' which has been omitted from Table 4.4(b), since its very low percentage of ≪e≫ spellings (4 percent, or only 2 of 48 instances) may reflect an attempt to avoid confusion with another common spelling for 'her', *here*. See Kurath and Kuhn 1956–, *hir(e)*.) Yet the rankings by word frequency reveal that, for the long vowel at least, the least frequent words have clearly changed first: 62 percent of the spellings in the frequency range 1–10 contain the innovative ≪e≫, compared to only 21 percent of the most frequent words, those in the frequency range 91–400. No frequency effect was found for the short vowels.

Even if one looks at frequency rankings within word classes for this sound change, as displayed in Tables 4.5(a) and (b), the most frequent

Table 4.4(a) Middle English long /øː/ unrounding (Phillips 1983b: 490)

By word class	Number of headwords	Average % of ≪e≫ spellings
Numerals	2	0
Nouns	17	28
Verbs	23	67
Nonnumerical adjectives	7	70
Adverbs and function words	3	100
By word frequency	**Number of headwords**	**Average % of ≪e≫ spellings**
1–10	27	62
11–20	7	66
21–30	8	45
31–60	5	43
61–90	2	28
91–400	2	21

106

Table 4.4(b) Middle English short /ø/ unrounding (Phillips 1983b: 490)

By word class	Number of headwords	Average % of «e» spellings
Numerals	3	10
Nouns	8	55
Verbs	6	85
Nonnumerical adjectives	3	72
Function words*	3	100

By word frequency	Number of headwords	Average % of «e» spellings
1–10	14	68
11–90	6	57
90–347	3	69

* Omitting *he(o)re* 'her'.

Table 4.5(a) Frequency effects of long /ø:/ > /e:/ in the *Ormulum* by word class (Phillips 1984: 328)

Word class	Frequency	Words	Average % «e»
Adverbs and function words	12–51	sket, newenn, bitwenenn	100
Nonnumerical adjectives	2–8	seoc, freo, dreoriȝ, neow	66
	21–36	deop, deore, leof	76
Verbs	2–10	beodeþþ, forrbedeþþ, secnedd, nedenn, chesenn, fleȝhenn, cneolenn, wex, freollsenn, forrleosenn, (bi)reowenn, steorenn, dreȝhenn, forrseon	69
	11–47	leȝhenn, cneow, fell, fleon, heold, ȝede, streonenn	68
	69	seon	52
	355	beon	41
Nouns	1–8	breostlin, derrlinng, þeos, leo, fend, wheol, heowe, fe(hh), freond	49
	21–47	deor, leom, treo, streon, leod	6
	68–82	preost, þeod	4
	158	deofell	1

Lexical Diffusion and Word Class   107

Table 4.5(b)   Development in the *Ormulum* of short /ø/ > /e/ (Phillips 1984: 328)

Word class	Frequency	Words	Average % «e»
Function words	1–347	bineþenn, sellf, hemm	100
Verbs	1–39	clepenn, herrcnenn, werrpenn, ȝeorrnde, berrȝhenn, forrweorrpenn	85*
Nonnumerical adjectives	2–15	feorr, þeorrf, fele	72
Nouns	1–2	berrhless, deorrf (like), berrme, sede(full)	75
	26–90	weorrc, weorelld, heorrte	46
	154	heofenn	6
Numerals	2–5	seofenntiȝ, seoffnde	10
	46	seofenn	9

*This percentage would be much higher if *ȝeorrnde* were omitted; only 1 of its 9 attestations (11%) contains the innovative vowel. All the other verbs, except for one of the 38 instances of *forrweorrpenn*, consistently contain the innovative «e».

words still tend to be the leaders – especially evident in the data for the most numerous word classes, that is, nouns and verbs containing the long vowel. Specifically, among the nouns with long vowels, those with low frequencies – that is, occurring less than 10 times in the *Ormulum's* 10,000 lines of verse – contain the innovative vowel 49 percent of the time, whereas more frequent nouns contain the vowel much less often (on average less than 6 percent of the time). Verbs with the long vowel display a steady decrease as frequency increases: 69 percent for the least frequent group (1–10), 68 percent for the next most frequent (11–47), versus 52 percent for the frequent *seon* 'see' and 41 percent for the very frequent *beon* 'be.' Among the words with short vowels, for which there are fewer word forms overall, the largest group, nouns, show the same progression: very infrequent nouns contain the innovative «e» 75 percent of the time, more frequent nouns 46 percent of the time, and the most frequent noun, *heofenn*, only 6 percent of the time.

In Chapter 3 it was suggested that this sound change affected the least frequent words first because its implementation required access to the language's segmental constraint disfavoring front rounded vowels. On the other hand, what this change shares with the other changes that affect function words first – the shift of Old English /an/ to /on/

108 *Word Frequency and Lexical Diffusion*

and /t, d/ deletion in Modern English – is that they are all weakening processes, that is, assimilations, deletions, or unroundings of front vowels.

4.1.3 Function words changing last but most frequent words first

In contrast to the sound changes examined thus far, changes that affect function words last appear to be strengthening processes. For instance, for a commonly recognized strengthening process, the High German Consonant Shift – whereby initial, doubled, and postconsonantal voiceless stops became affricates, medial and final voiceless stops became fricatives, and voiced stops became voiceless – Barrack (1976: 171) notes that in the Old High German *Isidor*, the change from /d/ to /t/ occurred first in only very frequent content words such as *fater* 'father,' *muoter* 'mother,' and *got* 'God.' And, according to Schirmunski (1956: 217), in Middle Franconian another part of the shift, that of /t/ > /s/, noticeably affected all words except such function words as *dat* 'that,' *wat* 'what,' *et* 'it,' *dit* 'this,' *alt* 'as,' *at* 'all,' *up/op* 'on,' *mōt* (Ripuarian) 'must,' and *lēt* (Ripuarian) 'let.'

Similarly, the spread of a Dutch vowel strengthening process from Amsterdam to neighboring villages has affected function words last (and provides a good contrast to Goeman et al.'s (1993) study of the diphthongization of WGmc. /î/ discussed above). Gerritsen and Jansen (1980) argue for the shift in Dutch of [ɛι] > [ɛ̯] and [αι] > [aː] as a strengthening, despite the fact that it includes the loss of a glide element, on the basis of its other characteristics: the vowel is lengthened and, in the case of [αι] > [aː] tensed; reduction would be more likely before consonants; whereas these innovative forms also occur word-finally; and the new variants occur preferentially in stressed syllables (p. 36). Although they consider the possibility of this being a dialect borrowing, or "unnatural change," only three of the locations they sampled met their requirements for considering this an unnatural change (i.e. little or no evidence of diphthongs at an earlier stage which might have developed naturally into the Amsterdam variant) (p. 44), and in those the change affected the most frequent nonpronominal words first, just as it did in the numerous vicinities exhibiting a "natural change" (p. 50). For example, the "most frequent non-pronominal form in spoken Dutch" containing the vowel in question, the verb *krijgen* 'to get,' was far more likely to contain the innovative vowel than were other nonpronominal forms, such as *blijven* 'to stay' and *kijken* 'to look' (p. 52). They omitted

Lexical Diffusion and Word Class 109

unstressed forms of the pronoun and the preposition *bij* from their survey, since unstressed forms are subject to reductive processes. But they found that, when stressed, pronouns were the most resistant to the change, changing last if ever. Gerritsen and Jansen, therefore, were able to set up the following implicational scale: "all dialects with pronominal variants changing to Amsterdam [aː] or [ɛᵧ] have changed throughout their lexicons; all frequent and infrequent words have an Amsterdam variant, too. All dialects with infrequent words changing to the Amsterdam variants have Amsterdam variants in their frequent words, too" (p. 44).

The disproval of one hypothesis that Gerritsen and Jansen made about this sound change highlights the danger in assuming that the path of reductive versus strengthening sound changes is determined by functional considerations in the speech act. Reductions, they reason, being based in ease of articulation for the speaker, cause "indistinctness of lexical items," but they are accepted in frequent words because "it is easier for a listener to understand indistinct words which he hears every minute, than indistinct ones which he never or only very seldom hears" (p. 37). Logically, then, one might expect words undergoing a strengthening sound change to affect the least frequent words first: "The rationale behind this hypothesis is that a speaker emphasizes a lexical item in order to direct the listener's attention to that item, arguing (correctly or incorrectly) that the information contained in the item is not expected by the listener" (p. 37). Yet this proved not to be the case in the strengthening of Dutch diphthongs. Instead, this sound change fits with other sound changes discussed in Chapter 3 which affected the most frequent words first, namely it does not require analysis of the lexical entry beyond the phonological encoding. And it affects pronouns last because it is a strengthening process.

4.1.4 Function words changing last and most frequent words last

A change which affected last both the function words and the most frequent words within grammatical categories is the Old English lengthening of vowels before homorganic voiced consonant clusters of the type -*nd*, -*ld*, -*rd*, etc., as reflected in spellings in the *Ormulum* manuscript (*c.* 1180). In Chapter 3 it was shown that within those categories for which sufficient measurable data exist, the most frequent words had changed first, as reiterated in a succinct version in Table 4.6. For each environment, the average frequency listed in the "Changed"

110   *Word Frequency and Lexical Diffusion*

Table 4.6 Low-frequency words changing first in vowel lengthening before homorganic consonant clusters in the *Ormulum, c.* 1180

Environment	Average word frequencies		
	Changed	Variable	Unchanged
Verbs in -*e(o)nd*	13.3	27.5	38.0
Verbs in -*and*	31.5	–	80.0
Nouns in -*and*	19.4	48.0	–
Verbs in -*ing*	2.2	–	26.0
Verbs in -*e(o)ng*	6.25	4.0	–
Verbs in -*ang*	2.0	–	11.5

column is significantly lower than that listed in the "Variable" and/or "Unchanged" columns.

A complete list of the spellings on which this table and the next are based is reproduced in Appendix D, where the complete tables from Phillips (1983b: 495–9) appear. Table 4.7, where function word classes appear in ALL CAPITALS, summarizes the influence of word class on this lengthening.[2] If the word class contains more than one example, the plural is used (e.g. PREPOSITIONS); if there is only one example for a particular word class, the singular is used (e.g. PREPOSITION). Since two-syllable nouns ending in -*err*, -*errn*, and -*ell* (e.g. *wullderr* 'glory,' *unnderrn* 'the third hour of the day,' *enngell* 'angel,' etc.) consistently resisted lengthening, they are not included. Also excluded, in the "Variable" column, are two words for which the less frequent variant represented less than 3 percent of the forms, e.g. *findenn* (74)/*finndeþþ* (1), *sindenn* (2)/*sinndenn* (81) 'are' and *word* (255)/*worrd* (1) 'word.' Note that a word class may appear in more than one category if separate words within it exhibit different effects. For instance, for words where the vowel in question is followed by -*nd*, some verbs have changed completely (*attwindenn, bindenn, blendeþþ, bundenn, endenn, findenn, fandenn, fundenn, grindesst, lendenn, wand, wundenn*), some verbs exhibit variation (*shendenn/shennd, wendenn/wenndenn*), and some verbs remain unchanged (*brennd, senndenn, stanndenn, unnderrstanndenn, wiþþstanndenn*). With respect to function words, however, it is clear that they have overwhelmingly resisted this lengthening. The only exception is prepositions ending in -*ng*, which all indicate lengthened vowels – (*a)mang* (55), *bilenge* (1), *lang* (1) – whereas adverbs, for instance, vary between *wrang* (14) with the lengthened vowel and *forrlan_nge* (13) and *lannge* (13) with the short vowel.

Lexical Diffusion and Word Class 111

Table 4.7 Precluster vowel lengthening in the *Ormulum* (*c.* 1180) by word class

Environment	Changed	Variable	Unchanged
-ld	nouns, verbs, adjectives, adverbs		AUXILIARIES
-nd	nouns, verbs, adjectives	nouns, verbs	verbs, adverbs, AUXILIARY, CONJUNCTION, PREPOSITIONS
-mb	nouns, verb, adjectives	adverb	PREPOSITION
-ng	nouns, verbs, adjectives, adverb, PREPOSITIONS	verbs	verbs, adverbs
-rd	nouns, verbs		verbs, noun, adjectives, adverbs, AUXILIARY, PREPOSITIONS
-rþ	noun, verb, adjective	adjective	verbs, adjective, adverbs, AUXILIARY
-rn	nouns, verbs, adjectives, adverbs	noun, adjective, adverb	nouns, verb, adverb, AUXILIARY
-rl	nouns		nouns, verb

Since the evidence above reveals that when function words are affected first, the sound change is invariably a weakening process, it seems logical that their low sentence stress is most likely responsible for their resistance to this vowel strengthening via lengthening. That this is true may also be seen from the behavior in Table 4.7 of adverbs, which are also less prominently stressed than the other content word classes. Not only do adverbs often occur in the "Unchanged" column, but for no phonological environment have adverbs undergone the strengthening involved in Old English vowel lengthening unless nouns, verbs, and adjectives had undergone it as well. In fact, in the "Changed" column, adjectives do not appear unless verbs do, and verbs do not appear unless nouns do. Hence, there appears to be a continuum nouns > verbs > adjectives > adverbs > function words. This ranking is not meant to be universal but may reflect stress patterns in the language at the time. Berg (2000), for instance, finds that for Modern English, adjectives pair more often with nouns than with verbs, and appeals to Kelly and Bock's (1988) argument that the preponderant stress pattern within each word

112 *Word Frequency and Lexical Diffusion*

class is largely determined by the rhythmic patterns of sentences in the language.

4.1.5 Summary

In sum, grammatical class and word frequency are totally independent effects and should not be confused. Function words can change first even when the least frequent words within other word classes change first, and they can change last even when the most frequent words within other word classes change first. That this should be possible is due to the different characteristics of word frequency and word class. The effect of word frequency is determined by the strength with which the word is entrenched in the mental lexicon, as argued in Chapter 3. The fact that function words typically undergo weakening processes first, on the other hand, is probably due to their low sentence stress. The word classes that constitute the general class of function words are not the only word classes, however, that behave independently.

4.2 Other word class effects

Other word class effects may sometimes hinge on their phonological characteristics, but these cannot account for all such behavior. Given the findings on speech perception and production, this should not come as a surprise. As Bunger (2002) notes, in speech perception, "we have early access to the higher-level lexical information associated with grammatical category, as well as to acoustic-phonetic neighborhood information and statistical lexical information (word frequency), and . . . we may use all of these cues to facilitate word identification." Models of speech production agree that different levels must be accessed separately in real time, however rapidly, with the retrieval of syntactic information occurring before that of phonological information. Turennout et al. (1998), for instance, report that grammatical information about words is accessed about 40 ms before information about their sounds. This finding does not invalidate interactive views of the lexicon; as summarized in Bock (1999), proponents of interactive models (e.g. Dell et al. 1997) argue that partial information from one stage may affect the next in a CASCADE effect and even that information from later levels may influence higher processing levels (FEEDBACK effect).

Evidence from brain imaging techniques even reveal a difference between word classes in language processing. For example, the following summary, provided by Kutas and Schmitt (2003: 186–7), of such research on measurements of electrical activity in the brain ("ERPs") makes it clear that word class and word frequency effects observable in language change correlate with measurable activity in the brain:

> On the face of it, ERPs [event-related brain potential] to different word classes do differ. The responses to function and content words differ from one another, as do the responses to nouns versus verbs and pronouns versus articles, among others.... In fact, no one denies that different lexical classes are associated with different ERP patterns. They do, however, disagree over what this means about how their members are represented in the brain and/or how they are accessed. It is difficult to answer this question because content and function words vary in important ways, such as word length and word frequency, which are in and of themselves known to have big effects on a word's processing.
>
> For example, both reaction time and eye movement testify to the fact that longer words take more time to access than shorter words and that frequently used words are understood and produced more quickly than rare words (Jescheniak & Levelt, 1994; Just & Carpenter, 1980). These differences alone could account for the observed differences between the ERPs to content and function words, as function words are typically much shorter and of much higher frequency than content words (Gordon & Caramazza, 1985; Thibadeau, Just, & Carpenter, 1983). In fact, we have found that frequency does account for one of the proposed ERP differences between the two word classes (King & Kutas, 1995, 1998). ...[W]e find that taking into account the frequency of a word reveals that the ERPs to all words include a negativity at left frontal recording sites. Thus, regardless of lexical class, the ERPs to all words contain a negativity somewhere between 250 and 400 msec, whose latency varies with a word's frequency of usage.

It is not surprising, then, to find both frequency and word class routinely affecting sound changes, for in order to produce language, speakers must access words from their mental lexicon.

One simple example of the influence of word class comes from the laxing of Middle English /uː/ to Early Modern English /ʊ/. Data from Bronstein and Sheldon's (1951) survey of dictionaries from the last quarter of the eighteenth century reveal that verbs tended to change before nouns, as did the adjective *crooked* and its derivatives. Details are presented in

114 *Word Frequency and Lexical Diffusion*

Table 4.8 Middle English /uː/ > Early Modern English /ʊ/ (> /ʌ/) (based on Bronstein and Sheldon (1951))

Environment	Words	Frequency	Dictionary dates				
			1771	1788	1789	1796	1798
-f	roof (n)	998	u	ʊ	u	u	u
	hoof (n)	137	u	u	u	u	u
	woof (n)	3	u	u	u	u	u
	loof (n)	0	u	u	u	u	u
	loof (v)	0	u	ʌ	ʌ	ʌ	ʌ
-k	book (n)	7,780	u	ʊ	u	u	ʊ
	hook (n)	679	u	ʊ	u	u	ʊ
	crook (n)	104	u	ʊ	u	u	ʊ
	brook (n)	79	u	ʊ	u	u	ʊ
	rook (n)	33	u	u	u	u	ʊ
	nook (n)	24	u	u	u	u	ʊ
	flook (n)	0		u	u	u	ʊ
	took (v)	46,180		ʊ	ʊ	ʊ	ʊ
	shook (v)	41,417	u	ʊ	ʊ	ʊ	ʊ
	look (v)	24,165	u	ʊ	ʊ	ʊ	ʊ
	cook (v)	1,284	u	ʊ	ʊ	ʊ	ʊ
	crooked (adj.), -ly (adv), -ness (n)		u	ʊ	ʊ	ʊ	ʊ

Table 4.8, where frequency figures have been taken from the Lemma Frequency given in the CELEX database. Not included are words with the vowel before /p, m/ since all vowels in such words resisted the change. Nor are words ending in /t/ or /d/ included, since the only verb in this group is *stood* and the nouns (*root* and *soot*), by ending in /t/ and not /d/, do not form near-minimal pairs with it.[3] Most revealing are the data for vowels preceding /k/, where all the dictionaries record the innovative lax vowel in all four verbs, whereas only the most recent dictionary (published in 1798) records the lax vowel in all of the nouns.

A more complex example of the influence of word class comes from data on word-final [ɔ] tensing in French, which has affected adverbs last. A survey of 14 dictionaries dating from 1768 to 1973, carried out by Morin et al. (1990), revealed that, whereas the tensing of [ɔ] is "almost non-existent" in the first four dictionaries, in the last three, the only word not yet tensed is the adverb *trop* (p. 517). This sound change is particularly interesting because it is a change that earlier was morphologically conditioned by plurality in nouns and adjectives,

Lexical Diffusion and Word Class 115

then generalized to affect all nouns and adjectives regardless of number (singular or plural), and finally generalized to adverbs. Since the change is a strengthening of the vowel (through tensing), it seems appropriate, given our findings above for function words, that a word class that typically draws lower stress, even in French, has resisted this change.

Another example from French comes from Hansen (2001), who could not find a clear word frequency effect for the raising of [$\bar{a}$] to [$\mathfrak{I}$], but who did find a clear word class effect. That is, in stressed position, adverbs (especially adverbs ending in -*ment*) were affected before verbs and nouns. The pronoun, *en*, had progressed even further, often (18 percent of the time) even exhibiting a sound approaching nasalized [$\tilde{\varepsilon}$], the only word class with more than 1 percent such pronunciations (p. 243). Two words which had not undergone this change but had denasalized the vowel instead were the adverbs *quand* and *enfin* (p. 245). In general, she found that "the word classes that favor the new rounded realization of /$\bar{a}$/ are all lexical words (i.e., words with a high information load), whereas the word classes that lag behind roughly coincide with grammatical words, which are semantically more empty" (p. 244). This effect held even within phonetic environments. For instance, after a labial consonant Hansen found the following percentages of variable pronunciations: "in adjectives, 76 per cent; in adverbs, 65 per cent; in nouns, 65 per cent; in verbs, 51 per cent; in prepositions, 50 per cent; and in pronouns, 33 per cent" (p. 244).

Toon (1992: 439) summarizes the development of yet another change that involved both word frequency and word class, including a clear statement of the impact of such findings on the neogrammarian versus lexical diffusion issue:

Wang (1969) has proposed that sound changes can diffuse gradually through the lexicon – a serious challenge to the neogrammarian hypothesis that sound changes are sensitive only to phonetic environment. The Northumbrian development of West Germanic */ɑ/ before nasals offers an extremely important case in point. In all three tenth century Northumbrian glosses to *Li*, *Ru1* and the *DurRit*, the sound is always spelled ≪o≫ *except* in the preterite singular of class III strong verbs, where it is spelled ≪a≫ without exception. This is an important example of constrained lexical diffusion. A single grammatical class accounts for the entire residue of an otherwise completed sound change. But this residue is not unrelated to the earlier resistance, as seen above, to the sound change before homorganic clusters with a nasal. Most of the verbs of strong class

116 *Word Frequency and Lexical Diffusion*

III contain a homorganic consonant cluster. We have a lexical class based both on a shared ablaut alternation and a shared phonological environment. The resistance to sound change has been transferred from the phonological environment to the grammatical class. Even the verbs of class III which do not contain a homorganic cluster are resistant to the change (*wann, blann, ingann*, etc.) while the cluster outside of this grammatical class is subject to the phonological regularity. The resistance has not spread to other strong verbs; we find the regular phonological development in class VI and preterite present verbs which contain West Germanic */a/ before a nasal, even a nasal homorganic cluster.

Phonological theories which adhere to a strict modular, process approach have difficulty accounting for such intricate relationships between phonetic and grammatical generalizations, despite the fact that speakers regularly make such connections. Bybee (2001: 121–5), for instance, discusses a number of productive generalizations speakers have made based on "gang effects," a familiar example being the productivity of the strong verb pattern of such words as s*ing, sang, sung*, which can even lead to the creation of nonce forms such as *splang* for a suggested base form of *spling*. A phonology that allows for bidirectional connections between grammatical generalizations and phonological forms, however, easily incorporates such effects.

4.3   Frequency effects within word classes

One question that still needs to answered, however, is why word frequency effects tend to be working **within** word classes. Findings on speech production help to explain this behavior.

All theories of language production posit a lemma level separate from a word form level, whether production is seen as a strictly one-way process (Levelt et al. 1991, 1999; Levelt 2001; Schriefers et al. 1990) or as allowing connections between levels to be maintained (Dell and Reich 1981; Dell 1986b; Dell and O'Seaghdha 1991, 1992; Jurafsky et al. 2002). The lemma contains semantic and syntactic information, whereas the word form contains phonological material.[4] In very simplistic terms, Aitchison (2003: 104) explains why word-level semantics and word class should meet in the lemma:

> Word class categorization is not arbitrary, and in origin arose out of semantic categories. Prototypical nouns tend to be people and things,

Lexical Diffusion and Word Class 117

and prototypical verbs tend to be actions.... From the point of view of the mental lexicon, this suggests that we should not regard meaning and word class as separate ingredients which need to be attached, but as integrated. In brief, we should regard words as coins, with meaning and word class together on one side, a combination sometimes called the *lemma*, and the sounds on the other. So, for example, choice of a word meaning "daisy" automatically brings with it a metaphorical label of noun, and selection of a word meaning "jump" inevitably involves a label of verb.

The amount and kind of information concerning pronunciation contained at the word form level are subject to debate, but evidence is growing that there must be considerable phonetic detail available at that level (Pisoni et al. 1985; Pisoni 1997; Cleary and Pisoni 2001; Lachs et al. 2003).

Evidence for the autonomy of the two levels, lemma versus word form, include tip-of-the tongue phenomena, speech errors, the behavior of aphasics, as well as frequency effects on gender-determined articles and on blends. For instance, in the common phenomenon known as tip-of-the-tongue, the lemma has been accessed, but the speaker has trouble accessing the lexeme – that is, the speaker knows what he/she wants to say but cannot find the right word form. Since this includes knowing the grammatical class of the word without knowing the phonological form (Miozzo and Caramazza 1997; Vigliocco et al. 1997), grammatical class is seen as information contained within the lemma. Similarly, certain aphasic patients can access the meaning and the syntactic features of words, yet cannot produce the word forms (Henaff Gonon et al. 1989). In slips of the tongue, verbs are less susceptible overall and adjectives are more susceptible to semantic group slips (Hotopf 1980: 107). In addition, although frequency effects have been reported for both lemma and lexeme access in perception (Hogaboam and Perfetti 1975; Simpson 1981; Simpson and Burgess 1985; Li and Yip 1996), word frequency effects in speech production have been found only at the lexeme level and not at the lemma. For instance, in studying the behavior of blends, Laubstein (1999) found that only those with phonological overlap exhibited a word frequency effect. Rather than treat blends as splices of two words of equal status, Laubstein interepreted a blend such as *snickering/chuckling → snickeling*, where much of the phonological material is shared, as a target (*snickering*) which has been subjected to a process of "sublexical substitution" by an intruder (*chuckling*). One reason for taking this approach is that

118 *Word Frequency and Lexical Diffusion*

such blends never involve more or fewer syllables than either of the two participant words – *nullifies/negates* can yield only a two- or three-syllable word, not a one- or four-syllable one. That is, the intended target "provides all the features of the word, including its metrical structure, foot and syllable structure, and its segmental makeup. The intruder provides only one subsyllabic constituent (or affix)" (p. 138). Such phonological information occurs only in the lexeme. Of the blends of this kind in her study, 61 percent of the targets were more frequent than their intruders (p. 139). In contrast, blends which involved semantic similarity but not phonetic overlap, such as *yes/right* → *yight*, showed no frequency effect, reflecting their production at the lemma level (p. 141).

Other frequency effects have been found in naming tasks. Oldfield and Wingfield (1965), for instance, found that subjects took longer to name pictures of objects with low-frequency names (e.g. *syringe*) than pictures with high-frequency names (e.g. *basket*), with Wingfield (1968) verifying that this effect was due to lexical differences (i.e. at the lexeme level), not to the speed at which the objects were recognized (which would occur at the lemma level). That morphological information is also registered at the lemma level has been shown by studies eliciting gender assignment. For instance, Jescheniak and Levelt (1994) replicated Oldfield and Wingfield's (1965) results and added an experiment eliciting gender decision for Dutch words, *het* (neuter) versus *de* (feminine or masculine). Since gender is not phonologically encoded in that language, a decision about gender should involve a search for information available as part of the lemma. Although they found that the gender-appropriate article of more frequent words was accessed more frequently in the initial task, this effect was not robust over repetitions: "whereas the frequency effect amounted to 54 ms [between high- versus low-frequency words] at the first presentation, it shrank to 15 ms in the second presentation" (p. 834). In contrast, in the replicated naming task involving lexemes, the frequency effect remained robust over repetitions, being just as robust even on the third trial as on the first. Jescheniak and Levelt attribute the dissipation of the frequency effect in the gender-naming task to a recency effect. That is, "the connection strength between a lemma and its gender node ... increases every time the word's gender information is used and decays slowly thereafter" (p. 835). Thus, the gender of infrequent words was accessed more quickly the second time around because the connection had just been made shortly before – as part of the lemma. If gender were encoded in the lexeme, the effect of frequency should have remained constant across repetitions.

Lexical Diffusion and Word Class 119

More evidence that during production frequency effects occur only at the lexeme level comes from studies of substitution errors. When the substitution is meaning-based, as in *shoe* for *boot*, the intruding word is just as likely to be less frequent than the target as it is to be more frequent. When the substitution is form-based, however, as in *shoe* for *zoo*, the intruding word is usually more frequent than the target word (Viso et al. 1991; Hotopf, 1980). Other studies have also shown that low-frequency words are more prone to speech errors than high-frequency words (Dell 1988, 1990; Stemberger 1984; Stemberger and MacWhinney, 1986), on which the notions of entrenchment and lexical strength are based. That is, with each encounter, high-frequency words become more and more entrenched in the lexicon, making them less susceptible to error and to certain types of change, such as analogy (Bybee 2001: 136).

Yet, contrary to one-way process models such as Levelt's (2001), the production of word forms must still allow for some "leakage" and look-back features, as well as connections between lexemes. In particular, mixed-error word substitutions support a model that allows some bidirectional interaction between the lemmas and word forms. Dell and O'Seaghdha (1992: 296) give examples of errors that contain both semantic and phonological similarities to their targets, as in *start → stop* or *cat → rat*, and summarize the evidence accumulated by Dell and Reich (1981), Harley (1984), and Martin et al. (1989): "The important point about mixed errors is that they are much more likely than would be predicted from the independent contributions of phonological and semantic similarity. ... Therefore, mixed errors suggest an interactive influence of semantics and phonology in lexical selection." They describe their "interactive two-step hypothesis" as follows:

> Activation is predominantly semantic during lemma access, and activation is predominantly phonological during phonological access, but there is some activation of phonological information during lemma access, and some activation of semantic information during phonological access. Typically, this interactive view is implemented through spreading activation. (p. 289)

Other evidence that there must be some interaction between levels comes from Miozzo and Caramazza's (1997) tip-of-the-tongue experiment, which found that grammatical class and the initial phoneme of

120 *Word Frequency and Lexical Diffusion*

a word were equally likely to be retrieved before the full phonological form. Perhaps Saffran (2003: 273) expresses it best:

> The assumption that there are regions of specialization within the language system does not entail the assumption that these subcomponents must operate independently of one another, as some theorists have claimed (for example, Fodor, 1983). Evidence for the interaction of various forms of linguistic information (e.g., Dell et al, 1997; MacDonald et al, 1994) indicates that at least some components must be highly interconnected.

Further evidence that the relationship between lemmas and lexemes is more complex than originally conceived comes from studies of homophones. Of particular interest is the finding that a less frequent homophone benefits from its more frequent partner. Dell (1990), for instance, found that a low-frequency word such as *wee* was just as likely to trigger a phonological error as its high-frequency homophone, *we*. And Jescheniak and Levelt (1994: 838) found that when Dutch speakers proficient in English were given a task in which they had to translate an English word, the low-frequency Dutch lexemes (e.g. *bos* 'bunch') benefited from their high-frequency homophones (e.g. *bos* 'forest') so that in the speed of access, they behaved like the words in the high-frequency control group. Jescheniak et al. (2003) replicated Jescheniak and Levelt's (1994) experiment, yielding the same result, and conducted a similar experiment with speakers of German, which confirmed their conclusion. In a more recent study, Cohn et al. (2005) measured the duration of homophones which varied in degree to which their word frequencies differed: homophones with large frequency difference were *time/thyme* and *way/whey*; with medium difference *beach/beech*, *pain/pane*, *gate/gait*, *night/knight*, *sign/sine*, and *birth/berth*; with no difference *sun/son*, *loot/lute*, *peace/piece*, *knave/nave*, *chord/cord*, and *poll/pole*. They found no significant difference between the three categories. And Labov (1994: 460–5) reports no frequency effect in the data collected by Hindle (1980) on the pronunciation of the vowels /u/ and /o/ in the homonyms *two/too* and *know/no* in a speaker from Philadelphia, where the vowels are shifting. He concludes that "We fail to find any evidence for lexical diffusion in these two changes in progress; all available data point to phonetically conditioned, gradual sound change in the spirit of Neogrammarian proclamation" (p. 465). In the light of the other studies reported above, however, Labov and Hindle's finding is not surprising, since they were looking at homophones from different word classes (and

Lexical Diffusion and Word Class 121

hence lemmas) which share a common word form. What their findings and others' have done is to firmly locate frequency effects at the word form or lexeme level.

On the other hand, we know that homophones may follow independent paths during historical change, as in tone shifts in Chinese. Chen (1972: 491), for instance, reports that in the Choazhou dialect "fully 58 per cent of the original 491 homonym sets [in Middle Chinese] have undergone divergent developments." Chen's suggestion that one explanation might be literary and colloquial pronunciations coexisting side by side could account for homonyms in the same word class, but it does not address homophones of different word classes, and clearly more research needs to be done in this area. For instance, Jescheniak et al. (2003: 437) suggest that some languages might be more susceptible to frequency inheritance in homophones. They observe that "Dutch and German have relatively few homophones and revealed frequency inheritance effects (Jescheniak & Levelt, 1994, and the present study). Chinese has relatively many homophones but did not show an inheritance effect (Caramazza, Costa, et al., 2001)." Although they raise questions about the latter article's results, they conclude that "[p]erhaps frequency inheritance in homophones is more likely to be observed in some languages than in others" (p. 437) and see this as a field for further research.[5]

Among the sound changes presented in this book, the discussion in Chapter 2 of stress shifts in English requires the split of homonyms such as *convíct* (noun or verb) into *cónvict* (n.) versus *convíct* (v.). That is, two lemmas which originally linked to a single word form, /kən'vɪct/ became linked to separate word forms, /'kɑnˌvɪkt/ for the noun and /kən'vɪct/ for the verb. Recall that the motivation behind this split was the preponderance of disyllabic nouns in English having initial stress and disyllabic verbs having final stress. Therefore, the creation of the innovative form *cónvict* (n.) relied on the same generalization about English stress that the creation of a totally new lexeme would rely on. It was the low entrenchment, the low lexical strength of the connection between the noun lemma and its word form that allowed the creation of the new word form with initial stress. The implementation of this shift required the same process to occur in individual speakers' production; that is, weak connections between infrequent forms were overruled by the new pronunciation that conformed to the general behavior of nouns in English.

The opposite pattern, exhibited by stress shift in words ending in *-ate* affecting the most frequent words first, is probably due to the different prosodic contexts of the word forms, as is, no doubt, the

122 Word Frequency and Lexical Diffusion

development of adjectival forms with schwa in their final syllable rather than full vowels, as in the pronunciations of *alternate* as /al-tər-nət/ for the adjectival versus its earlier pronunciation, which is now reserved for the verb /al-tər-net/. That is, pronunciation differences due to varying prosodic contexts might lead to lexicalization and thus, in turn, to the split of homophones into "multiple lexemes." Jurafsky et al. (2002), for instance, found that "the frequent partitive sense of *of* was more likely to have a deleted coda than the less frequent genitive or complement senses" but that "the relativizer sense of *that* is shorter and has more coda deletion than the equally frequent complementizer sense of *that*" (p. 27). They acknowledged that meaning (at the lemma level) and frequency were not directly linked in production, but searched for an explanation for the productions of *of.* Their solution was that diachronic splits of homonyms could arise due to factors other than frequency, such as prosodic prominence within the clause, which leads the differing pronunciations to become lexicalized – making it seem at times that a change, such as reduction, is associated with more frequent lemmas (p. 27). Their proposal led them to posit a multiple lexeme model which includes fine phonetic detail in lexical entries:

> Perhaps, for example, ..., all lemmas for *of* are linked to the word-forms [ʌv] and [ʌ], but the genitive or complement *of* is linked more preferentially to the wordform [ʌv], while the partitive *of* is linked more preferentially to [ʌ]. Similarly, the relativizer sense of *that* could be preferentially linked to [ðæ], while the complementizer sense of *that* could be preferentially linked to [ðæt]. (p. 28)

Such a view might well explain the results of Guion's (1995) study on homonyms as well, which showed a difference in behavior between citation forms and sentence-embedded forms. She found that for pairs such as *whey/way* and *knead/need,* "the citation forms showed no difference in either duration or second formant frequency. The words in the sentences did, however, show systematic differences in duration and second formant frequency" (p. 112).

Thus, it appears that homophones of even closely related word classes might split through a lexification of subtle phonetic differences in natural speech. Such an interpretation also fits well with the overwhelming evidence, summarized in Lachs et al. (2003), that speakers store in implicit memory fine phonetic detail of variations in the speech signal. Such evidence strongly supports the position that word forms are not stored as sequences of autonomous phonemes but as wholes,

Lexical Diffusion and Word Class 123

including both linguistic and extralinguistic information, compatible, they say, with current exemplar theory (Lachs et al. 2003: 225). Thus the "extensiveness and pervasiveness of homonym splits" that Chen (1972: 492) cites may not be so difficult to explain after all.

4.4 Conclusion

Often it is indeed difficult to tease apart the disparate influences at work on a particular sound change. Carr (1991: 52), for instance, reports on a weakening of the consonant /t/, which is influenced both by word class and by phonetic environment in different ways in different stages and geographical locations:

> The rule of Weakening is common in accents in the middle and far north of England, according to Wells (1982: 370), who states that it applies **only where the preceding vowel is short**. This is parallel to the claim made by Wright (1892: 87) for the West Yorkshire dialect of Windhill, which, like present day Tyneside, had Weakening **in the word *what*, and in verbs where the vowel in question was short**. Wright presents no cases of word-final /t/ in nouns undergoing Weakening, and in fact cites an example where **Weakening applies to a word-final /t/ in a verb** and then **fails to apply in a noun**, in *get a bit of time*, where Weakening applies to the /t/ in *get* but not to the /t/ in *bit*. Petyt's (1985: 151–152) examples for industrial West Yorkshire are limited in number but show Weakening applying **only in monosyllabic verbs and in *what***. It would appear that in Tyneside, this restriction to the word *what* **spread to other non-lexical words such as *that*, *not*, and *but*,** and that application in verbs spread from those with a short vowel to **all verbs with the stress on the final syllable**, regardless of vowel length. [my bold]

In order to help sort out the many influences on the course of sound change, this chapter has attempted to present more straightforward examples of the effect of word class on lexical diffusion. In general, we have found that weakening sound changes tend to affect word categories with low sentence stress, such as function words, whereas strengthening sound changes have the opposite effect. In addition, word frequency effects have been shown to be clearest inside of word classes – as one might expect, since in production word class is accessed before the word form and its phonetic encoding. Therefore, word frequency effects are often clearest within grammatical word classes.

5
Analogy, Borrowing, and Lexical Diffusion

5.0 Introduction

Exceptions to sound changes have often been "explained" by reference to borrowing or analogy. In their introduction to *The Handbook of Historical Linguistics*, Janda and Joseph (2003a: 115), in fact, justify their failure to accord lexical diffusion a discussion of its own on the grounds that "diffusionary effects in the spread of phonological change through the lexicons of speakers...are actually epiphenomenal, being the result of already-needed mechanisms of analogical change and dialect borrowing." Such opinions are shared by such linguists as Hale (2003: 356), who sees "apparent" lexical diffusion as borrowing between dialects, and Kiparsky (1995: 647–51), who conflates analogy and lexical diffusion. Analogy and borrowing, however, are not sufficient to account for the behavior of lexically diffused changes, and the purpose of this chapter is to demonstrate why lexical diffusion must be an independent phenomenon. In particular, that borrowing and traditional notions of analogy are not commensurate with lexical diffusion will be shown by the fact that changes typically labeled as either borrowing or analogy can be diffused lexically in very different word frequency patterns. Thus, neither an appeal to borrowing nor to analogy can account for the lexical progression of a change.

Crucially, the difference between MOTIVATION, INNOVATION, and IMPLEMENTATION of a change must be understood and maintained. Speakers innovate. Any sound change must begin with a particular speaker or group of speakers introducing a new, variable pronunciation, a point which J. Milroy (1992c: 77) emphasizes when he says that the distinction between innovation and change involves a "distinction in principle between *speaker* and *system*" and the "associated distinction – the distinction between speaker *innovation*, on the one hand, and linguistic *change*, on the other. Innovation and change are not conceptually the same thing: an innovation is an act of the speaker, whereas a change is manifested within the language system. It is speakers, and not languages, that innovate." The **motivation** for a change may be internal (coarticulation, reanalysis, analogy, etc.) or it may be external (such as borrowing based on the prestige of another dialect or language). But whatever the motivation, the innovation, to gain larger currency, must spread to other speakers. This **implementation** of the change can only be accomplished through borrowing from speakers by speakers. The **ordered heterogeneity** described by Weinreich et al. (1968: 100) also extends to the lexicon: simultaneous with the social and phonetic diffusion of a change, it is also spreading within each speaker's internal lexicon through the network of connections between similar words and the pronunciation of those words is being shared with other speakers. Whether from a source external to the speech community or from one internal to it, as a new pronunciation becomes more and more productive, it spreads through the lexicon by affecting the most frequent words first if it requires no deeper analysis than access to the phonetic detail in its word form. If, in production, the implementation requires deeper analysis – say, access to the word's grammatical class or phonotactic structure – it affects the least frequent words first. Analogy and borrowing may provide the motivation behind many sound changes, and phonetic analogy and conceptual analogy are no doubt involved in the progression of a change through an individual's lexicon, but that progression is via lexical diffusion, one or more words at a time, not all words simultaneously.

5.1 Lexical diffusion and analogy

The most noted proponent of lexical diffusion as a subset of analogical changes is Kiparsky, who argues that lexical diffusion is "not an exceptional type of sound change, nor a new, fourth type of linguistic change, but a well-behaved type of analogical change. . . . [G]enuine instances of 'lexical diffusion' (those which are not due to other mechanisms such as dialect mixture) are *all* the result of analogical change" (1995: 641). By identifying lexical diffusion with analogy, he attempts to maintain the tripartite division of linguistic change into "sound change," "analogy," and "borrowing." And "sound change" he identifies only with regular, neogrammarian changes.[1] Kiparsky (1995: 643), in a section entitled "It walks like analogy, it talks like analogy. . . ," claims that lexical diffusion "behave[s] like lexical *analogy* in every respect." Using the example

126 *Word Frequency and Lexical Diffusion*

of the shortening of English /u/ in words like *took* and *should*, he explains,

> the direction of phonemic replacement is determined by the rule, and its actuation is triggered jointly by the generalization of the rule to new contexts, and by the item-by-item simplification of lexical representations in each context. When idiosyncratic feature specifications are eliminated from lexical entries, the features automatically default to the values assigned by the rule system, just as when the special form *kine* is lost from the lexicon the plural of *cow* automatically defaults to *cows*. (p. 644)

Kiparsky identifies exceptionless sound changes as affecting the postlexical phonology, whereas lexical diffusion and analogy he sees as working within the Lexical Phonology, reflected in the "quantal" item-by-item nature of the two processes. We have shown in numerous examples in Chapter 3, however, that many changes are both phonetically gradual and lexically gradual. This alone negates Kiparsky's identification, within his own system of lexically diffused and analogical changes, since lexically diffused changes are not necessarily "quantal," that is, abrupt.

Even within the generative paradigm, Hale (2003: 352–4) takes issue with Kiparsky's identification of morphological analogy with phonological regularization. He points out that it is easy to imagine a scenario whereby a child does not have a lexical item *kine* and no exception marker on *cow* that signals the plural is *kine*, leading the child to produce *cows* as the default plural. He adds, "The same scenario cannot hold, however, for a phonological representation. To fail to acquire the underlying phonological representation of a given lexeme is to lack that lexeme altogether" (p. 353). As he concisely sums up the problem: "Morphological representations are derived representations, whereas underlying phonological representations are input representations." A similar point is made by Reiss (2003: 150) in his critique of Kiparsky's argument that "analogical change is grammar optimization." Reiss points out that this view requires learners "to first correctly acquire the target grammar (so they can evaluate its complexity), and then to replace the acquired grammar with a simpler one. Such a view requires the child to successfully acquire one of the ambient languages, then to reject it as too complex, despite the fact that some of the speakers in the environment do have such grammars." Reiss argues, in fact, that since language change is part of E-language (externalized language) in the

Analogy, Borrowing, and Lexical Diffusion 127

sense of Chomsky (1986) and since E-language "involves idealization over abstract entities like speech communities" whereas phonological theories in the generative paradigm, whether rule-based or constraint based, focus in I-language (internalized language), there is no sense in which generative phonological theories can speak of language change: "[T]he term 'language change' is a misnomer. This is because there is no meaningful sense in which the mental grammar in one speaker's mind turns into the grammar instantiated in another speaker's mind" (p. 148).

From the viewpoint of lexical diffusion, however, especially troubling in an identification of lexical diffusion with morphological analogy is the assumption that all lexically diffused changes behave the same with regard to word frequency. They do not. In the case of morphological substitutions, analogical changes have been shown to affect the least frequent words first. Noting that analogical changes occur "when memory fails," Hooper (1976), for instance, shows that the diffusion of the regular past tense suffix affects the least frequent words first. Frequent words such as *be, come, do, give* remain irregular because they are more entrenched in memory. This means that if lexical diffusion were identical to morphological analogy, one would expect lexically diffused sound changes to affect the least frequent words first. But only a subset of lexically diffused changes behave in this way. Three sound changes which have affected the least frequent words first are glide deletion in Southern American English, unrounding of Middle English /ö:/, and stress shift in diatonic words such as *address* and *convict* (Phillips 1984 and Chapter 3 above). Yet far more frequent – certainly more frequently documented – are changes which affect the most frequent words first, as Schuchardt (1885: 58) initially suggested: "Rarely used words drag behind; very frequently used ones hurry ahead." Many changes of this type are discussed in Chapter 3 above and include, for example, the raising of Old English /a/ to /o/ before nasals (Phillips 1980), Modern English schwa deletion (Hooper 1976), intervocalic spirantization in Ethiopian languages (Leslau 1969: 182–3), and Modern English stress shift in words ending in *-ate* (Phillips 1998c). In fact, Ogura (1987: 173) has shown that Kiparsky's own example of English /ū/ becoming /ʊ/ affected the most frequent words first. In addition, Phillips (1983c) investigated the lexical diffusion of Middle English diphthongization of vowel + glide sequences, a change which began before consonants but was extended by phonetic analogy to word-final position and then to intervocalic position. It was found that this change in its later stages did not behave like other analogies, affecting the least

128 *Word Frequency and Lexical Diffusion*

frequent words first, but just the opposite. Even in the extended environments, the most frequent words were affected first (p. 20).

It is noteworthy that an analogical approach to language does exist that incorporates word frequency. Skousen's model (1989, 1992; Skousen et al. 2002), in fact, works much like interactive accounts. And Skousen (1992: 5–6) contrasts his approach with rule-based models of structural linguistics, finding among other differences, that

> rule descriptions are virtually incapable of describing the probabilistic behavior characteristic of language variation. In fact, the correct description of non-deterministic behavior may ultimately require a separate rule for every different set of conditions. Taken to its logical conclusion, this would mean that each rule would represent a single occurrence since probably no two occurrences are completely identical (given enough textual specification). ... Most importantly, analogical models are dynamic alternatives to the static descriptions of rules.

Skousen (1992: 7) notes the similarity of his model to interactive models, and such models are, in fact, the only current models in linguistics that can account for frequency effects. As Bybee (2001: 110) proposes, "what determines whether a morphologically complex form is stored in memory is its frequency of use, not its classification as regular or irregular." And the same is true of morphologically simple forms. That is, it is the degree of entrenchment, or lexical strength, which is based on frequency of use that determines whether an item can be retrieved in production easily and without recourse to deeper analysis than the phonetic shape of its stored word form. Changes, both morphological and phonological, that affect the least frequent words first do so because such forms are not deeply entrenched in memory, necessitating retrieval of generalizations such as word class or preferred phonotactic shape, which influence the pronunciation of these word forms.

5.2 Lexical diffusion and borrowing

Two very different approaches to borrowing are presented by Kiparsky (1995: 643) and J. Milroy (1992c, 1999). Kiparsky sees borrowing as a type of change distinct from regular (i.e. neogrammarian) change, analogy, and lexical diffusion. Borrowing proceeds item by item, is quantal (not gradual), occurs as a result of contact, and is rapid. Lexically

Analogy, Borrowing, and Lexical Diffusion 129

diffused changes, he claims, share the first two qualities, but are "endogenous" and slow. The characteristics Kiparsky attributes to borrowing follow Bloomfield's (1933: 390) account, which uses as an example the replacement of the tongue-tip trill by the uvular trill in various European language varieties. Bloomfield says, "Aside from its spread by borrowing, the new habit ... could have originated only as a sudden replacement of one trill by another. A replacement of this sort is surely different from the gradual and imperceptible alterations of phonetic change." Milroy (2003b: 214–15) takes issue with this statement of Bloomfield's, however, and points out, among other things, that what Bloomfield calls a change is a *speaker innovation* and that "an innovation is not in itself a change. ... Here, linguistic change (change in the system) is defined as a separate phenomenon from speaker-based innovation, and the problem becomes one of explaining how innovations that are constantly taking place feed into the system only at particular times and places" (p. 215). As Milroy (1992c: 88) makes clear, however, all change involves borrowing: "[W]e have no criteria for determining absolutely that there is an axiomatic distinction between sound change and borrowing (or contact change) because ... all changes must arise from contact between speakers." Milroy's position echoes those of Wang and Lien (1993: 356) that "there is no conflict between lexical diffusion and borrowing" and of Schuchardt, whose position Vennemann (1972: 171) summarizes as follows: "The mechanism of spread of sound change is borrowing by imitation....There is no difference in principle between borrowing among individuals and borrowing among dialects."

Explanations that appeal to borrowing from an external dialect even for the innovation stage of a change without confirming independent evidence, of course, should always be met with a healthy dose of skepticism. In addition to the tendency to treat borrowing as a "waste-basket" category for exceptions that have no clear explanations, Chen (1972: 462–5) lists other shortcomings inherent in a facile appeal to dialect borrowing. For one thing, in most cases, it is impossible to rule out the possibility of dialect borrowing: "[D]ialect mixture is a partially vitiated hypothesis to the extent that it cannot define what would constitute counter-evidence. A hypothesis which admits of no counter-evidence is not a well-formed hypothesis" (p. 465). Also, perhaps even more importantly, the notion of "dialect" itself is fuzzy. It is unclear where a dialect begins and where it ends. As Paul (1880: 390) points out, if we start from the proposition that each individual has his/her own idiolect, then as soon as two people talk with each other, dialect mixture (*Sprachmischung*) has occurred.[2] Indeed, Chen concludes, linguists who

130 *Word Frequency and Lexical Diffusion*

adhere to the philosophy that the object of linguistic description should be an ideal speaker-hearer in a completely homogeneous speech community have no other way of accounting for exceptions, since every person's speech is a composite of their interaction with other speakers and groups of speakers. Thus, we are brought back to the inevitable conclusion that the implementation of all sound change must be through borrowing, from speaker to speaker, whether within the same dialect or across dialect or language barriers. J. Milroy (2003b: 215), again, makes the point clear in his discussion of the replacement of the tongue-tip trill with the uvular trill in Europe:

> [I]f we accept Bloomfield's distinction, we may be inclined to believe that we can locate the "original" innovation in some specific community at some particular date, when there can be no guarantee at all that this is the original "sound change" (or innovation) – the *Urquelle* of all the "borrowings". We cannot be certain that it had not previously been imported from somewhere else where it was "more original" – and so on backwards ad infinitum with the origin continuously receding and eluding our grasp. In general, therefore, the distinction on which Bloomfield depended (true sound change vs. borrowing) is difficult to maintain here, and the internal/external dichotomy is again at issue. The implementation of this *change* seems to involve a process that has been called *borrowing*: if so, this process is part of the (internal?) *sound change*.

Johanson (2002: 309) expresses a similar position when he says he is "inclined to conceive of internal factors as tendencies that may become the object of external causation." Such a case may well be the influence of Low German on open-syllable lengthening in High German. Becker (2002) presents evidence for a possible influence but admits that, as a phonetically natural change, the influence of Low German may be an illusion (p. 51). Certainly, even if the innovation in High German is motivated by imitation of lengthening in Low German, at every stage of the implementation, the imitation of particular words from Low German to High German or from High German speaker to High German speaker must be part of the spread of the change.

Also inexplicable in a theory that equates borrowing with lexical replacement or phoneme substitution is the behavior of what Trudgill (1986: 59–61) calls FUDGED DIALECTS. In such dialects "the accommodation is incomplete by being partial *phonetically*" (p. 61); that is, in dialects of Southern England one finds innovative [ʌ] in words such as *cup*, *butter*, *love*, and *come*, whereas in Northern dialects one finds conservative [ʊ]. *Fudged dialects* are those located between the two that in these words produce an intermediate vowel [ɤ]. Trudgill grasps the importance of this fact for the debate between neogrammarian and lexically diffused changes: "Note that fudged dialects force a redefinition of *lexical diffusion* which, in that it focuses on the spread of changes through the lexicon, is usually characterized (see Wang, 1969) as being 'phonetically sudden but lexically gradual'. Clearly fudging is both phonetically *and* lexically gradual" (p. 61).

In discussing the spread of a pronunciation, one must, of course, take into consideration the different types of contact between speakers. On a very simplistic level, one must at least distinguish contact between speakers of different languages, contact between speakers of different varieties of the same language, and contact between speakers of a homogeneous language or dialect. But as Thomason (2003: 697) suggests, "Change resulting from code-switching between different languages does, of course, differ from change via diffusion from another register and dialect borrowing; but ... the differences are a matter of degree, not of kind." In contact situations with other languages, many factors determine the number and type of words borrowed and whether their pronunciations are adopted or adapted to the borrowing language. Very often the choice of words is determined by semantic fields, as in the number of French words borrowed into Middle English from the fields of government, architecture, and the arts. In contact between dialects of the same language, it is also true that sociological factors often determine the number and types of words borrowed and which pronunciations are imitated; for instance, there is probably a sociological reason why teenagers in Terre Haute, Indiana, occasionally are heard to say "Oh, man!" with a tensed [Æ] in *man*, a sporadic borrowing that has not led to a spread of the tense vowel to other lexical items. Similarly, the sporadic pronunciation in the United States of *either* with an initial diphthong [aɪ] in both cultivated and uncultivated dialects is most likely "a recent adoption from British English" (Kurath and McDavid 1961: 149), one which has developed no productivity.

Indeed, deciding when a change has occurred is not a simple matter. There is, in fact, much disagreement on the point at which one may say a *change* has taken place. As Andersen (2001a: 228–9) notes,

> "change" is a pretheoretical notion with no fixed extension. This is why it is sometimes an issue whether a given historical event sequence in a tradition of speaking is to be understood as a series of changes, as one

132   *Word Frequency and Lexical Diffusion*

> single change, or as part(s) of a change.... [E]very change in a tradition of speaking is analyzable into smaller events...*subchanges*, sometimes understandable as a single act of *innovation*, but mostly composed of a stream of numerous, practically identical acts of innovation, made in speech acts by individual speakers and hearers. Changes of different type consist of distinct combinations of subchanges, logically consecutive, but in actuality always overlapping in time.

As Schuchardt pointed out many years ago, "Every stage of a language is a transitional stage" (1885 [1972]: 53). Since diffusion of a change through the lexicon occurs neither at the beginning – innovation – nor at some arbitrary later point in time, but during the entire **implementation** of the change until all the possible words have been affected, this may seem to be a nonissue. But it is for this reason, if for none other, that the idea that neogrammarian changes represent the end result of lexically diffused changes (Lass 1984: 326–7), although totally congruent with the position taken in this book, does not answer the debate about how changes are implemented. The evidence regarding that debate is becoming ever stronger that sound changes spread through the lexicon, affecting one or several words at a time until, perhaps, all the words with a particular phonological structure have been affected.

Nonetheless, the complexity of the implementation phase is immense. Many of the issues are discussed, for instance, by Wolfram and Schilling-Estes's recent contribution to the *Handbook of Historical Linguistics* (2003), who make it clear that, among other influences, a change becomes propagated through social groups, through phonological and morphological environments, and through the lexicon. All of these happen simultaneously, and even within individuals variation is to be expected. As Wolfram and Schilling-Estes explain: "the notion of variability ... applies to both intra-speaker and inter-speaker variation. In other words, an individual speaker will go through a period of fluctuation between the old and new variant, and speakers within a given speech community will show variation from speaker to speaker with respect to the use of the new and old variant" (p. 717). (See Andersen 2001a for examples of morphological change progressing according to morphological and semantic criteria.)

It is also difficult to know sometimes, even when a change has occurred, whether it is an independent development or the result of the influence of another dialect/variety. For example, J. Milroy (1992a: 58–9) looks into the development of *back* varieties of /a/ in Belfast English,

Analogy, Borrowing, and Lexical Diffusion 133

where "one common local belief ... is that upper-middle-class people tend to front-raise /a/ (as in *bat*) towards the conservative RP value: [æ]." But Milroy finds that, although the realization in Belfast English of /a/ as a long, back vowel in such words as *dance* and *bath* does seem to mimic RP speech, there is a difference between the two varieties in the pair *can, can't*: Belfast *can* has long a *back* vowel and *can't* has a short *front* vowel – whereas RP has the opposite pattern. As he says, "on a superficial view we may...be tempted to believe that speakers are adopting this external norm. ... Of these environments, however, only the voiceless fricative and /r/ environments coincide with the backing environments of RP, so we are clearly dealing with a different /a/-backing rule." The rule of /a/-raising is also different in the two dialects, with the raising in Belfast being limited to prevelar environments, as other Ulster varieties also attest. Milroy concludes:

> RP thus has no direct effect on the convergence pattern displayed by middle-class speakers; therefore, if we start with the RP norm and derive these speech community patterns from it, we can falsify the situation totally. In this case the main falsification would be that hundreds of thousands of inner-city speakers who are not remotely interested in RP have "borrowed" back [ɑ] from RP. (p. 59)

At other times, the influence of another variety is clear, but the behavior of the borrowing dialect regarding phonological environment is quite different from that of its source. A good example is Wolfram and Schilling-Estes's (1996) account of the adoption of the unglided Southern pronunciation [aː] for the traditional pronunciation [ɔɪ] in Ocracoke, North Carolina. They find that "Southern [aː] is making its way into the Ocracoke dialect in a phonetically implausible manner. Whereas other dialects of Southern English favor Southern [aː] before voiced segments (e.g. *tide*), particularly nasals (e.g. *time*), Ocracoke favors its incidence before voiceless segments (e.g. *light*)" (p. 70), suggesting that "Southern ungliding is clearly being resisted where the [ɔɪ] associated with the traditional Ocracoke brogue is most strongly entrenched – before voiced obstruents" (p. 77). In this regard, it differs from the borrowings we will investigate below. They consider it an incipient change, since "it is characterized by low frequency usage levels (less than 10 per cent of all potential unglided phonological environments are actually unglided) and lexical constraints on its variability (for example, a major item for ungliding is the lexical item *Carolina*)" (p. 80). (Unfortunately, they do not list other words that exhibit either

134 *Word Frequency and Lexical Diffusion*

pronunciation.) On the basis of such sound changes, Wolfram and Schilling-Estes (2003: 720) suggest that "the role of the lexicon in phonological change is more prominent at the incipient and cessation stages of a change than at its midpoint" and that in the typical S-curve trajectory of such a change, "irregularity and lexical diffusion are maximized at the beginning and the end of the slope and phonological regularity is maximized during the rapid expansion in the application of the rule change during the mid-course of change." Their use of the term "maximized" here is well taken. At every point, both phonological conditioning and lexical diffusion are active, but it does seem true that lexical leaders and lexical exceptions are most noticeable at the beginning and at the end of a sound change, whether it begins as a borrowing from another dialect or from within the speech community itself.

The particular role of word frequency in changes that clearly have their basis in imitation of other dialects or varieties has also been disputed. For instance, Bybee (2000b: 82) suggests that a certain change "is a dialect borrowing or accommodation to the standard dialect. Words learned at the mother's knee, so to speak, would be the most conservative, while the least frequent words would be affected first." Gerritsen and Jansen (1980), on the other hand, attribute to dialect borrowing a sound change that affected the most frequent words first:

> In the case of unnatural change, i.e. dialect borrowing, the following is to be expected. . . . In all probability, dialect speakers will hear and recognize the Amsterdam variants first in highly frequent words. It is acceptable, therefore, to assume that in the subsequent process of unconscious imitation of the new variant, the dialect speaker will use Amsterdam variants first and foremost in the words he frequently heard pronounced with the Amsterdam variants, thus in highly frequent words.

These functional explanations clearly contradict each other.

The discussion of borrowing and lexical diffusion below will focus on changes that clearly have as their source imitation of an external dialect. It will become clear that, with regard to word frequency, natural changes that have been adopted into a speech community from an external variety behave much as changes that have their impetus within the speech community. For example, the changes discussed in section 5.2.2 below involve a natural realignment of articulatory gestures, and speakers of the borrowing dialect produce the new pronunciation first in the more frequent words. Many other borrowings from other dialects affect the less frequent words first, particularly when the change involves the imitation of "unnatural" changes, such as the reversal of an earlier phonetically natural change through imitation of a standard dialect. In addition, the CULTURAL BORROWING of words from select semantic fields seems to affect the least frequent words, since everyday terms are rarely included in such borrowings. Whether the change involves just a few words or represents a later stage in which it has developed productivity within the borrowing speech community, the propagation of the change always involves imitation of other speakers.

5.2.1 Borrowings which affect the least frequent words first

Bloomfield (1933: 444) distinguishes between "*dialect borrowing,* where the borrowed features come from within the same speech-area (as, *father, rather* with [a] in an [ɛ]-dialect), and *cultural borrowing,* where the borrowed features come from a different language," a distinction that he admits "cannot always be carried out," although his concern seems to be mainly with locating the boundary between such languages as French and Italian or Swedish and Norwegian (pp. 54, 444). We will not be discussing borrowing from other languages here, so we will modify the term to create CULTURAL DIALECT BORROWING for borrowings from another dialect which most noticeably affect special parts of the vocabulary, such as learned, literary, or technical words. Wang and Lien (1993), for example, give a complex example of the interweaving of literary and colloquial strata in Chinese, but without reference to word frequency. Cultural borrowings tend to be drawn from certain semantic fields or higher levels of formality, however, so it is not surprising that less frequent words tend to be associated with them. This is no less true of so-called "reversed changes" motivated by the imitation of a standard dialect as of newly introduced pronunciations from a more prestigious variety. Sometimes word frequency is invoked in such changes, but most frequency effects seem secondary to the borrowing of these pronunci-ations into certain styles or semantic fields. Note that many of these cultural borrowings are also phonetically unnatural – e.g. the restitution of word-final consonants or the introduction of a tense vowel where the phonetic environment has contributed in the past to laxing of the vowel. For that reason, no doubt, they do not normally achieve the sort of productivity typical of many other sound changes that were motivated by imitation of another dialect. Indeed, such borrowings are best seen as LEXICAL REPLACEMENTS, close synonyms that exist in separate registers. The results of such replacements may be seen in DOUBLETS such as *varmint* ~ *vermin, critter* ~ *creature, vase* [ves] ~ *vase* [vɑːz], where

136 *Word Frequency and Lexical Diffusion*

the second lexeme is a lexical replacement from the standard or more prestigious variety.

5.2.1.1 Reversed changes

Many of the studies on dialect influence have been of changes which appear to have reversed course due to influence of standard languages or neighboring dialects. In such cases, frequent words seem the most resistant to the reversal, which is really a lexical replacement from another dialect. For instance, Lippi-Green (1989) reports on a change in progress in a rural village in the Alps. The dialect had already undergone the shift of Middle High German short /a/ from [ɑ] to [ɔ], which had become part of the village's identity. At the time of her investigation, the original change was being reversed under the influence of dialects that had not undergone the shift. As she describes it, "The change displays established characteristics of lexical diffusion (Labov 1981:296): It is discrete, shows exceptions to the lexical category involved, and is neither predictable nor learnable, and it shows some rough phonetic conditioning" (p. 221). It is limited to very formal and infrequent words, but "[a]ll stylistically marked lexical items showed a greater degree of [ɑ] innovation whether or not they were in the lowest frequency ranking" (p. 222). That is to say, the frequency of the words was not really as important as the stylistic marking.

Bakken (2001) reports similar behavior in the restitution of earlier forms in dialects of southern Norway and notes that the true reversal of a change requires that there still be older phonetic/phonotactic patterns that can form the basis for such a reversal. In the case of her Norwegian data, the earlier change appears to have been fully implemented before borrowing reintroduced earlier pronunciations. She identifies several groups resistant to restitution of /l:/ (for /d:/) and /l/ (which had been lost before certain consonants):

(a) word forms which "seem to have a special status within the dialect vocabulary; they are somehow perceived as independent words without links to cognates in neighboring dialects" (e.g. words for 'holiday,' 'follow,' '-self,' 'silver ornament,' 'shallow valley,' 'grassy elevation in an otherwise flat field,' 'merry').
(b) word forms that "never occur in the expected dialectal form," most of which are probably very early restitutions, late loans, or reintroductions.
(c) the words for 'mountain,' 'people,' 'sled,' 'milk,' 'turn over,' and 'cave' (p. 65).

Analogy, Borrowing, and Lexical Diffusion 137

On the role of frequency, Bakken reports that many of the resistant forms are among the most frequent words, although the most frequent word, the pronoun *alle* 'all'

> does not stand out compared to words like *fjøll* and *elleve* 'eleven' that are much less frequent according to a word frequency count for Norwegian (Vestbøstad 1989). Moreover, words that in Vestbøstad (1989) appear to be very infrequent, such as *heller* 'cave', *eismall* 'alone', *kjelke* 'sled', and *talg* 'tallow' are among the last to be restored. (p. 66).

Of course it is clear that Bakken has not controlled for fine phonetic environment or word class. The point here, however, is simply that frequent forms seem especially resistant to the restitution of earlier forms from the influence of other dialects, but because of their associations with the local culture, not because of their token frequency.

Confirming this pattern is Janson's (1977) study of the reintroduction of forms in final /d/ in Modern Swedish, apparently before the original sound change deleting this consonant had been completed. Common words resist the reintroduced /d/ forms, as is well demonstrated in lexical splits where the meaning within a common phrase or expression has diverged from the earlier meaning revealed in the restored forms:

> *Det var syn(d)* That is a pity
> *Han begick en synd* He committed a sin
> *Jag har inte rå(d)* I have no means (or I cannot afford)
> *Ge mig ett råd* Give me advice (p. 261)

5.2.1.2 Other cultural borrowings based on prestige

Similar to reversed changes are those which are based on other borrowings from a more prestigious variety, prestige admittedly being a cover term for many factors, including "usefulness in communication," "function in social advance," and "literary-cultural value" (Weinreich 1974 [1953]: 75–9). To take an example from a non-Indo-European colloquial variety being influenced by a quite different standard variety, Abd-el-Jawad and Suleiman (1990: 294) point out that in the colloquial Arabic variety spoken in north Jordan, speakers substitute standard spoken Arabic [k] in words which otherwise would have [č]. Table 5.1, based on their data, presents phonologically comparable forms which

138   *Word Frequency and Lexical Diffusion*

Table 5.1 Borrowed pronunciations in north Jordan from Standard Arabic (based on Abd-el-Jawad and Suleiman 1990: 94)

Variation	Invariable borrowings from Standard Arabic
kars ~ čars 'belly'	*karaasi* 'chairs'
ʕ il(i)k ~ ʕ ilič 'chewing gum, a name of plant'	*sil(i)k* 'wire'
samak ~ samač 'fish'	*fašak* 'cartridges'
dahak ~ dahač 'he crushed'	*masak* 'he caught'
farak ~ farač 'he rubbed'	*tarak* 'he left'
Haka ~ Hača 'he spoke'	*ʔakal* 'he ate'
Haki ~ Hači 'speech'	*ʔakil* 'food, eating'

nonetheless behave differently. Abd-el-Jawad and Suleiman (1990: 295) find they are led

> to agree with Holes (1983: 442) that if native speakers want to make some purely dialectal lexical items sound "more educated" or "more standard", they will replace these words with completely different S[tandard] A[rabic] words (lexical substitution) with the same meaning rather than applying phonological modification or substitution. This may be true in the case of what is called "paired items" in diglossic languages. However, it is quite common for speakers to modify the COL[loquial] items phonologically only in their attempt to make these items more standard. For example, the local variant [č], the socially marked non-standard form, is often substituted with SA [k] in what may be categorized as local words, such as /čaHHasti/ "box of matches" which corresponds to SA /kibriita/; however, both /kaHHaati/ and /čibriiti/ ~ čabriiti/ do often occur.

In all of the borrowed changes Abd-el-Jawad and Suleiman investigate, however, there is a core set of "items which refer to domestic and local objects and concepts" that maintain the colloquial variant (p. 298). In this way it seems that the most frequent words have been last to change, but in reality it is a semantic category that just happens to occur more frequently that has resisted the change.

These examples are actually quite similar to the familiar example from Bloomfield (1933: 329–31) of isoglosses for the words for *mouse* and *house* in the dialect area overlapping the Netherlands and Germany. Bloomfield reports that in several districts speakers produce the conservative vowel [uː] in *mouse* but innovative [yː] in *house*. Bloomfield argues

Analogy, Borrowing, and Lexical Diffusion 139

that the pattern favors an interpretation of Hollandish influence over North German Hanseatic since

> the word *house* will occur much oftener than the word *mouse* in official speech and in conversation with persons who represent the cultural center; *mouse* is more confined to homely and familiar situations. Accordingly, we find that the word *house* in the upper-class and central form with [y:] spread into districts where the word *mouse* has persisted in the old-fashioned form with [u:].

In this example, it seems that the two words are probably both very frequent, although Kloeke (1927: 190–1) suggested that *muis* was the less frequent and the CELEX database for Dutch lemmas lists the frequency for *muis* as 899 and *huis* as 26,719. Mice, however, were probably more often a topic of conversation in earlier centuries than they are today. In brief, it is difficult to know in such restricted examples whether word frequency or social indices are responsible for the pattern of diffusion.

Clearer is Andersen's (1973) example of adaptive change in certain dialects of Czech. In what he calls the Teták dialects, Proto-Slavic *p *b *m became /t, d, n/, a change which Andersen argues is an EVOLUTIVE change, "entirely explainable in terms of the linguistic system that gave rise to it" (p. 778). The replacement in these dialects of /t, d, n/ by /p, b, m/ was an ADAPTIVE change, "not explainable without reference to factors outside the linguistic system in question" and typically goal-oriented, in this case the outside factor being "the Peták dialects, with whom the Teták speakers came into closer contact as communication improved during the 19th century" (p. 778). Since the Teták pronunciation had become a marker of social inferiority, those speakers imitated the pronunciation of the Peták dialects, with the result that the offending /t, d, n/ now occur "in a small and diminishing number of very common lexemes, e.g. /koutit/ (Standard Czech *koupiti*) 'buy', /tekňe/ (*pěkně*) 'nicely', /di:lej/ (*bílý*), /dežet/ (*běžeti*) 'run', /dřemeno/ (*břemeno*) 'burden', /ni:t/ (*míti*) 'have', /nesto/ (*město*) 'town'" (p. 765).

A number of examples present themselves from the history of French and Spanish. For example, Penny (2000: 70) points out that in the *Atlas linguistique de la France* (1903–10),

> The isoglosses which reflect the advance of /ʃ/ at the expense of /k/ do not coincide exactly, and are sometimes markedly divergent, and it is evident that the rate of advance is more rapid in words associated with supralocal concerns and least rapid in the case of words closely

140 *Word Frequency and Lexical Diffusion*

related with local lifestyles, such as names of farm implements and farm activities.

He follows this with an example from Spanish of "a similar word-by-word retreat of /h/ in western Andalusia": "The isogloss which, in Cantabria, separates retention of initial /h/ in *hacer* 'to do, make' from its deletion (i.e., the isogloss which separates /haθér/ from /aθér/) is to be found further to the west than the isogloss which separates these two pronunciations in *hacha* 'axe' (Penny 1984)" (pp. 70–1).

The complexity of cultural dialect borrowings may be seen in Holder's (1990) study of borrowings in the history of French. The fluctuation between [ɔ] and [u] in Modern French can be traced back to French borrowings from Latin during the Renaissance, borrowings with [ɔ] where French had developed an [u], some examples being "*collection, collège, colosse, copieux, object, volume.*" Sometimes doublets resulted, such as *soleil/souleil* and *brossaille/broussailles*, which eventually chose one vowel over the other, modern *soleil* and *broussailles*. As Holder explains, "The main candidates for *relatinisation* of this sort were words which fell within the learnèd, literary, and administrative sphere, but the innovation spread to familiar vocabulary as well. It was eventually rejected at this level no doubt because of its association with the upper layer of vocabulary" (p. 75). Therefore, the impression is that the [ɔ] pronunciation is limited to less frequent words, but this effect is not due to lexical diffusion by word frequency.

Another case from French involves a complicated relationship between different geographical and social dialects. Holder (1990: 77–80) reports on the borrowing of the *oi* [wɛ] (with a "popular variant" [wa]) from the eastern dialects of France into Paris, which originally patterned with western varieties in developing the reflex *ais* [ɛ]. In the sixteenth century -*ais* mainly subsisted in the imperfect/conditional ending and in geographic adjectives, with "-*ois* ... favoured by the educated classes, whereas -*ais* was distinctly working class Parisian" (p. 77). The -*ais* pronunciation nevertheless itself also developed some prestige within courtly circles since it was associated with being Parisian as opposed to being from the provinces. It is within the geographical adjectives that word frequency effects were noted by French grammarians as early as the eighteenth century. That is, the borrowing of -*ais* from the vernacular into courtly circles affected more frequent words such as *anglais* 'English' and *français* 'French' over the less frequent *suédois* 'Swedish' and *danois* 'Danish.' These pronunciations have become standard usage in French. Holder suggests that word frequency might not have been the primary

Analogy, Borrowing, and Lexical Diffusion 141

factor behind the distribution of these endings, however; for instance, he notes that country names ending in -*land* invariably take the -*ais* ending, regardless of frequency (p. 80).

A final example of the complexity resulting from the imposition of prestigious, prescribed usage comes from Beal's (1999) study of eighteenth-century English pronunciation: "he [Kenrick 1773] writes, that it "would now appear affectation" to pronounce *boil, join*, otherwise than *bile, jine*, but that same pronunciation in *oil, toil* is 'a vicious custom' which "prevails in common conversation" (Kenrick 1773 quoted in Jespersen 1909–49: 330)" (pp. 67–8).

5.2.1.3 *Ideologically motivated vs. ideologically free changes*

Those familiar with Labov's work will recognize these cultural dialect borrowings as examples of CHANGE FROM ABOVE, identified by him with "borrowings from other systems" and acknowledged as subject to lexical diffusion, which he also identifies with "a high degree of social awareness" (1994: 542). He uses the term "lexical diffusion" here, however, in a loose sense and seems to refer to the effect of such changes on a set of readily identifiable words from select semantic fields. Since it is very likely that all sound changes proceed through the lexicon word by word, as argued in the preceding chapters – and that the spread of all change crucially involves spread by borrowing from speaker to speaker – it is not surprising that these socially highly marked borrowings have affected individual words, but this is a narrow, albeit not insignificant, subset of changes that languages undergo. It is not the orderly progression of words through the lexicon that is typical of lexical diffusion as a method of implementing sound change in general. In fact, the "changes from above" discussed in this section seem truly "sporadic" regarding which words are affected. That is, most of the examples above seem to affect infrequent words because they affect learned or formal vocabulary and are often not phonetically natural.

Another factor probably contributes to cultural dialect borrowings affecting the less frequent words first. We know that speakers store fine phonetic detail in exemplars they have for words (Lachs et al. 2003), and Johnson (1997) proposes that the phonological representation consists of a generalization over a group of such exemplars. As Kirchner (1999) notes, "speaker-specific properties of tokens of words remain part of the representation of these words in long-term memory," but he adds the following: "In the case of higher frequency words, however, the individual exemplar does not stand out from its

142 *Word Frequency and Lexical Diffusion*

neighbours to the same extent, because activation of the one also activates a much larger cohort of similar exemplars." That means that the phonetics of a lower-frequency word spoken by a higher-status person would have a better chance of remaining in long-term memory, and thus being activated when the speaker wanted to produce that lexical item.

Such socially indexed changes may best be identified with IDEOLOGICALLY MOTIVATED changes, as described by L. Milroy (2003). She references Silverstein's (1979: 193) definition of *language ideologies* as "sets of beliefs about language articulated by users as a rationalization or justification of perceived language structure or use" and notes that "language ideologies may be viewed as a system for making sense of the indexicality inherent in language, given that languages and language forms index speakers' social identifies fairly reliably in communities.... Typically, social actors associate a linguistic form or variety (accurately or otherwise) with some meaningful social group" (p. 161). Thus language ideologies include, among other things, beliefs about standard languages and their use, and "operate as constraints on global changes" (p. 166). Global changes, on the other hand, are those whose "effect on a wide range of speech communities is similar and cannot readily be explained with reference to local social structure" and are identified with IDEOLOGICALLY FREE changes. She contrasts her divisions with the distinction between CHANGE FROM ABOVE and CHANGE FROM BELOW identified by Labov (1994):

> Labov's long-standing distinction between "changes from above" and "changes from below"... refers simultaneously to levels of social awareness and positions in the socio-economic hierarchy (Labov 1994: 78). The characterization of "change from above" as diffusing from a relatively high-status group of speakers is problematic, since the social semiotics underlying ideologically motivated change are clearly not thus restricted. (p. 168, fn. 3)

Milroy's divisions are more useful in our discussion of lexical diffusion because changes which having strong social indices may begin as ideologically motivated but, if the social conditions change, they may develop in the same way as ideologically free changes. Such "ideologically free" behavior seems to typify the changes we will look at next.

5.2.2 Borrowings which affect the most frequent words first

An example of a sound change that seems to have begun as ideologically motivated imitation of another dialect but which clearly is following

Analogy, Borrowing, and Lexical Diffusion 143

a path of orderly lexical diffusion is the Dublin Vowel Shift among "socially conscious urbanites from outside Dublin" – or "detached participants" (Hickey 1999: 278). The vowel shift itself involves the raising of [ɒ(ː)] to [ɔ(ː)] (the long vowel sometimes raising further to [oː]) and the retraction of [aɪ] to [ɑɪ] and of [ɒɪ] to [ɔɪ] or [oɪ] (p. 275). For "fashionable Dubliners" – or "motivated participants" – the shift affects all words, but for the "detached participants" Hickey (pp. 278–9) describes a highly salient word leading the change, with very frequent words being the next to change:

> [T]he first word to show the Dublin Vowel Shift is *Ireland* and its derivative *Irish*. This is almost a test case, a keyword, for those speakers who are beginning to participate in the shift. The keyword view of lexical diffusion is closely linked to the notion of salience with certain words. Often the words are used as carrier forms for a characteristic pronunciation of a group; common items with this function are the keywords *Irish* and *Ireland*, the numerals *five* and *nine* along with various frequently occurring adjectives like *wild, mild, kind;* nouns like *time, mind, side;* verbs like *rise, drive, hide,* etc.

In a similar vein, the following sections will detail the development of two sound changes which clearly originated in other dialects and which show clear evidence of the influence of word frequency in their diffusion. Both are like the Dublin Vowel Shift in that they are low-level phonetic changes affecting the most frequent words first, just as predicted from the behavior of other sound changes discussed in Chapter 3. Thus, the motivation behind the shifts – imitation of another variety – is not what determines their implementation. The key factors in their propagation through the lexicon are, instead, phonetic similarity and word frequency. The first example originated as a borrowing into American English from British, and the other affected one dialect of Old English before spreading to another.

5.2.2.1   *The spread of broad /aː/ to the United States*

According to Wells (1982: 232), by the middle of the eighteenth century in England, short [æ] had lengthened and developed into [aː] (later [ɑː]) before voiceless fricatives and certain nasals in words such as *bath, past, laugh, craft, sample,* and *can't*. There were many lexical exceptions, however, including in modern RP *math, aster, gaff, Taft, ample,* and *cant.* Apparently from the beginning of this change – and certainly from

144 *Word Frequency and Lexical Diffusion*

the earliest attestations we have of it – it has had lexical exceptions. Beal (1999: 106) notes, "The first writers to give evidence of a long vowel distinct from ME /aː/ are Daines (1640), Coles (1674), and Cooper (1685, 1687)." Cooper, she says, is "the first to show evidence of the new long vowel occurring before voiceless fricatives, specifically stating that *past* (= *pass* + *ed*) has a long vowel but *pass* (as in *pass by*) a short one. Cooper also shows the long vowel in *path*, but does not suggest that this is generalized to other words in which ≪ a ≫ is followed by /θ/." For Modern English, Beal reports "RP speakers having /æ/ in *cant, rant, finance, romance, expand, random*, but / aː/ in *can't, plant, dance, demand*" (p. 107).

For Modern British English, Trudgill (1983: 48) describes the transition zones that characterize dialects in England that have participated in the development of the vowel, the more northerly dialects having maintained the vowel [æ]. He says, "If we draw an isogloss for every relevant word contained in the SED [*Survey of English Dialects*, Orton et al. 1962–69] materials we get a bundle of isoglosses, giving an impression of a continuum, because no isogloss for a particular word coincides absolutely with any other isogloss for any other word." The sound change is moving northward, and

in the transition zone most speakers alternate between the two vowels, but:

(a) the /aː/ vowel is more common in middle-class speech than working-class speech.
(b) the /aː/ vowel is more common in formal styles than informal styles;
(c) the /aː/ vowel is more common in the speech of younger than older speakers;
(d) the /aː/ vowel is more common in some words than others;
(e) the /aː/ vowel is more common in some phonological environments than others;
(f) the /aː/ vowel is more common in the south of the transition zone than in the north.

Thus, this sound change is a good example of the simultaneous lexical, phonological, and social diffusion of a single change.

This sound change also appeared in the United States, "probably as a fashionable import from Britain in the eighteenth or nineteenth century," where it survives in some New England dialects (Wells 1982: 205). Phillips (1989 [1993]) has shown that the pattern of "broad *a*"

Analogy, Borrowing, and Lexical Diffusion 145

Table 5.2 Distribution of innovative "broad *a*" (Phillips 1989 [1993])

"Eastern US" and RP share "broad *a*" ("Eastern US" [a, ɑ] and RP [aː])	*calf, giraffe, laugh, staff; aft, after craft, daft, draft, draught, graft, laughter, raft, shaft, Shaftesbury, bath, path; aghast, avast, blast, cast, castor, disaster, disastrous, fast, last, mast, master, nasty, past, pastor, plaster, vast; clasp, gasp, grasp, rasp; ask, bask, basket, cask, casket, flask, mask, task; castle; fasten, ass, brass, class, glass, grass, pass; advance, answer, chance, chancel, chancellor, dance, enhance, France, Frances, Francis, glance, lance, prance, trance; advantage, aunt, can't, chant, chantey, chantry, chanty, enchant, grant, plant, shan't, slant, supplant; blanch, branch, stanch; chandler, command, demand, remand; example, sample*
"Eastern US" and RP share [æ]	*gaff; ascot, casque, gasket, mascot; tassel, vassal, Masson; amass, bass, crass, cuirass, gas, lass, mass, morass, passage; cancel, cancer, expanse, fancy, manse, romance*
"Eastern US" has [æ] for RP [aː]	*haft; aster; rascal; vantage; ranch, stanchion; Alexander, Flanders, slander*
"Eastern US" has [a, ɑ] for RP [æ]	*alas*

borrowing into what Kenyon and Knott call "Eastern US" (EUS) English follows a word form by word form borrowing of the more frequent words that had undergone the shift in British English. Table 5.2, based on that work, reflects data in Wells (1982), Jones (1977), and Kenyon and Knott (1953). It shows that there are several words whose innovative pronunciations were not borrowed (*haft; aster; rascal; vantage; ranch, stanchion; Alexander, Flanders, slander*), but only one (*alas*) that underwent the shift in the US but not in England. This study therefore supports Trudgill's (1986: 58) observation that during accommodation people "modify their pronunciation of *particular words*, ... with some words being affected before others," which implies that the spread of a sound change from one group to another must of necessity proceed via lexical diffusion, affecting some words before others.

Table 5.3 divides the words by phonetic environments and displays their average frequency according to Carroll et al. (1971), using their estimated frequency-per-million tokens rounded off to the nearest hundredth. This table reveals that, within each phonetic category, the change has affected the most frequent words first in both RP and EUS. That is, the numbers under [aː] are consistently higher than the numbers under [æ] for each phonetic environment.

146   *Word Frequency and Lexical Diffusion*

Table 5.3   Average frequencies by phonetic environment (Phillips 1989 [1993])

	British RP		"Eastern US"	
	[aː]	[æ]	[aː]	[æ]
[-f#]	94.31	0.15	76.58	0.45
[-ft]	101.46	0.00	110.68	0.00
[-θ]	45.52	2.65	45.52	7.72
[-st]	71.93	1.47	71.93	1.47
[-sp]	3.74	0.00	3.74	0.00
[-sk]	26.59	0.09	29.65	0.50
[-səl]	37.56	0.13	37.56	0.20
[-sən]	14.33	0.00	14.33	0.00
[-s]	123.80	21.24	89.58	21.24
[-ns]	44.12	4.79	47.27	4.79
[-nt]	31.86	0.16	36.71	3.12
[-ntʃ]	16.69	4.50	14.23	10.85
[-nd]	6.98	61.10*	10.92	64.80*
[-mp]	179.42	1.63	179.42	1.63

*Not including *and*.

A second point is also important, however; namely, of the subset of (already frequent) words that had the innovative vowel in British English, EUS English borrowed the most frequent (see Table 5.4). In fact, the most frequent word that was affected in British English but not EUS English, *Alexander* (frequency = 10.272) is less frequent than any phonetic group average that changed in both dialects (frequency 10.92 and above). And the one word that has changed in EUS English but not RP, *alas* (frequency = 6.22), has a frequency higher than any of the other unchanged words.

There is reason to believe that this change did not develop true productivity in the dialect Kenyon and Knott (1953) labeled EUS. First, if the change were independently productive in the Eastern US, one would not expect it to affect *exactly* the same words in both dialects. That is, even though we can look at the average frequency of words and say the most frequent words have changed first in each dialect, occasionally there are individual words that do not follow the general pattern. To take an example of words where the vowel precedes [ns], the word *chancellor* has a much lower frequency (0.91) than the word *fancy* (16.69), but *chancellor* has the innovative pronunciation, and *fancy* does not. (Of course they are also of different word classes, which may well make a difference, as pointed out in Chapter 4.) Second, only one word, *alas*, shows the innovative pronunciation in American English

Analogy, Borrowing, and Lexical Diffusion 147

Table 5.4 "Eastern US" [æ] ~ RP [ɑː] in comparatively infrequent words (based on Phillips 1989 [1993])

EUS words in unchanged [æ] for RP [ɑː]	Frequency of unchanged words	Average frequency of EUS changed words before that cluster
haft	0.00	110.68 (before -*ft*-)
aster	0.16	71.93 (before -*st*-)
rascal	1.22	29.65 (before -*sk*-)
vantage	0.75	36.71 (before -*nt*-)
*stanchion**	0.24 (*stanchions*)	14.23 (before -*nt ʃ*-)
Alexander	10.27	10.92 (before -*nd*-)
Flanders	1.47	
slander	0.40	

* *ranch* frequency 36.371, omitted, since it is a nineteenth-century borrowing from Spanish.

but not in British. And third, the "sound change" has never been very productive in English in this form. Kenyon and Knott (1953: xl) and Laferriere (1977) both note that it is in decline.

This change may well have led to the development of a more productive change in other Northern cities, however, as discussed in Labov (1972: 47–95) and Ferguson (1972). This change is usually described as having involved two stages, beginning with the lengthening of [æ] to [æː], which subsequently became [ɑː]. Ferguson (1972: 217) suggests that the borrowing into EUS took place at the /æː/ stage, and it is this vowel which has been tensed in Philadelphia. A significant sign of this productivity is that in this dialect, the tensing has affected, in general, all the /ɑː/ words of British RP *plus* additional ones. Laferriere, on the other hand, sees the raising of the vowel in Boston as an independent development competing with a "still active, although restricted" backing rule (1977: 106). Both of these are entirely plausible developments. To return to L. Milroy's (2003: 166) discussion of "ideology-free" and "ideologically motivated" changes, the cultural dialect borrowings discussed above were identified with ideologically motivated changes. The shift to "broad *a*" in the EUS may have started as an ideologically motivated change, but as she points out, such changes can lose their external social markings and become ideologically free. The latter type of changes include both internally motivated changes and dialect leveling and "appear to operate globally, in the sense that their effect on a wide range of speech communities is similar and cannot readily be explained with reference to local

148 *Word Frequency and Lexical Diffusion*

social structure"; they "do not appear to be socially mediated in the sense that they cannot readily be mapped on to images of salient local social categories, and they occur independently in speech communities widely separated by space and time." Important to this approach is the observation that a change may be constrained by social indices at one point, but once the linguistic distinction loses its local social relevance, it is free to follow the trajectory of an ideology-free change.

5.2.2.2   *Old English an > on before nasals*

The development of /a/ before nasals in Old English is a classic example of a sound change that began in one dialect (Mercian), but which spread into another dialect, West Saxon. It is especially interesting because the original /a/, which had been maintained in some West Saxon words, was later borrowed back into Mercian[3] (in *Rushworth 1).* The early history is summarized by Nielsen (1992: 640–1):

> It has sometimes been supposed that the rounding of *a* before nasals was a shared Old English/Old (East) Frisian isogloss, but as Toon has recently shown (1983: 90–118) *a* did not begin to change into *o* before nasals until after 700, a change which started in the North, gained acceptance and prestige in most of England during the period of Mercian supremacy in the 8th and early 9th centuries, and declined with the West Saxon political domination later in the 9th century.

Hogg (1982) discusses the possible phonemic versus allophonic status of the supposed [ɔ] sound represented by ≪o≫, but it suffices here to note that the scribes clearly grouped the sound with others represented by the grapheme ≪o≫, and for that reason in the discussion below the graphemic symbol will be used.

Toon (1983) investigates this change in several early Mercian gloss-aries: the *Epinal Glossary* (*c.* AD 700) has *o* for expected *a* only once in 59 words containing historical *a* before a nasal; the *Erfurt Glossary* (*c.* AD 750) has an *a* : *o* ratio of 32 : 33; the *Leyden Glossary* (AD 754–800) shows an *a* : *o* ratio of 5 : 11; the *Corpus Glossary* (*c.* AD 800) shows a ratio of 38 : 95; and the *Vespasian Psalter Gloss* (*c.* AD 830)[4] has only forms in *o*. Toon also finds the progression of the vowel shift in these manuscripts to be phonetically conditioned, as expressed in variable rules which are displayed in tabular form in Table 5.5. Since the *Corpus Glossary* is a copy of some sources that are shared with the *Erfurt Glossary* and some sources that are not, only the unshared section is included in the table.

Analogy, Borrowing, and Lexical Diffusion 149

Table 5.5 Progression of $a \rightarrow o$ before nasals in early Mercian glosses (Toon 1983: 100–6)

Phonetic environment	Percentage «o» spellings		
	Erfurt (c. 750)	*Corpus (unshared)* (*c.* 800)	*Vespasian Psalter (c.* 830)
—— m	41	94	100
—— n	53	74	100
—— ŋ	60	66	100

Toon also separates out the data for the environment of /n/ and /m/ followed by a homorganic consonant, but I have combined those here with the other data for /n/ and /m/.

Toon's data strongly support his conclusion that the change of prenasal $a > o$ in Mercian was a phonetically gradual shift that was also lexically gradual. As Toon remarks,

> Of particular interest is the consistency with which individual lexical items are treated [in the *Corpus Glossary*]. Eight words occur two or more times: *gegangend* (2X), *ongong* (2X), *fromlice* (3X), *stom* (2X), *hond* (2X), *condel* (2X), but *mand* (2X) and *suan* (2X). None of these words varies in its spelling; thus, it is not the case that the variable rule is applying consistently across the lexicon, sensitive only to phonetic environment. (p. 105)

He also points out that *Corpus* and *Erfurt* behave differently with respect to some words, which dispels the notion of spellings based on scribal training: "Both have *o* in 21 glosses, but *Erfurt* has *a* in 17 cases where *Corpus* has *o*, and, conversely, *o* in 8 cases where *Corpus* has *a*. This observation is to be emphasized as it provides evidence that the variation in these texts represents synchronic variations in the language of the scribes rather than dialect mixture stemming from the textual tradition" (p. 105).

It is also important to realize that scribes' spelling was not as fixed as one might imagine. As Hogg (1992b: 77–8) describes it,

> even if the alphabet [in Old English] was fixed, spellings varied to a much greater extent than they do today, albeit to a lesser extent than in Middle English. One major reason for this was that the cultural and educational infrastructure for a standardization of spelling simply did

150 *Word Frequency and Lexical Diffusion*

not exist for much of the time. We must also remember that scribes were making individual copies of manuscripts for a tiny and generally locally restricted audience. This meant that each scriptorium at any one time would have its own spelling conventions, which would differ from the conventions both of other scriptoria and of the same scriptorium at some other time. In part this would be a matter of dialect, for at least in the earlier period scribes probably attempted to represent in a recognizable form the speech of those around them. But it has also to be remembered that the concept of "correct" spelling is a modern one. For the Anglo-Saxon scribe it would not necessarily have been "incorrect" to spell a word one way in one line and another way in the next.

Toon (1986: 285) offers an explanation for the willingness of scribes to vary between ≪a≫ and ≪o≫ in prenasal position:

"Because /o/ when it occurred before nasals had been raised to /u/ in Germanic times, Old English /a/ and /o/ could not be contrastive in prenasal positions. The raising of [ɑ] to [ɔ] then involves a subphonemic change; an allophone of /a/ is becoming an allophone of /o/. At the stage of uncertainty between *a* and *o*, the scribes were recording sub-phonemic variation.

This explanation has been reinforced by recent work on exemplar theory, according to which

people have detailed long-term memories of particular percepts, and these are stored as locations on the map [of articulatory/acoustic space]. . . . For example, the set of exemplars labelled with /i/ implicitly defines the region of the formant space which corresponds to that vowel; at the center of this distribution, the exemplars are numerous whereas towards the margins of the distribution, the exemplars become much sparser. (Pierrehumbert 2002: 113)

The set of exemplars for a particular label, say /a/, called an EXEMPLAR CLOUD, may overlap with another exemplar cloud, say /o/, producing the variation shown in Old English *an* ~ *on* spellings. The overlap between /ɑ/ and /ɔ/ is particularly common before nasals and may therefore be considered a natural, articulatorily or auditorily based sound change. The phonetic and perceptual underpinnings of this change are elaborated in Beddor et al. (1986: 199), who note that low nasal vowels

Analogy, Borrowing, and Lexical Diffusion 151

typically undergo raising, as in such diverse languages as "Breton, Haida, Narna, Seneca, and Zapotec." An example of its phonetic and lexical effects in Modern English is provided by Thomas (2001: 53), who states:

> Merger of /ɑ/ and /ɔ/ only before nasals, as in *Don* and *dawn*, is reported by Labov, Ash, and Boberg (2005) from some parts of the North. Lexical-specific variation between /ɑ/ and /ɔ/ before nasals, as in *on* and *long*, is well known (e.g., Kurath and McDavid 1961). These alternations are due to the damping effects of nasality on the first oral formant, which make the height of the vowel less certain for listeners.

Spellings in «on» also appear in dialects neighboring Mercia. According to Toon (1978b: 360),

> A study of the early charters written in Kent reveals an influx and retreat of Mercian spellings (and hence probably pronunciations) which parallels the rise and fall of Mercian political fortunes. West Germanic *a was regularly written *o* [before nasals], but the name of the people of Kent and their major city, *cantuariorum* and *cantuar-abyrg*, resisted the change.

In the mid-eleventh-century *Kentish Glosses*, Toon (1978b: 360) finds the "fluctuation much the same as that found in the charters (about 65% *a*)" and notes that it is "remarkable how consistent words which occur more than once are in the shape of their vowel: *mon* (4×), *ponne* (9×), *gestrangad(e* (4×), *fra(m* (4×), *manegn* [sic] (2×)." He concludes that the consistency of "*mon* and the weakly stressed *ponne*" is "strongly suggestive of lexical diffusion." This is the pattern one would expect in an assimilation, as shown in Chapter 4, that is, very frequent function words have changed first, or in this case, most consistently. So, despite the ideological motivation behind the imitation of Mercian pronunciations, this shift behaves just like an ideologically free change in its effect on function words.

The same pattern is found in the shift of «a» to «o» before nasals in the West Saxon dialect. Again, these pronunciations must have been "borrowed" into that dialect through imitation of Mercian speakers. As Sweet (1871–72 [1958]: xxii) notes,

> The labialization of *a* before nasals which appears in every stage and dialect of O.E. is so strongly developed in early W.S. as in many

152 *Word Frequency and Lexical Diffusion*

words almost to exclude the original sound and constitute a special characteristic of the period. Such forms as *monig, monn, ond, long* occur in every line of the Pastoral and Orosius, while in Elfric and Wulfstan the original *manig, mann, and, lang* reappear....The change is, however, by no means universal in early W.S.: such forms as *mann, manig, land* occur now and then in the best MSS., while in some words the *a* is almost exclusively used. The general rule seems to be that **the commonest words have *o*, the rarer *a*.** Thus in all MSS. of Alfred's time the form *ond* occurs exclusively, never *and*....In the same way *monn, monig* are much more frequent than *mann, manig*, while a rarer word, such as *panne, ramm*...is almost always written with *a*. [my bold]

Spellings in «o» found in the lengthy Hatton 20 Manuscript of Alfred's translation of Gregory's *Pastoral Care*, detailed below, support Sweet's statement. Although it is the work of several scribes, it is nonetheless contemporary, *c.* AD 900, with the original translation by Alfred (Potter 1948: 120–1). In addition, it is "the most complete of all Alfred's translations and it is therefore one of the longest pieces of continuous writing in our older literature, exceeded only slightly by the Old English versions of Bede's *History* and Gregory's *Dialogues*" (p. 118). Text information from the York–Toronto–Helsinki Parsed Corpus of Old English Prose[5] lists the word count of Sweet's (1871–72 [1958]) edition as 68,556. It is described as "a close translation" of the original Latin, and its style as "literary ... lack[ing] the colloquial expressions which are characteristic of Werferth's *Dialogues* and which appear in King Alfred's other translations of Orosius, Boethis, and Augustine" (Potter 1948: 117). Thus, this text might not be the best choice for an investigation of English syntax, but for our purposes, such characteristics should not detract from its philological value. For one thing, we do not have to be concerned with differences that may be attributable to style or register. And the translation of such a long, learned work should produce infrequent words which might not appear in shorter, more colloquial works, while words that are frequent in speech should also be, relatively speaking, frequent in a written text as well.

The specific data presented below are taken from Phillips (1978, 1980) and are based on the concordance prepared during the creation of the *Dictionary of Old English*, of Sweet's edition, plus corrections made by Kim (1973). Inflectionally related forms are represented by just one of the lexeme's word forms, as are forms related closely by both form and meaning, such as *spananne* and *forspananne*, both meaning 'entice.' The full list of forms appears in Appendix E.

Analogy, Borrowing, and Lexical Diffusion 153

Table 5.6 Progression of WGmc. a → «o» before nasals in early Mercian gloss-aries (Toon 1983: 100–6), plus early West Saxon *Pastoral Care*

Phonetic environment	Percentage «o» spellings			
	Erfurt (*c.* 750)	*Corpus* (unshared) (*c.* 800)	*Vespasian Psalter* (*c.* 830)	*Pastoral Care* (*c.* 900)
—— m	41	94	100	79
—— n	53	74	100	93
—— ŋ	60	66	100	68

Table 5.6 shows how the occurrence of «o» in the *Pastoral Care* also varies by phonetic environment and by lexical diffusion; that is, even though the percentages by phonetic environment differ across the texts, for each text (except, of course, the *Vespasian Psalter*) within each phonetic environment, some words have changed before others.

Another factor that has affected the diffusion of «o» in the *Pastoral Care* has been word class, as outlined in Table 5.7, where adverbs and function words have been grouped together because most of the adverbs containing «a» or «o» before a nasal are also used as func-tion words, for example, *ærðon(ðe)* 'before, formerly,' *ongemang* 'among, meanwhile,' *forðon* 'because, therefore,' *ðon* 'then; he (sg. instru.),' and *ðonne* 'then, when.'

The overall effect of word frequency is the most obvious influ-ence, however, as Table 5.8 displays. That is, a gradual increase in the percentage of «on» spellings strongly corresponds to an increase in word frequency, regardless of word class. Only the 91–400 group is aberrant, and it contains only three words – the adjective *manige/monige* 'many' (67 percent «on»), the verb *manian/monian* 'to warn' (26 percent «on»), and the article *ðane/ðone* 'the, masc. sg. acc.' (99 percent «on»).

Table 5.7 *Pastoral Care* progression of «o» before nasals by word class and phonetic environment

	Nouns	Adjectives	Verbs	Adverb/function
—— m	40	–	33	81
—— n	85	70	28	99.9
—— ŋ	86	57	43	53

154 Word Frequency and Lexical Diffusion

Table 5.8 Word frequency and ≪on≫ spellings in the *Pastoral Care* (Phillips 1980: 21)

Frequency group	Average % of ≪on≫ spellings
1–10	39.4
11–20	49.4
21–30	51.3
31–60	55.3
61–90	95.0
91–400	64.0
Over 400	97.8

Thus, if these spellings indicate a shift in West Saxon pronunciation due to the influence of Mercian (i.e. "borrowing" from Mercian), the more frequent words' pronunciation has been borrowed first. Indeed, that this was a true change in West Saxon – and not just due to habits ingrained in Mercian scribes – is shown by the fact that two of these words, *from* and *on*, never reverted to their earlier *-an-* spellings (Brunner 1965: 21). Also, if scribes were taught certain spellings in their training, there is no reason why scribes might remember the spellings of nouns better than that of verbs. Therefore, this sound change appears to have crossed dialect boundaries while maintaining phonetic and lexical diffusion very similar to that which characterized earlier stages of the shift.

It happens that a later manuscript shows what happens when the opposite influence pertains; that is, when West Saxon /a/ is imitated by a speaker of Mercian. *Rushworth 1*, the Mercian portion of the interlinear gloss to the *Rushworth Gospels, c. 975*, contains spellings with ≪a≫ based on West Saxon dialects that retained /a/, West Saxon having grown by then in political influence as Mercian influence had waned. Toon (1983: 117) therefore attributes its ≪a≫ spellings to "Farmon's tendency to hypercorrect," and that the replacement of /a/ with /ɔ/ never developed productivity in the *Rushworth 1* dialect area may be seen in the fact that in Middle English one distinguishing characteristic of manuscripts of that area (West Midlands) is prenasal ≪o≫ spellings. The full list of ≪a≫ versus ≪o≫ spellings is given in Brown (1891: 18–19), who concludes that *Rushworth 1* has a ratio of 122 ≪a≫, mostly before ≪ng≫, to approximately 800 ≪o≫. Table 5.9 displays Toon's (1983) results, including his separate tabulations for stressed and unstressed syllables containing the alveolar nasal, /n/. The point that Toon emphasized in these data was that "clearly, the lexicon is not affected uniformly on the basis of phonetic environment. The language

Analogy, Borrowing, and Lexical Diffusion 155

Table 5.9 Percentage of «o» versus «a» in *Rushworth 1* (Toon 1983: 105–6)

Phonetic environment	Rushworth 1 (*c.* 975) percentages of spellings	
	«o»	«a»
—— m	98	02
—'— n	96	04
—— n (unstressed)	84	16
—— ŋ	09	91

is changing one word at a time; Farmon's spellings show that he retains and loses certain West Saxon pronunciations on a word-to-word basis" (pp. 117–18).

However, the words for which Farmon uses West Saxon «a» are different from those for which the *Pastoral Care* scribes used Mercian «o», some of which may be attributable to the incomplete progression of the original change to /ɔ/ in the Rushworth dialect (before the velar nasal – where most of the «a» spellings occur) or resistance to /ɔ/ on the basis of morphological class (as in the appearance of /a/ in the past tense of class III verbs).[6] The influence of word frequency can be seen in the behavior of the vowel before /n/ in nouns, however: one finds single spellings of *candel-* 'candle-,' *panne* 'pan,' *ingann* 'entrance,' but otherwise «o»: *hona* 'cock,' *monde* 'basket,' *sond* 'sand,' *wona* 'lack,' and always in the very frequent words *hond* 'hand' (30×), *lond* 'land' (27×), and *mon(n* (113×) (Toon 1983: 116). That is, Farmon is incorporating the West Saxon «a» into less frequent nouns. This pattern is more reminiscent of sound change reversals under the influence of a standard dialect, discussed above in section 5.2.1.

5.2.3   Phonetic discreteness vs. gradualness in borrowed changes

The results of borrowed changes have generally been distinguished from sound change by their discreteness or phonetic abruptness (e.g. Schogt 1961: 92), a position summarized by Harris (1985: 2–3) in his discussion of changes which involve phoneme redistribution across the lexicon:

> Strictly speaking, this [i.e., phoneme redistribution] doesn't constitute phonological change proper (although it may eventually have phonological consequences). The phenomenon generally occurs in response to exonormative pressures and in traditional terms would

156 *Word Frequency and Lexical Diffusion*

be called borrowing. However, the latter term with its connotations of sporadic superficial change is hardly appropriate for describing the massive adaptive redistribution that is to be observed in conservative dialects whose phonemic incidence is markedly different from standard patterns (see especially J. Milroy 1980). ... [T]he two types of change are qualitatively different and clearly distinguishable while they are in progress. Sound change proper is typically reflected in variation across phonetic continua; phonemic redistribution typically involves alternation between phonetically quite discrete variants.

On the basis of such reasoning, borrowed changes have been linked with lexical diffusion. But most changes are much more complex, with borrowing being a necessary method of implementation even within homogeneous dialects and lexical diffusion evidenced both in "variation across phonetic continua" (phonetically gradual changes – see Chapter 3) and in "phonemic redistribution" (phonetically abrupt changes – see Chapter 2).

In this section we have specifically seen instances of the spread of changes from one dialect to another all the while exhibiting the same pattern of lexical diffusion. In this way, the evidence supports J. Milroy's (2003b: 215–16) distinction between INNOVATIONS, VARIATION, and SOUND CHANGE:

[I]nnovations may be endogenous or exogenous, and they lead to *variation* within the community; *sound change*, however, as distinct from variation, requires some kind of external trigger. To return to Bloomfield's example: the abrupt movement from alveolar to uvular [r] is an innovation, which attests to variability, but which may not always lead to change. Bloomfield's "spread by borrowing", however, is a necessary constituent part of a language change (the borrowing process is from person to person and subsequently group to group). To that extent language change is necessarily exogenous.

Typical of the complex relationship between internal and external factors in the spread of a change lexeme by lexeme is Rivierre's (1991: 429) description of final consonant loss in New Caledonia:

Alongside a number of internal factors which have contributed to this [Final Consonant] loss, the role played by contact appears to have been considerable since, on the whole, the closer the languages in question are to the centre of propagation, the more strongly they are affected by this process. The process of loss of any one consonant is in itself gradual, in two respects: the new pronunciation, without the F[inal] C[onsonants], seems to be initiated by a small number of speakers in a limited number of lexemes, then, step by step, the innovation gains on the community as a whole and gradually spreads to all the vocabulary concerned by the change.

Such an interplay of factors is altogether expected in a usage-based phonology. Since borrowing (i.e. imitation of other speakers) is inherent to the spread of an innovation from speaker to speaker within a speech community, and lexical diffusion is inherent in the spread of an innovation from one word to another in the spread of an innovation, both are inherent to sound change. However, there is no need to identify lexical diffusion with borrowing.

5.3 Conclusion

This chapter has presented evidence for the recognition of lexical diffusion as a method of implementation of sound change, independent of analogy or borrowing. Following J. Milroy (2003a, b), borrowing from speaker to speaker is viewed as inherent to linguistic change and thus not a separate branch of change at all. In the context of sound change, analogy is argued to be the application of emergent generalizations on individual word forms within an interactive, connectionist lexicon. Its effect on the least frequent words first, in both morphological change and in sound change, is a reflection of the importance of frequency of use for all lexical representations, expressed through the notion of **lexical strength**. Since word forms are stored in phonetically detailed representations based on exemplars, changes which directly affect the production of word forms without access to generalizations that have emerged from these word forms – that is, changes such as assimilations and reductions – affect the most frequent words first. Changes which require access to such generalizations as phonotactic constraints or connections between word class and stress patterns affect the least frequent words first, for those are the ones most similar to analogical changes in morphology – being based on generalizations extracted from word forms and accessed only when word forms are not strongly entrenched in memory because of their infrequency.

6
Applications of Lexical Diffusion

6.0 Introduction

The purpose of this chapter is to demonstrate how an understanding of lexical diffusion can contribute to studies of other sound changes, both in interpreting manuscript variation and in determining the motivation behind a particular sound change. Lexical diffusion has also been enlisted to reconstruct the diachronic path that led to the synchronic variation in earlier stages of the language. Principled arguments for the role of lexical diffusion in the progression of particular sound changes have been made, for instance, by Barrack (1998: 209–13) for Siever's Law and by Salmons and Iverson (1993) for the variation between «þl» and «fl» in Gothic. Barrack was able to discard Seebold's (1972) theory of two suffixes -iya- and -ya- in Vedic Sanskrit and to explain two types of "skewed variation" involving the shift of -iya- to -ya- from pre-Vedic to Classical Sanskrit:

> In every case the degree of denuclearization in light and heavy stems forms a staggered pattern: Denuclearization in light stems always advances in a roughly proportional manner over the analogous loss in heavy stems of the same morphosyntactic category. Thus the theory of lexical diffusion provides a credible, unitary account of the anomaly of skewed variation. (pp. 212–13)

Salmons and Iverson's (1993) strongest evidence for the likely lexical diffusion of the sound change *fl-* > *þl-* in Gothic is that *þl-* is found in the more frequent words but not in the less frequent. "The *þl-* forms represent four different roots, which show ten distinct derivational variants ... and 37 total tokens in the Gothic data. The *fl*-forms also occur

Applications of Lexical Diffusion 159

in four different roots, but they involve only five derivational variants ...and each of the five forms only occurs once." Although they admit there is no way to rule out dialect mixture, they doubt such appeals because all of the five items derivationally related to *þliuhan* "to flee" have «þ», and lexical borrowing often introduces a new form, "just as English shows *tooth, toothless, toothy,* but also *dental*" (p. 93).

The three previously published papers reproduced below add to such studies and demonstrate in detail how an appropriate understanding of lexical diffusion can enhance the interpretation of otherwise recalcitrant data. The first (Phillips 1995) demonstrates how the lexical diffusion of the sound change reflected by the variable spellings in «eo» ~ «e» in the *Ormulum* manuscript (NE Midland, *c.* 1180) can aid in interpreting similar spellings in the "Continuations" section of the *Peterborough Chronicle* (East Midlands, 1122–54).The second (Phillips 1997) applies the same technique to the same manuscripts in the interpretation of the development of the Early Middle English diphthongs. The third (Phillips 2002) uses the pattern of lexical diffusion of the Early Modern English shortening/laxing of /uː/ to /ʊ/ to argue that this change must have primarily been a laxing of the vowel rather than a shortening. These articles are reproduced as in the originals, with only minor changes, mainly regarding formatting and the numbering of footnotes.[1]

6.1 Lexical diffusion as a guide to scribal intent*

For those who attempt to understand the precise nature of Old and Middle English dialects – their origin, interrelationship, and the status of sound changes that distinguish them – a major frustration arises from a (no doubt often well-placed) mistrust of scribal spellings as reflections of the scribe's own dialect. This is especially true for manuscripts written after the establishment of a West Saxon standard orthography around the year 1000.

This mistrust is typified by Bennett and Smithers, *Early Middle English Verse and Prose* (1968: 374), when they say regarding the continuations of the *Peterborough Chronicle* (1122–54), that their "philological value...is reduced by a slight admixture ... of forms from the standard written

---

* By permission of the publisher, this section, originally published in *Historical Linguistics 1993: Selected Papers from the 11th International Conference on Historical Linguistics, 16–20 August 1993,* edited by Henning Andersen (John Benjamins, 1995), is reprinted here with minor changes.

160 *Word Frequency and Lexical Diffusion*

language of late O[ld] E[nglish], which was W[est] S[axon], and by a disordered system of spelling." Such variation has of course more recently been found to reflect "orderly heterogeneity" within a dialect – variation based on phonetic, lexical, or social conditioning. Early documents have proved the easiest to work with, since early scribes did not have a standard system to adhere to. Toon (1976a, b, 1978b, 1983, 1992), for instance, has shown fine phonetic conditioning of variation in early Mercian manuscripts, and Phillips (1980) has revealed lexically conditioned variation in Alfredian West Saxon. The question I want to focus on in this section is whether variation in a later manuscript can also reliably reflect a sound change in progress.

The manuscript I have chosen to work with is the Laud MS containing the *Peterborough Chronicle*, specifically the years 1122–54, the very work referred to above as having a "disorderly system of spelling." According to Mitchell (1974: 133–4), "Only two scribes ... worked on the Laud MS. The first scribe copied the annals up to 1121, adding some twenty insertions of local interest. He then wrote new entries at intervals from 1122 to 1131. The second scribe did his work in one block, some time in 1155, and thus completed the annals from 1132 through 1154." Therefore, an investigation of the annals from 1122 to 1154 will reveal the patterning in a work known to be by two scribes from the East Midlands area. As Clark (1970: xlv) remarks, "the Peterborough Continuations are, in spite of influence from the *Schriftsprache* both on spelling and on grammar, strongly marked by the East-Midland dialect of the district where they were written. This is no less true of the First Continuation than of the Final one, whose East-Midland character seems never to have been questioned."[2]

The variation I am investigating is that between ≪eo≫ and ≪e≫ because an earlier investigation (Phillips 1984) revealed a very regular frequency- and word-class-ranked diffusion of ME [ö(:)] becoming [e(:)] reflected in spellings of ≪eo≫ vs. ≪e≫ in the *Ormulum*, composed in the author's own very regular spelling system only 25–50 years later in the same dialect area, Northeast Midlands *c.* 1180 (Parkes 1983: 125). The less frequent the word, the more likely it was to contain the innovative ≪e≫ spelling; and word classes varied greatly in their percentage of innovative spellings. The *Peterborough Chronicle*, in the same general area only a generation or two earlier (East Midlands 1122–54), also shows variation in the spelling of words with OE /e(:)o/ and is therefore an ideal document for testing the value of lexical diffusion studies to the identification of dialect mixture vs. scribal pronunciation.

Applications of Lexical Diffusion 161

Even Clark (1970: xlvi), in the introduction to her edition of the *Chronicle*, does not recognize internal dialect variation as a possibility when she says that for both long and short *eo*, "*e*-spellings are common beside traditional *eo*, and for the long sound they predominate. ... In both cases traditional spellings still occur, but inverted spellings (*feonlandes* 1070, *geseogen* (past p[article]) 1122, *leong* 1123, etc.) suggest that there is no longer any phonetic distinction between old spellings and new."

Yet her final statement is precisely what I wish to test – whether there was still any phonetic distinction between *eo* (presumably [ö(:)]) and *e* [e(:)].[3] If there was, then we will also be forced to reconsider the existence of inverted spellings as conclusive evidence for the completion of a sound change.

The data taken from the *Peterborough Chronicle* for the years 1122–54 are presented in Tables 6.1 and 6.2. These tables include only those tokens actually spelled with either ≪e≫ or ≪eo≫. I have chosen to omit the few spellings where ≪æ≫ and/or ≪ea≫ appear. The inclusion of such spellings actually makes a difference in only one word group (see note 7 below). For now we will just consider the variation between orthographic ≪e≫ and ≪eo≫.[4]

The data in Tables 6.1 and 6.2 have been arranged by word class and, within each word class, by word frequency, from the least frequent

Table 6.1 Reflexes of OE *ēo* in the *Peterborough Chronicle*, 1122–54[5]

	Forms	Frequency	% ≪e≫	Average % ≪e≫
Prepositions (Average: 100% ≪e≫)	*betwenan/betwenen*	3	100	
Adjectives (Average: 100% ≪e≫)	*neuuœ*	1	100	
	undep	1	100	
Verbs (Average: 86% ≪ e≫)	*iedon*	1	100	
	beheld(e)	2	100	
	behet	2	100	
	cesen	2	100	
	se(o)þ	2	50	
	þestrede	2	100	
	underþed(en)	2	100	
	herd(e)/herdon/geheord	5	80	92
	be(o)n	10	80	80
	held(e)(n)/heold(en/on)	23	48	48

162

Table 6.1   (Continued)

	Forms	Frequency	% «e»	Average % «e»
Nouns	*beon "bees"*	1	0	
(Average:	*deoules*	1	0	
32% «e»)	*feond*	1	0	
	þefas	1	100	
	underþeodnysse	1	0	
	leodbiscopes	2	0	
	preostes	2	0	
	wefod	2	100	
	der(fald)	3	100	
	fre(o)nd	5	100	
Numerals	*feowerti*	1	0	
(Average:	*feorþe*	1	0	
27% «e»)	*feower*	3	0	
	þre(o)	5	80	

Table 6.2   Reflexes of OE *ĕo* in the *Peterborough Chronicle*, 1122–54[6]

	Forms	Frequency	% « e »	Average % « e »
Adverbs and	*bene(o)þen*	2	100	
function words	*þe(o)nen/þe(o)non*	5	40	70
(Average: 67%	*he(o)re/heora*	20	85	
«e»)	*he(o)m/he(o)mself*	42	43	64
Verbs	*clepeden*	1	100	
(Average: 56%	*ieornden*	1	0	
«e»)	*segon/geseogen*	3	67	
Adjectives	*se(o)lue/selua*	3	67	
(Average: 71% «e»)	*fela/fe(o)le*	8	75	
Nouns	*clepunge*	1	100	
(Average: 24%	*weorkes*	1	0	
«e»)	*weoruld*	1	0	
	heouene	2	0	
	eorldom	3	0	
	fe(o)rd	3	67	
	erthe/eorþe/ eorþdyne/dine	4	25	27
	eorle(es)	53	0	0
Numerals (Average: 75% «e»)	*twe(o)lf(e)*	4	75	

Applications of Lexical Diffusion   163

words at the top of each class to the most frequent words at the bottom. Since the *Peterborough Chronicle* over the dates I am investigating covers only 20 pages in Clark's (1970) edition, conclusions regarding word frequency are especially hard to draw. (The *Ormulum*, in comparison, is much longer, consisting of 20,000 lines of verse which take up two volumes in the EETS edition.) The word groups for which we have the largest number of tokens have been divided for their average percentages at frequency 1–5, 6–10, and over 10. For example, in Table 6.1, verbs with the frequency 1–5 are spelled with «e» 92 percent of the time; *be(o)n*, with 10 occurrences, is spelled *ben* 8 of those times, or 80 percent; and the various forms of *he(o)lden* are spelled with «e» 48 percent of the time. Thus, these verbs do seem to follow the same frequency pattern found in the *Ormulum*, with the least frequent words having the greatest number of spellings in «e». And in Table 6.2, the adverbs and function words and the nouns follow the same pattern, although there is only one truly frequent noun, *eorl*, and the adverbs and function words may be subdivided into the less frequent prepositions and adverbs (*beneþen* is used both ways) and the more frequent pronouns.

Far more impressive when one compares the *Peterborough Chronicle's* spellings with the *Ormulum's* is the parallel overall percentage of «e» spellings according to word class. The two documents are compared in Table 6.3.

Only the numerals with short *ĕo/ĕ* in this table seem to defy the pattern in the *Ormulum* – and that is based on only one numeral, *twe(o)lf*, which in four occurrences had «e» 75 percent of the time. Otherwise the percentages are – to my eye, at least – impressively similar, especially the large gap between the first three word classes and the nouns.[7]

What this patterning leads me to conclude is that rather than having a "disordered system of spelling" or "an admixture of Anglian forms," the variable spellings in «e» and «eo» in the investigated annals of the *Peterborough Chronicle* represent a true sound change in progress – the unrounding of /ö(:)/ to /e(:)/.

A second conclusion may be drawn from the consideration of inverse spellings mentioned by Clark above. They do exist: for the long vowel, *ceose* occurs (1×) for 'cheese' (also *cæse* (1×)); *eom* (1×) for *eam* (1×) "uncle"; *feorde(n)* (3×) and *fordfeorde* (1×) for usual *ferde(n)*, *ferd(o)n* (32×) and *forþferde* (8×); and *ongeon* (1×) in place of expected *ongean*. For the short vowel, *leong* occurs once for *leng* (2×) (*lang(e)* also occurs, 3×) and *geoldes* occurs once for expected *geld*.

But do these inverse spellings necessarily negate the findings in Tables 6.1–6.3? I do not think so, even though scholars often use inverse

164   *Word Frequency and Lexical Diffusion*

Table 6.3   Comparison of lexical diffusion by word class

Word class	Average % innovative «e» spellings	
	Ormulum	*Peterborough Chronicle*
(a) Old English *ēo*		
Adverbs and function words	100	100
Nonnumerical adjectives	70	100
Verbs	67	86
Nouns	28	32
Numerals	0	27
(b) Old English *ĕo*		
Function words	76	67
Verbs	85	56
Nonnumerical adjectives	72	71
Nouns	55	24
Numerals	10	75

spellings as proof that a sound change has been completed. Recent work on mergers and near-mergers suggests that reality is not that neat. Labov et al. (1991: 42), for instance, report that the speech of all three of their informants from Tillingham in Essex showed near-merger of /ay/ and /oy/. For one speaker, they say, "One /oy/ word appears to have crossed over into the /ay/ class—*joined*. Otherwise, we can draw a boundary between the two classes: basically, a separation of peripheral from nonperipheral." In addition, Faber (1992: 66) has shown that in the merger in Utah English of tense and lax vowels before [l], "speakers must be supplementing or maintaining the contrast... with some feature not generally associated with English vowels." Strikingly, "in two instances, subjects consistently differentiated between the members of a tense–lax pair, but labeled them in reverse: the nucleus for *peel* was marked /ɪ/ and that for *pill* /i/" (p. 66). Similar confusion and crossover of individual words may well have arisen during the vowel merger we are investigating.

In addition, similar evidence for inverse or hypercorrect spellings in an Old English manuscript has been given by Toon (1978b: 361). He presents evidence that in the Mercian Rushworth Gospels and in the Northumbrian Lindisfarne Gospels the loss of /h/ before sonorants is variable, depending on which sonorant follows: /h/ is lost most frequently before /n/, next before the liquids, and least often before /w/.

Applications of Lexical Diffusion 165

Yet Toon notes that 'while the data would at first seem to point to a sound change in its earliest stages, the very careful (and hypercorrecting) scribes give additional testimony to the intensity of the change" (1978b: 361) and then gives examples from the Lindisfarne Gospels of hypercorrect, nonetymological ≪h≫: *hnett, hniþriga, hniþrung, hracentig, hraeca, hlaet, hleafa,* etc. This is precisely the same situation we have in the *Peterborough Chronicle,* that is, a sound change in progress where inverse or hypercorrect spellings nonetheless appear.

Therefore, I would submit that the existence of a few inverse spellings should not override findings of orderly variation such as we have found for ≪e≫ and ≪eo≫ in the *Peterborough Chronicle.* They certainly cannot in and of themselves reliably indicate that a sound change has reached completion.

As a final argument for taking these variant spellings at their face value, i.e. as representing variation within the dialect, I refer to a statement by Toon (1992: 445):

> The strongest argument for taking manuscript variation seriously is certainly the facts of the internal structure of that heterogeneity. On those who will reject the orthographic variation as random lies the onus of otherwise explaining those regularities and their close resemblance to kinds of phonetic conditioning being discovered in contemporary studies of sound [change] in progress.

I believe this is equally true for lexical conditioning and Middle English manuscripts, even those written when and where a standard orthography existed.

6.2 The *Peterborough Chronicle* diphthongs*

Standard handbooks such as Mossé (1952: 27–8) tell us how all the Old English diphthongs became monophthongs in Middle English, and how a new set of diphthongs arose from combinations of vowel plus following semivowel, and later from vowel plus one of the spirants [x, ç, γ]. (See also Lass 1992b: 49–53.) In an article on the treatment

---

* By permission of the publisher, this section, originally published in *Studies in Middle English Linguistics,* edited by Jacek Fisiak (Mouton de Gruyter, 1997), is reprinted here with minor changes.

166 *Word Frequency and Lexical Diffusion*

of diphthongs in the *Ormulum* – *c.* AD 1180 according to Parkes (1983: 125) – I discovered an orderly progress of phonetic and lexical diffusion of the new diphthongs from vowel-plus-semivowel combinations (diphthongs from other combinations not yet having appeared in his dialect) (Phillips 1983c). Of course, the *Ormulum* is an ideal document for such an investigation, being written in the author's own spelling system. The question I have chosen to investigate here is whether or not such regularity can be found in a Middle English manuscript uninfluenced by such a spelling reform agenda. Such a manuscript may be found in the same general dialect area (East Midlands) only a generation or two earlier in the *Peterborough Chronicle*, especially if one concentrates on the uncopied sections of it, namely those encompassing the years 1122–54. Specifically, if the spellings for diphthongs and potential diphthongs in the Continuations of the *Peterborough Chronicle* for the years 1122–54 parallel the development in the *Ormulum*, then we will have further support for the proposition that the spellings in the *Peterborough Chronicle* do not represent dialect mixture of East Anglian plus influence from the *Schriftsprache*, as suggested by Clark (1970: xlv) or a "disordered system of spelling," as suggested by Bennett and Smithers (1968: 374). Rather, variant spellings may be taken as indications of variation within the scribes' own speech. . . .

According to my earlier investigation of diphthongs in the *Ormulum* (Phillips 1983c: 12), all the new diphthongs derived from vowel + semivowel combinations had appeared in preconsonantal position. Next most often was diphthongization word-finally. Least frequent were intervocalic diphthongs, as one might expect. It is in this order, then, that the data are arranged in the tables below. I followed Luick (1914–21: 366) in considering a diphthong as represented orthographically by a sequence of vowel plus ≪ww≫ or ≪ȝȝ≫. Starting with the development of OE *æg* into ME *ai*, in the *Ormulum*, this OE combination is invariably written as a diphthong in all environments, spelled ≪aȝȝ≫, for example, *daȝȝ/daȝȝess, faȝȝre/faȝȝerr, naȝȝlenn*, etc. (Phillips 1983c: 12–14).

As for the *Peterborough Chronicle*, I followed Lass's (1992b: 49) suggestion that ≪ei≫ for OE ≪eg≫, ≪æi≫ for OE ≪æg≫, and so forth, indicate diphthongs. I included the entries from both Continuations, that is covering the years 1122–54, although two scribes were responsible (the first for the years 1122–31, the second for 1132–54). Although the scribes do have some orthographic differences (see, for example, Kniezsa 1988), I found that those did not appear salient in my search for diphthongal spellings, and both scribes are clearly East Midland speakers (Clark 1970: xlv). Nonetheless, to assuage any doubts, in the

Applications of Lexical Diffusion 167

tables below the spellings of the first scribe are given in lowercase letters and those of the second scribe in uppercase letters. I chose not to include the Interpolations, since they are generally copies of earlier, albeit Anglian, material and might retain archaic spellings for that reason. The data for the Continuations are given in Table 6.4, which shows that in the *Peterborough Chronicle*, written 30–60 years earlier than the *Ormulum*, only a handful of words show no diphthongal spelling – but they are all intervocalic: *dœges* (3×), *Hœge* (1×), and *sœgen* (2×).[8] All others show diphthongization.[9]

Diphthongization of OE /e(:)j/ also appears to be complete preconsonantally and word-finally in Orm, as in *eȝȝlenn, leȝȝd, reȝȝn, aweȝȝ, leȝȝ,* etc. (Phillips 1983c: 12). Intervocalically, it is lexically diffused, with the more frequent words having diphthongized first: for the short vowel, we find diphthongized *aweȝȝe* 'away' (1×, cf. *aweȝȝ* 14×), *eȝȝe* 'fear' (10×), *leȝȝepp* 'lay' (2×), *weȝȝe* 'way' (58×) versus unchanged *forrleȝenn*

Table 6.4 ≪ai≫ and ≪æi≫ in the *Peterborough Chronicle*, 1122–54

Preconsonantal	Word-final	Intervocalic
≪æi≫	≪æi≫	≪æi≫
dæirime	*dæi* (10×)	*ÆIE*
LÆIDE	*Eastrendæi*	*dæies* (10×)/*DÆIES* (2×)/*DÆIES* (3×)
LÆIDEN	*FRIDÆI*	
sæide (3×)	*læi* (2×)	
sæidon (3×)	*mæi* (2×)	*Ramesæie*
SÆIN	*MASSED/Ellmessedæi* (2×)	*Sunendæies*
pæines	*MIDDÆI*	
Iohan of Sæis	*Sunendæi/SUNNENDÆI*	
	Tywesdæi	
≪ai≫	≪ai≫	≪ai≫
BLAIS	*LAI*	*daies*
PAIS (4×)	*MAI*	
FAIR	*Mai* (2×)	
	≪æig≫	≪æig≫
	messedæig	*dæiges*
	Monendæig	
	Fridæig	
		≪æg≫
		dæges (3×)
		Hæge (1×)
		SÆGEN (2×)

168 *Word Frequency and Lexical Diffusion*

'having committed adultery' (3×), *forrleȝermesse* 'adultery' (3×). For the long vowel, diphthongized *beȝȝenn* 'both' (1×) and *tweȝȝenn* 'twice' (70×) contrast with unchanged *feȝedd* 'joined' (4×) and *wreȝenn* 'accuse' (8×) (Phillips 1983c: 14–15). Similarly, in the *Peterborough Chronicle* Continuations, word-finally and preconsonantally, we find ≪ei≫ (or ≪eig≫) consistently, with the single exception of *heglice*. In contrast, intervocalically, we find both ≪ei≫ and ≪eg≫. See Table 6.5.

Thus far, then, diphthongization has proceeded just as one might expect it would in a manuscript shortly preceding the *Ormulum*.

The diphthongization of vowels before /w/ is a little more complicated. In the *Ormulum* all /a/ + /w/ combinations have diphthongized: *clawwstremann, clawwess, strawwenn, tawwenn* (Phillips 1983c: 12, 14). In the *Peterborough Chronicle*, on the other hand, the sequence ≪au≫ appears preconsonantally only in Latin names, except for the single *saule* (1×); and it, or rather its apparent equivalents – ≪eau≫ and

Table 6.5 ≪ei≫ and ≪eg≫ in the *Peterborough Chronicle*, 1122–54

Preconsonantal	Word-final	Intervocalic
≪ei≫	≪ei≫	≪ei≫
Alein	*DEI*	*BEIEN*
Gerueises (5×)	*MESSEDEI*	*EIE*
Gode'f'reiþ/Godefreith	*SEI*	
Luuein	*Wodnesdei*	
Peitowe(2×)/*Peitou*/*PEITOU*		
Seintes		
onleide		
reilþein		
seide (3×)/*seidon*		
seiþ		
swein		
þeines		
UUREIDE		
≪eig≫	≪eig≫	
þeignes (2×)/*þeignas*	*deig*	
		≪eg≫
		adylege
		bradegede
		manege
		PRIULEGIES
		RACHENTEGES
		twegen
		penegas

Applications of Lexical Diffusion 169

≪æu≫[10] – appear word-finally only in *Angeau* and *fæu*. Otherwise, the ≪w≫ spelling remains. (See Table 6.6.) This still fits perfectly with the pattern we might expect in a manuscript predating the *Ormulum*, but I would caution that intervocalic spellings in *eau* (in the First Continuation, 1122–32) and *æu* (in the Second Continuation, 1133–54) do exist, but except for one use of ≪æu≫ for the diphthong (*læuede*), they invariably involve ≪u≫ as a symbol for [v], so there might have been an independent orthographic reason for the scribes to avoid this combination. Observe such spellings as *geauen* (1×) and *heaued* (1×) in the First Continuation, and *æue[r]* (1×), *æuez* (1×), *æure* (3×), *æuric* (3×), *hæued* (1×), *næure* (3×), *ræuede* (1×)/*ræueden* (2×), and *ræueres* (1×) in the Second Continuation.

As for the development of OE *eow*, Orm shows two directions. The development into *oww* seems influenced by Old Norse (see

Table 6.6 ≪au≫ and ≪aw≫ in the *Peterborough Chronicle*, 1122–54

Preconsonantal	Word-final	Intervocalic
≪au≫	≪æu≫	
Audoenus	*ANGÆU*(2×)	
Augusti (2×)	*FÆU*	
FAURESFELD		
Laudamus		
Laurentius		
Paules		
Raulf		
SAULE		
≪aw≫		≪aw≫
sawle		*blawen*
		fraward
		hornblaweres
		lawed
		scawe
		≪æw≫
		læwed
		≪eaw≫
		feawe
		Gleawecestre/Gleawceastre/Gleawecestrescire
		≪æuu≫
		læuued
		≪æu≫
		læuede

170 *Word Frequency and Lexical Diffusion*

Phillips 1983c: 17 for argumentation): *fowwerr/fowwre, fowwerrtiʒ, trowwe, trowwenn, trowwþe,* and their various inflections and derivatives. The *Peterborough Chronicle* also contains the spelling *fower* (1×) vs. *feower* (3×) and *feowerti* – all in the First Continuation. Other words in the *Peterborough Chronicle* with intervocalic ≪ow≫ are *toward* (perhaps undiphthongized because of its stress [or morphological] pattern) and the proper nouns *Bricstowe, Bristowe,* and *Peitowe.* Again, an intervocalic spelling in ≪ou≫ might have been misinterpreted as [ov], so I am hesitant to draw any conclusions from these spellings. Preconsonantally, however, and word-finally, there is variation, and it is not unlikely that ≪ou≫ stands for the diphthongized pronunciation (note French placenames such as *Peitou/Peitowe,* and *Angeo/Angeow*). See Table 6.7. The spelling *nouther/nouþer* goes back to OE *nāwþer,* retaining the OE diphthong.

In the *Ormulum,* variation between *e(o)ww* and unchanged *e(o)w* – *eo* /ö/ was at this time unrounding concurrently to /e/ – occurs both word-finally and intervocalically. Word-finally, one finds diphthongized *þe(o)ww* 'servant' next to undiphthongized *hew* 'form,' *ne(o)w* 'new,' and *cne(o)w* 'knew.' Intervocalically, within nouns the more frequent words seem to have diphthongized first, witness *þe(o)wwess, tre(o)wwess,* and *cnewwe* 'knee' versus *he(o)we, hewenn,* and *larewess.* Within verbs, the diphthongization is lexically determined, but there being only the two verbs *chewwenn* and *cnewe* 'knew,' one cannot tell why one preceded the other. (Certainly *cnewe* would be the more frequent one.) The single adverb and adjective have not diphthongized: *newenn* and *ne(o)we* (Phillips 1983c: 12–13, 18).

Table 6.7 ≪ou≫ and ≪ow≫ in the *Peterborough Chronicle,* 1122–54

Preconsonantal	Word-final	Intervocalic
≪ou≫	≪ou≫	
Eourard	*ANGOU*	
GLOUCESTRE/GLOU[C]ESTRE/GLOUCESTRE	*PEITOU*	
Windlesoure		
NOUTHER/NOUÞER		
	≪ow≫	≪ow≫
	Angeow (7×)	*fower/feower*(3×)
		feowerti
		toward
		Bricstowe
		BRISTOWE
		Peitowe (2×)

Applications of Lexical Diffusion 171

The *Peterborough Chronicle*, on the other hand, uses the symbols ≪eu≫ for the new diphthong preconsonantally and word-finally in *Gleucestre/ Gleucæster, treuthe(s)*, and *nareu* (see Table 6.8). Intervocalically, only ≪ew≫ and probably the equivalent ≪euu≫ appear: *blewen* and *neuuæ*.

The preceding findings for all the diphthongs have been summarized in Table 6.9, which indicates that the *Ormulum* is consistently further along in the diphthongization process than is the *Peterborough Chronicle*. Only for word-final [eu] – the group for which we have the fewest number of tokens in the Continuations – does the process seem to be complete in the *Peterborough Chronicle* but shows up as lexically diffused in the *Ormulum*. Intervocalically, where diphthongization has not occurred in the *Peterborough Chronicle*, it has either affected all the words in the *Ormulum* a generation or two later ([au] and [ou]) or it has at least begun

Table 6.8 ≪eu≫ and ≪ew≫ in *Peterborough Chronicle*, 1122–54

Preconsonantal	Word-final	Intervocalic
≪eu≫	≪eu≫	
Gleucestre(2×)/ *Gleucæstre*	*NAREU*	
TREUTHE(S) (2×)		
		≪euu≫
		NEUUÆ
		≪ew≫
		blewen

Table 6.9 Summary

Diphthong	Preconsonantal		Word-final		Intervocalic	
[au]	O	PC	O	PC	O	PC-no
[ou]	O	PC	(O)	PC	O	PC-no
[eu]	O	PC	O-ld	PC	O-ld	PC-no
[ei]	O	PC	O	PC	O-ld	PC-ld
[ai]/[æi]	O	PC	O	PC	O	PC-ld

O – the diphthong is found in all words in this position in the *Ormulum*.
PC – the diphthong is found in all words in this position in the *Peterborough Chronicle* Continuations (although some words may be variably spelled – e.g. *Fridæi* alongside *Fridæig*).
O-ld – diphthongization is lexically diffused in this position in the *Ormulum* (e.g. *beʒʒen* alongside *feʒedd*).
PC-ld – diphthongization is lexically diffused in this position in the *Peterborough Chronicle* Continuations (e.g. *dæies* vs. *sægen*).
PC-no – only nondiphthongal spellings occur in this position in the *Peterborough Chronicle* Continuations (e.g. *blewen*).
(O) – this position is unattested in Orm but has been surmised from the occurrence of full diphthongization in the other two environments.

172 *Word Frequency and Lexical Diffusion*

(i.e. it is lexically diffused) ([eu]). Again, intervocalically, where diph-thongization has only begun (i.e. is lexically diffused) in the *Peterborough Chronicle*, the *Ormulum* reveals the process as being still lexically diffused (for [ei]) or as completed (for [ai]/[æi]). To reiterate, the pattern seems clear that the *Ormulum* is further along in the process of diphthongiza-tion than is the *Peterborough Chronicle* – as one would expect. The point here is simply that the spellings show this progression quite faithfully.

In conclusion, I wish to argue that the very regularity of the spellings in the *Peterborough Chronicle* and their orderly correspondence with spellings in the *Ormulum* suggest strongly that the *Peterborough Chronicle* spellings are actually reflections of the scribes' tendency to incorporate their own dialect into their writing. Variant spellings need not be attrib-uted to influence from the *Schriftsprache* (Clark 1970: xlv) nor to a "disordered system of spelling" (Bennett and Smithers 1968: 374). They are more than likely fairly faithful renderings of the scribes' own East Midland dialect.

On a more general level, I would like to think that this investigation has strengthened the argument that lessons we have learned about the orderly progression of sound change through the lexicon can help us distinguish dialect mixture in a manuscript from orderly heterogeneity within a dialect due to change in progress. By our using such tools as lexical diffusion, cautious investigation of Middle English texts may reveal more about Middle English pronunciation than we once thought possible. As Milroy (1992b: 192) suggests, "in general, variable texts can become more valuable for our researches than relatively uniform ones."

6.3 Lexical diffusion and competing analyses of sound change*

A little over 100 years ago, in 1885, Schuchardt planted the seeds of modern lexical diffusion theory when he noted that during a sound change "rarely used words drag behind; very frequently used ones hurry ahead" ([1972]: 58). In 1969, Wang picked up Schuchardt's idea and expanded it, introducing the term "lexical diffusion" to describe the gradual effect of a phonological rule as it spreads to more and more

---

* By permission of the publisher, this chapter, originally published in *Studies in the History of the English Language: a Millennial Perspective*, edited by Donka Minkova and Robert Stockwell (Mouton de Gruyter, 2002), is reprinted here with minor changes.

words in the lexicon. Since then, a number of articles have found that word frequency does indeed influence the lexical diffusion of a sound change, many finding that the most frequent words have changed first (e.g. Leslau 1969; Fidelholz 1975; Hooper 1976; Phillips 1980, 1983c, 1998c; Rhodes 1996). Phillips (1984), however, also documented several sound changes which affected the least frequent words first and has subsequently refined the theory of word frequency and lexical diffusion, most recently in Phillips (2001). The purpose of this section is to demonstrate how an understanding of the relationship between word frequency and sound change can be used to help choose between competing analyses of a given sound change, specifically the shift of Early Modern English /uː/ to /ʊ/ in such words as *good, stood, book, took,* and *foot*.[11]

6.3.1 Description

The change of Early Modern English /uː/ to/ʊ/ noticeably involves both a change in vowel quantity (i.e. shortening) and vowel quality (i.e. laxing[12]), not surprising since vowel length and quality were apparently mutually dependent (Stockwell and Minkova 1990). Yet was the motivation between this process primarily to make the vowel shorter? Or was the motivation a change in vowel quality? That is, was it primarily a quantitative adjustment or a qualitative one? Dobson (1968: 497), Wells (1982: 197), and Lass (1999: 90) all describe this change as a shortening. In contrast, Pyles and Algeo (1993: 171–2) treat it as a laxing of the vowel: "Middle English [ō], as in *ro(o)te* 'root,' became [u]. Laxing of this [u] to [ʊ] has occurred in *book, foot, good, look, took,* and other words; in *blood* and *flood* there has been unrounding in addition to laxing, resulting in [ə] in these two words."

The choice seems arbitrary until one looks at the lexical diffusion of the shift, which has been documented by Ogura (1987) and which allows us to compare her findings with two theories about the origin of the shift – Ogura's own and Görlach's (1991) – both of which depend upon its characterization as a quantitative adjustment motivated either by higher-order syllable structure or by analogy.

6.3.2 Evidence

Using the orthoepical evidence given by Dobson (1968), Ogura (1987: 147) investigates the lexical diffusion of the "shortening" of ME /oː/ from the sixteenth century through the seventeenth century, within each of eight environments: "1 before [d], 2 before [t], 3 before [θ], 4 before [v], 5 before [f], 6 before [k], 7 before other consonants,

174   *Word Frequency and Lexical Diffusion*

8 after [Cl]" (Cl = cluster). Frequency counts were based on *The Harvard Concordance to Shakespeare* (Spevack 1973), which contains 884,547 tokens (Ogura 1987: 145). Dobson's sixteenth-century data were based on 10 orthoepists, including Cheke, Smith, Hart, Bullokar, Mulcaster, and Coote; the 1600–50 data were based on works by Tonkis, Robinson, Gil, Hayward, Sherwood, Butler, Daines, Johnson, *The English Scholemaster*, and Hodges; and the 1650–1700 data were based on works by 14 orthoepists of that period (Ogura 1987: 189–90).

Ogura discovered that phonetic conditioning played an important role, that is, that the shortening

> took place first before [d], then spread before [v], and lastly before [t, θ, k], and that within a given consonant, the vowel in the more frequent words and the vowel preceded by [Cl] changed first. That is, shortening was very common before [d], and fairly common before [v] in the 16th century, and before [t, θ, k] shortening became operative in the former half of the 17th century. (p. 145)

Ogura describes a rich interplay between phonetic conditioning and word frequency:

> Before [d] the shortening affected first *blood* and *flood* where the vowel is preceded by [Cl], and the more frequent words *good, (-)hood*, then *stood*, and lastly the less frequent word *food*. Before [v], *glove* when [Cl] precedes the vowel, and the more frequent words *(re)move* and *(ap)prove* changed earlier than the less frequent words *behove* and *hove*. Before [t, θ, k], the change corresponded roughly to an increase in word frequency. (1987: 145)

Ogura's evidence is, admittedly, not airtight. There are not a large number of words susceptible to this change, and they range over different word classes. The examples given above involving the same word class are especially more convincing – *(re)move* and *(ap)prove* vs. *behove* and *hove*. Ogura's example involving the words ending in *-ood*, on the other hand, may more appropriately be exemplifying differences between word classes. A better comparison would probably be the evidence that *food* according to one orthoepist could take the innovative vowel,[13] whereas there is no evidence the word *mood* has ever had that option. Another strong example in her corpus is the word *foot* (frequency 0.0200) showing the innovative vowel by 61.9 percent of the late seventeenth-century orthoepists versus no evidence of innovation in *root* (frequency 0.0053) or *boot* (frequency 0.0035). In current English, of course, *foot* generally contains [ʊ], *boot* generally contains [u], and *root* may vary.[14] Therefore, the general trend within phonetic environments and within word classes does nevertheless still support the more frequent words changing first.

6.3.3 Explanations

Within lexical diffusion theory, the implication of (within phonetic categories) the most frequent words changing first is clear: such sound changes always seem to be physiologically motivated.[15] For instance, sound changes which have been shown to affect the most frequent words first include unstressed vowel reduction and deletion, as in *mistook* with initial [ɪ] vs. *mistake* with initial [ə] (Fidelholz 1975) and two-syllable *nursery* vs. three-syllable *cursory* (Hooper 1976); t/d-deletion in American English (Bybee 2000b); Old English vowel raising before nasals (Phillips 1980); Middle English diphthongization of the type [ej] becoming [ei] (Phillips 1983c); and various assimilations and reductions in Ethiopian languages (Leslau 1969) – all of which can be attributed to the physical characteristics of the vocal mechanism and speech production.

In contrast, three changes have been documented (Phillips 1984) as affecting the least frequent words first: Southern American English glide deletion (e.g. /tjun/ > /tun/, /djuk/ > /duk/), which has as its impetus the reorganization of phonotactic constraints in English (as suggested by Cooley 1978); the unrounding of Middle English [ö(ː)] to [e(ː)], which has as its impetus the vowel system universal (or near-universal) that languages without high front rounded vowels do not have mid-front rounded vowels; and the stress shift in such words as *cónvict* (noun) vs. *convíct* (verb) from earlier *convíct* (noun or verb), which requires access of the lexical entry to determine the part of speech. None of these has as its impetus the physiological features of the vocal tract. Rather, they have their bases in syllable structure, language universals, and analogy based on word class. As detailed in Phillips (2001), all of these changes affecting the least frequent words first require lexical analysis; that is, they require accessing of information from the lexical entry before they can take effect. In contrast, changes affecting the most frequent words first ignore information in the lexical entry, allowing features of segments to blur, producing assimilations and reductions, or allowing stress rules to reset to default positions.

Yet Ogura (1987) and Görlach (1991) both posit explanations for what they call Early Modern English shortening that have to do with syllable

176 *Word Frequency and Lexical Diffusion*

structure and analogy, respectively – where one would expect the least frequent words to be changing first, despite Ogura's data exhibiting the most frequent words changing first.

6.3.4 Ogura's hypothesis

Ogura (1987: 150–1) hypothesizes that the impetus behind this change was an attempt to keep the duration of syllabic units relatively constant:

> Dobson (1968: §24) suggests that shortening is "essentially due to a general tendency to shorten the vowels of closed syllables," though "the consonants differ in their power to cause it." The assumption underlying this explanation is that the duration per syllabic unit is relatively constant, and there is a negative correlation or temporal compensation between the vowel and the following consonant. We may assume that the first factor that motivated the change is this temporal compensation within the monosyllabic word.

She hypothesizes that since vowels tend to be longer before voiced consonants, shortening took place first before [d] (p. 151). Note that this is precisely opposite the direction that one would expect articulatorily (Laver 1994: 446). By seeing this change as a shortening, she is led to an explanation whereby "ModE shortening was motivated by the higher-level articulatory unit, i.e., by the articulatory plan based on units larger than single segments" (p. 151). But not only would such a motivation most likely result in the least frequent words being changed first, there is also no supporting evidence that English in the sixteenth century was moving toward a system of equal weight per syllable. The movement in Middle English that Dobson (1968) mentions and that has been investigated more fully by Murray and Vennemann (1983) never attained fulfillment, largely because of the countermovement toward schwa loss, which created closed syllables where open ones had existed before. And so by the sixteenth century, a different motivation must be sought.

6.3.5 Görlach's hypothesis

Görlach (1991: 71) notes that "short vowels reflecting ME long vowel quantities are most frequent where ME has /ɛː, oː/ before /d, t, θ, v, f/ in monosyllabic words, but even here they occur only in a minority of possible words."[16] He suggests:

Applications of Lexical Diffusion 177

It is likely that the short vowel was introduced on the pattern of words in which the occurrence of a short or a long vowel was determined by the type of syllable the vowel appeared in (*glad* vs. *glade*). When these words became monosyllabic in all their forms, the conditioning factor was lost and the apparently free variation of short/long spread to cases like (*dead*). That such processes must have continued for some time is shown by words ending in -*ood*: early shortened forms (*flood*) are found side by side with later short forms (*good*) and those with the long vowel preserved (*mood*). (1991: 71)

Similarly, Strang (1970: 116) suggests, "There are changes of quantity, but their consequences in recent English are so confused that we must believe conflicting analogies have been at work." And Ritt's (1997: 69) appeal to semiotics to explain a preference for short /u/ before dentals also relies on speakers "check[ing] the mental dictionary" to resolve the ambiguity of the /d/ in /bluːd/, for example, being a past tense marker or not. Yet an explanation that requires comparison with other words in the lexicon is unconvincing since analogical changes affect the least frequent words first; that is, "infrequent words tend to regularize before frequent ones" (Bybee 1995: 236). Hooper's (1976: 99–100) study, for instance, found that more frequent verbs like *kept, left*, and *slept* resist being reshaped with an -*ed* suffix, whereas less frequent verbs like *crept, leapt*, and *wept* have developed the new forms *creeped, leaped*, and *weeped*. Although the environment of Hooper's example is morphological, it is similar to Görlach's, Strang's, and Ritt's proposals in that the shape of an infrequent morpheme is chosen through comparison with other morphemes. Frequent forms, in contrast, can even lose their connection to their own lexical content, as in *awful* no longer being connected to *awe*, *desperate* to *despair*, or *terrific* to *terrified* (Bybee 1985: 88).

6.3.6   An alternative explanation

So we are driven to search for a physiological motivation for this change. But are we looking for a motivation for shortening or for laxing? If the Early Modern English change were a true shortening, one would expect it to affect vowels before /t/ sooner than vowels before /d/, since languages generally have longer vowels before voiced segments, although not all languages have as great a difference as does Modern English (Laver 1994: 446). Similarly, one would least expect shortening of /uː/ before /d/, as Lehiste (1970: 20) explains in summarizing the work of Fischer-Jørgensen (1964) on the effect of a consonant's place of articulation on the length of the preceding vowel:

> The duration of a vowel depends on the extent of the movement of the speech organs required in order to come from the vowel position to the position of the following consonant. The greater the extent of the movement, the longer the vowel. This explains the fact that all vowels were shorter before /b/ than before /d/ and /g/: since two different articulators are involved in the sequence vowel + labial, there is no time delay in moving the articulator (i.e., the tongue) from the vowel target to the consonant target. On the other hand, /u/ was particularly long before /d/.

Judging from the phonetic evidence, alone, then, one would not expect this to be a vowel shortening. Therefore, the change is more likely to be a qualitative assimilation – which leads us to question what about the environment following a consonant-plus-[l] cluster and preceding [d] would lead to a qualitative change to [ʊ]. The diagrams in Figure 6.1, taken from Ladefoged and Maddieson (1996: 184, 303), demonstrate how the tongue position of [l] could encourage the shift in tongue position from [u] to [ʊ].

As for why the change would occur before dentals earlier than before other consonants, the articulatory basis might be that, as Ohala (1974: 265) notes, "although it is not necessarily the case that the back of the tongue is lower than usual for an [u] pronounced in the environment of dental consonants, it is frequently the case." Ohala (1974: 265) continues:

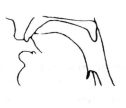
Lateral (German)

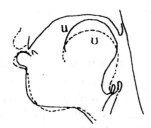
[u/ʊ] (German, after Bolla and Valaczkai 1986)

Figure 6.1 Tongue position of laterals and high back vowels (Ladefoged and Maddieson 1996: 184, 303). Reprinted by kind permission of Blackwell Publishers and the Hungarian Academy of Sciences

Applications of Lexical Diffusion 179

...velars have little effect on vowel quality, presumably because the lip configuration and the place of articulation of the "velar" can vary rather freely as a function of the contiguous vowel, second, ...labials have the greatest effect on front vowels (though not on [i]), mainly tending to centralize them, and third, ... dentals have the greatest effect on back vowels, notably high back vowels, and the effect again is to centralize them.

All that remains to explain is why the change would occur before [d] rather than [t], and there is some evidence that [d] can be seen as relatively lax compared to [t]. That is, while some phonologists reject the identification of voiceless consonants as tense/fortis and voiced consonants as lax/lenis, Ladefoged and Maddieson (1996: 96), in their discussion of the issue, find that "rates of articulator movement and muscular activation levels often do differentiate between phonological voicing categories." Although they warn that "as little is known about the articulatory dynamics of most languages, we would caution against making the assumption that phonological voicing differences are associated with articulatory strength differences in any particular case," they state:

Voiceless stops have a greater mean oral pressure than voiced stops, and also often have a greater peak oral pressure. Accordingly, the greater degree of articulatory activity in the formation of the closure may be an anticipation of this need to make a firmer seal. In principle, the parameters of voicing and gestural stiffness could vary independently. When they co-vary either one might be regarded as primary. (1996: 96)

So to suggest that less muscular energy is required before [d] than before [t] is not unreasonable. Therefore, I suggest that physiologically this sound change is a simple assimilation to the neighboring consonants. Only if we see it as primarily a qualitative change can we account for its behavior: its occurrence first after consonant + /l/ and before /d/, and its direction of diffusion from more to less frequent words.

6.3.7 Conclusion to /uː/ laxing

Our investigation of the laxing of Early Modern English /uː/ to /ʊ/ has served two purposes: to clarify the phonetic motivation behind this sound change, and to illustrate how lexical diffusion theory may guide historical linguists in evaluating competing analyses of a given sound

180 *Word Frequency and Lexical Diffusion*

change. The theory of lexical diffusion is still under construction, it is true, but it promises to be a powerful tool for future studies in historical phonology.

6.4 General conclusion

These three studies have demonstrated how work on manuscript variation and on determining the motivation behind particular sound changes can benefit from lexical diffusion theory as set forth in the preceding chapters. As Bybee (2001: 83) suggests, "lexical diffusion patterns can provide an additional and much-needed criterion for discovering both why and how sound changes take place."

7
Conclusions, Connections, and Implications

7.0 Introduction

The preceding chapters have presented data supporting a number of conclusions regarding the lexical diffusion of sound change, including the following:

- Phonetically gradual and phonetically abrupt changes are **both** lexically diffused.
- Whether the most frequent words or the least frequent are affected first in a sound change is dependent on the degree of **analysis** required in order to implement the change. Changes that affect the most frequent words require no analysis beyond the phonetic encoding. Changes that affect the least frequent words first require such analysis (word class, syllable structure, phonotactic constraints, etc.)
- Lexical diffusion occurs **within** phonological environments. There is therefore no dichotomy between lexically diffused changes and phonetically conditioned changes. A sound change usually proceeds through phonetic analogy, i.e. by making connections between phonetically similar portions in the phonological representations of lexemes.
- Word class and word frequency are independent influences upon the direction of a sound change. Lexical diffusion occurs within word classes, probably because word class is accessed in production prior to phonological form.
- Function words change first in weakening sound changes, whereas content words change first in strengthening sound changes.

181

- Lexical diffusion is one part of the **implementation** of a sound change. As a change is dispersing through the population and across phonological environments, it is simultaneously being diffused through the lexicon.
- Word frequency effects are found in production, not in perception.
- Lexical representations, including phonological representations, are linked in a connectionist network to other lexical representations, allowing generalizations to emerge which form the basis for the spread of the sound change to new words depending on phonetic or morphological resemblance.
- Connections between lexical items can also lead to generalizations based on morphology or semantics, resulting in so-called "gang effects" (as in the patterning together of *why, what, when, where* in the loss of /h/ before /w/).
- A usage-based, connectionist phonology best accounts for the varying routes of sound change. If words are stored in the lexicon and the phonology emerges from lexical connections, then the path of a sound change may be affected by any information in the lexicon, whether it be word frequency, word class, neighborhood density, semantics, or social correlates.

These findings have implications for other views on the motivation, actuation, and implementation of sound change, some of which are discussed below, including a final search for the locus of what has been called regular, neogrammarian change.

7.1 Apparent time effects

The finding that word frequency effects are rooted in production helps to explain why studies which use apparent time – such as our study in Chapter 2 of /j/-deletion in words like *tune, due*, and *nude* – show differences between age groups. That is, apparently people's production becomes less malleable as they age, even while their perception continues to adjust to new situations. For instance, in second-language acquisition, older speakers have a more difficult time producing new forms which they have no trouble in perceiving; and older speakers who move to a different dialect area are less likely to adopt the new dialect, whereas their children will adjust their production very rapidly.

Pierrehumbert (2003: 211) explains the near-merger findings of Labov et al. (1991) in the following way: "[S]ubjects whose productions display an acoustic difference between the vowels of such word pairs are

Conclusions, Connections, and Implications 183

unable to distinguish these words at above chance levels. This is true even if they are listening to their own speech" (p. 211). Her explanation is that "The subjects in the near-merger study must have been able to perceive a difference between *ferry* and *furry* at the time their production patterns were being established." That the subjects under discussion were unable to perceive the distinction even when their own speech was played back to them she attributes to the fact that the task

> was a word judgment task, hence involved access to the lexicon. Thus, one must consider not only the phonetic encoding in perception, but also the relationship of this encoding to the stored word-form. If subjects have learned, from exposure to the varied dialect community of Philadelphia, that vowel quality information does not reliably distinguish *ferry* and *furry*, then they can downweight this information as a perceptual cue in lexical access. They learn not to pay attention to a cue they cannot rely on. (p. 212)

She notes the superior malleability of the perceptual faculty as shown in a study by Schulman (1983) on the perception of the vowels in the words *sit, set, sat, sot* by bilingual Swedish–English speakers.

> The speakers were unable to hear the *set, sat* distinction when experimental instructions were delivered in Swedish, a language in which dialect diversity renders the distinction unreliable. However, they could hear the distinction when instructions were delivered in English. In short, this study indicates that the attentional weighting of different phonetic cues is not an entrenched feature of the cognitive system; instead, it can be varied according to the speech situation. (p. 212)

Again, such malleability of speech perception is not mirrored in adult production. In word frequency studies this becomes important because there is now abundant evidence that word frequency effects are found only in production, not in perception.

7.2 Child language

Our discussion of the role of production in the propagation of sound change has been exclusively on adult production, but studies have also been done of the lexical diffusion of acquired sounds in child phonological development. In fact, many such studies use the term "sound

184 *Word Frequency and Lexical Diffusion*

change" to refer to the acquisition of adult forms by children (as, for instance in Gierut and Storkel 2002: 122). Chen (1972: 493) encouraged such studies, suggesting that lexical diffusion in child language development might offer a "microchronic" version of historical sound change. And shortly thereafter, Ferguson and Farwell (1975) reported lexical diffusion in the first 50 words of seven children monolingual in English. As an example, they give the pronunciations of the words *baby, ball, blanket, book, bounce, bye-bye,* and *paper* by one child, "T," for sessions approximately one week apart, as outlined in Table 7.1. In one session, T has "the following words and initial-consonant variations: *baby* [b ~ β], *ball* [b], *blanket* [b], *book* [b ~ ∅], *bounce* [b], *bye-bye* [b ~ pʰ], *paper* [b ~ ∅]." At the next session, T exhibited the following pronunciations: "*baby* [b ~w~ p], *ball* [b], *bang* [b], *blanket* [b], *book* [b], *bounce* [b], *box* [b], *bye-bye* [b ~ β]; but *paper* [pʰ], *pat* [pʰ], *purse* [p]." Thus, the words did not pattern together in T's acquisition of the adult forms. The acquisition of the adult form in one word did not entail its acquisition in all words.

Berg (1993: 51) noted a similar behavior in his daughter's phonological development, that after she "began to pronounce the alveolar lateral in word-initial position at the age of 3:1, she continued to inconsistently use her favourite substitute [d] in a variety of words for a certain time." And other studies have confirmed the lexically gradual natural of the acquisition of adult phonemes (Beckman and Edwards 2000; Gierut 2001; Gierut and Morrisette 1998). Gierut and Storkel (2002), for instance, studied lexical diffusion and markedness, both positional and featural, in the acquisition of the fricatives /s/ and /f/ by preschool children, with the coronal /s/ considered unmarked and the labial /f/ considered marked. What they found was that "neither a child's presenting fricative inventory nor the markedness of fricatives being learned played a role in lexical diffusion. Rather, a consistent pattern of sound change in low frequency and high density lexical items was observed for postvocalic position" (p. 126). In prevocalic position, however, "the words that change were more variable in their frequency

Table 7.1 Acquisition of [b] "phone class" by T (based on Ferguson and Farwell 1975: 425)

	baby	*bye-bye*	*book*	*ball, blanket, bounce*
Session VI	b ~ β	b ~ pʰ	b ~ ∅	b
Session VII	b ~ w ~ p	b ~ β	b	b

Conclusions, Connections, and Implications 185

and density values" (p. 127). As they suggest, more research needs to be done in this area. If more studies support their finding that children are more likely to achieve the adult norm in low-frequency, high-density words, I would suggest the following possible explanation, namely, that children's production of high-frequency words has become fixed through their own use and their caregivers' probable acceptance of their "deviant" pronunciation. Low-frequency words in high-density networks, that is, with many similar words that could be confused with the target word, would provide greater motivation for the child to mimic the adult pronunciation as closely as possible.

Berg (1995) considers the connection between models of historical sound change and the behavior of his daughter's acquisition of German. Berg, for instance, found that at age three his daughter Melanie first produced the voiced [g] just hours after her first production of [k] (pp. 350–1). Yet she acquired [g] in *ganz* and *gut* fully four months apart, despite the words being essentially equally frequent. Indeed, her full mastery of word-initial velars took 15 months (p. 335). In explaining his daughter's phonological development, Berg finds inadequate the distinction between historical neogrammarian change, which locates change at the phonological level with no variation between words, and Malkiel's (1967) dictum that "Every word has a history of its own" (p. 353). As an alternative, he turns to a connectionist model: "[A]ll the changes that were observed during the data-collection period can be understood as changes affecting links. The phonological aspects of the change may be located in the associations between the feature and the segment level, and the lexical aspects in the associations between the segment and the word level" (p. 358). Part of the acquisition process for children is the development of "association strength" between linguistic units or "nodes":

A node representing a particular word may not yet function properly (or not exist at all). Secondly, the association between a segment and a word node may be so underdeveloped that an insufficient amount of information (or no information at all) reaches the recipient node. Thirdly, a segment node may be ill-developed (or lacking). Fourthly, the link between a segment and a feature node may be too weak. Fifthly, a feature node may not have reached the state of maturity or may not have been created yet. (p. 355)

Such considerations highlight the difference between lexical diffusion in child language and lexical diffusion of historical sound change. It is a truism that almost all children do attain adult proficiency.

186 *Word Frequency and Lexical Diffusion*

They may reanalyze the pronunciations they hear – each person's emergent grammar being of necessity nonidentical to their interlocutors' – but their output will conform with or at least very closely replicate the adult pronunciation (and the more they interact with other children, the pronunciation of their peers). That is, while studies of child language are interesting in the light they shed on the organization of phonology in the human brain, lexical diffusion in language acquisition need not replicate lexical diffusion in historical change. They are simply different phenomena. "Sound change" in phonological development is the acquisition of the adult pronunciation. Sound change in diachrony is a change in the adult pronunciation. This basic difference between the two must always be kept in mind.

The way that child development and historical sound change are similar is that they both depend upon the inherent structure of the human brain, which seems best modeled by an interactive connectionist framework, as Jaeger (1997) and Berg and Schade (2000) suggest for child language, and they both involve gradual restructuring of the lexicon, as Berg (1993: 51) describes the child's developing lexicon: "The restructuring of the lexicon is thus likely to be a gradual process and to take place within the constraints imposed by the general principles of information processing and storage." And his conclusion about the lexical diffusion of newly acquired phones in child language applies equally well to adult grammars: "If this restructuring does not affect the whole lexicon at the same time, it is even less likely that the reorganization of allophones into phonemes can be sparked off by the addition of a single word. This would require a window showing on the entire lexicon, which does not seem to be available" (p. 51). That is, the exemplar model of phonological encoding is supported both by child language development and by historical sound change.[1]

7.3 Age of acquisition

A separate yet related issue is the age at which a word is acquired. Certainly, it makes sense that words which are learned early might have a greater chance of developing long-term entrenched memory traces. And this would be especially true of highly frequent words, which makes it difficult to separate out the two influences. Barry et al. (1997: 577), however, find that the age of acquisition affected the labeling of a picture "mainly for names of low word frequency"; that is, the two factors "work together so that the fastest access will be for high-frequency, early-acquired names, whereas the slowest will be for low-frequency,

Conclusions, Connections, and Implications 187

late-acquired words." Gerhand and Barry (1998) review much of the research on the relative effects of word frequency and age of acquisition (AoA) in word processing, and also develop their own study of naming latencies in the reading by 33 British college students of 64 words, divided into the following 4 categories: "(a) early-acquired, high frequency (e.g., *win*, *cousin*); (b) early-acquired, low-frequency (e.g., *elf*, *rattle*); (c) late-acquired, high-frequency (e.g., *sex*, *union*); and (d) late-acquired, low frequency (e.g., *cue*, *marvel*)" (p. 269). Age of acquisition was based on Gilhooly and Logie (1980), and word frequency was based on Kučera and Francis (1967). They found that the two effects were not identical since they were "entirely additive: Participants were faster to read aloud early-acquired than late-acquired words and were also faster to name high-frequency than low-frequency words," leading them to suggest that "these two variables affect quite distinct stages of the word-naming processes" (p. 277). They proposed that the AoA affects the retrieval of a word's stored phonological representation, whereas word frequency "affects either the accessing of a word's stored orthographic representation . . . or the connections from word recognition to phonology (as suggested by Borowsky & Besner, 1993)" (p. 277).

In a follow-up article using the same four categories, plus an additional 64 nonwords, Gerhand and Barry (1999) studied lexical decision times (LDTs), with the result again that ". . . the **AoA** effect was reliable for **only low-frequency words**" (p. 598, my bold). In the serial model they follow, they suggest that

> [t]his interaction was interpreted in terms of frequency affecting lexical access and AoA affecting a postaccess decision, or checking, stage (of the kind proposed by Balota & Chumbley, 1984, 1985), in which phonological representations are consulted in order to make confident lexical decisions, particularly for low-frequency words. We propose that AoA affects the ease with which phonological information becomes available in this process in such a way that the phonology of late-acquired words is slower to be activated, and thus lexical decisions will be made more slowly to late-acquired than to early-acquired, low-frequency words. (p. 598)

However, Gerhand and Barry's findings could also fit with the kind of interactive lexicon that we have been envisioning. Rather than age of acquisition affecting "a postaccess decision" for low-frequency words, the early acquisition of these forms would make them more entrenched in memory and thus more likely to behave like high-frequency words.

188 *Word Frequency and Lexical Diffusion*

This conclusion seems consonant with findings from the lexical diffusion of historical sound change. For instance, words such as *heofenn* 'heaven,' *preost* 'priest,' and *deofell* 'devil' pattern with high-frequency words in the *Ormulum* manuscript (*c.* 1180) (Phillips 1984: 330). In ordinary usage, such words would surely be infrequent, and even Orm's age of acquisition must have been late, but as a monk, he would have encountered these words frequently. Thus, word frequency seems to be the significant factor in Orm's production of these forms and in the spellings he assigned to them. Similarly, reduced forms – reduction typically applying to high-frequency items – are often found in words used frequently only in particular occupations, as in *boatswain* /bosən/, *coxswain* /kaksən/, and *kiln* /kɪl/.

Both word frequency and age of acquisition, it might be added, contribute to a word's subjective familiarity, which Kreuz (1987: 159) found "more sensitive than printed frequency in measuring the underlying psychological construct of word familiarity." Certainly, since each of these constructs – age of acquisition and word frequency – is different for each speaker, printed word frequency lists are of necessity imperfect indicators of word familiarity, that is, of how entrenched a word's pronunciation is in memory. For that reason, it is sometimes hard to find clear word frequency effects in the speech of individuals, especially for sound changes that do not affect a large number of words of varying frequencies. As with so many fields of study, statistical significance is best sought over a large population, where idiosyncratic strong entrenchments of particular words cannot so easily skew the results. In any case, the findings on word frequency and age of acquisition confirm the influence of word frequency on adult production and the diffusion of sound change through adult populations.

7.4 Discourse strategies

Some writers have appealed to discourse strategies to explain the lexical diffusion of sound change – that is, speakers, consciously or unconsciously, modifying their speech to meet the needs of the hearer. For instance, Fenk-Oczlon (1989a, b, 2001) notes that in set phrases, called "freezes," like *knife and fork* or *now and again*, the higher-frequency word usually comes first. She comments, "What is familiar is easier for the speaker to call up and is more expectable and therefore more easily perceivable for the hearer" (1989b: 537). For her, frequency explains much of what Natural Phonologists such as Donegan and Stampe (1979) and Dressler (1984) attribute to phonostylistic variants in casual or rapid speech: "High frequency means . . . low information content. An element carrying a small amount of information can be processed within a shorter time. . . . [B]ackgrounding affects frequent words first and . . . token frequency is a key-factor for backgrounding processes" (2001: 436–7). However, while speakers surely participate in such discourse strategies, they do not in and of themselves explain the course of all sound change, or even of all seemingly reductive changes.

Work by Anderson et al. (1997), Bolinger (1963), Lieberman (1963), and Lindblom (1990) on reduced and clear speech processes is summarized by Wright (2003: 75): "In these studies talkers have been shown to produce more reduced speech when contextual information within the utterance or in the environment can aid the listener in recognising what is said, and to produce more careful speech when the talker is aware of conditions that may impede the listener's ability to understand what is said." Similar findings have also been found by Fowler and Housum (1987), Jurafsky et al. (2001), and Bradlow (2002). Wright (2003) tested the production of vowels in "easy" versus "hard" words, "easy" words being frequent forms for which few phonologically similar words exist and "hard" words being relatively low in frequency and having many phonologically similar words (p. 79). He found that "vowels from 'hard' words are more hyperarticulated than vowels from 'easy' words" (p. 84); that is, the vowels in "hard" words are produced with more acoustic distance from other vowels. This finding may help to explain why vowel reduction leads to more central vowels and other vocalic processes lead to more peripheral vowels, and even why vowel reduction affects the more frequent words first. But it does not explain why changes such as the diphthongization of Middle English /iː, uː/ also affect the most frequent words first, an effect we characterized in Chapter 3 as dependent upon the gradual change in the lexical exemplars which required no deeper analysis in lexical retrieval and production. Certainly, more work on the connection between neighborhood density and sound change needs to be pursued, since the number of phonologically similar words is crucial to Wright's study.

Berg (1998: 243) connects ease of articulation with discourse: "It has been empirically demonstrated that frequency speeds up the word-recognition process (Oldfield and Wingfield 1965). If speakers exploit this principle, they can be more sloppy about the pronunciation of high-frequency words than about that of low-frequency items, while still achieving the same degree of communicative success. In fact, this is precisely what speakers do: the higher the redundancy of a word, the less accurately it is articulated (Lieberman 1963)." This principle does seem to be true of reductive and assimilatory sound changes that affect the most frequent words first, but again does not account for other changes, such as stress shift in -*ate* verbs, which also affect the most frequent words first without affecting articulatory ease. Berg does distinguish between "two distinct areas where linguistic change may originate: on the one hand the processing network, which is subject to high-level constraints, and on the other the 'articulatory bottleneck', which is subject to low-level constraints" (p. 244), a distinction which sounds very similar to our division by level of analysis – the most frequent words being affected first when only "shallow" access of phonetic form is required in production, the less frequent words being affected first when further "analysis" is required to implement the change. But Berg's divisions do not follow this logic. He describes all changes as affecting the most frequent words first, with the only difference being that some proceed more quickly than others; that is, "those changes which crucially implicate the articulatory component, i.e. those which make articulation easier" correlate with **higher frequency** and **faster** change; "those which are independent of articulatory constraints, i.e. those which do *not* make articulation easier" also correlate with **higher frequency** but **slower** change (p. 244). It may well be true that the "faster" changes rooted in articulatory ease are the ones most likely to proceed so quickly as to *seem* to affect all the words at the same time and thus be labeled as neogrammarian or regular. But the prime example of neogrammarian change cited by both Labov (1994) and Kiparsky (1995) is the Northern Cities Shift. There is no reason why this unconditioned change should be based in ease of articulation. It apparently spreads very quickly, although, as we have seen in Chapter 1, there are lexical "stragglers," and speakers may even create hypercorrections. For example, a young hotel employee in Ann Arbor, Michigan, told me to park in the side parking lot or in the /bak/ (and, when asked to do so, repeated his instructions using the same pronunciation of *back*, /a/ having in most words apparently shifted to [æ] in his speech and /æ/ to [ɛ] – but not in the speech of many out-of-town guests).

In addition, we have seen that it is not just word frequency alone that governs which words undergo a change, but how word frequency interacts with lexical access in production. Support for this stance may be seen in the finding (in Chapter 3) that some seeming reductions, such as /j/-loss after /t, d, n/, do not affect the most frequent words first but last. This sound change turned out not to be due to "total assimilation" of the glide in casual or rapid speech. Rather it had its basis in generalizations concerning the phonotactic structure of English,

Conclusions, Connections, and Implications 191

which favored (in type frequency) glideless onsets over glided ones. And abrupt changes such as stress shifts (discussed in Chapter 2) are hard to explain using discourse strategies, yet some affect the most frequent words first and others the least.

7.5 "Neogrammarian" change as rapid dispersion through the lexicon

Two findings in the preceding chapters lead us to the conclusion that regular, neogrammarian change – defined as phonological change affecting all pertinent lexical items simultaneously – is unlikely to be found as a method of implementing sound change. First, lexical diffusion has been documented as affecting all types of phonological change – whether phonetically gradual or abrupt. Secondly, the word frequency effects on the lexical diffusion of those changes are a natural outgrowth of a model supported by numerous psycholinguistic studies, that is, a usage-based model of the mental lexicon in which the lexicon is central, with exemplar phonemes being based upon generalizations from phonetically detailed memory traces. Other current models of phonology fail to account for the patterns we have demonstrated of some changes affecting the most frequent words first and others the least frequent words first.

Why then do so many changes seem to be regular? For one thing, there are a number of situations which have led researchers to claim regularity, where lexical diffusion might still have been involved in the change:

- The sound change has already affected all the pertinent words.
- There are too few words meeting the phonetic description for lexical diffusion to be noticeable.
- The data under discussion do not include a wide range of words, especially words of different frequencies.
- There are "outliers," exceptional forms which do not undergo the change, but which proponents of neogrammarian change do not recognize as lexical diffusion.
- Writers assume that because there is detailed phonetic conditioning, there is no lexical diffusion.

Researchers should therefore take such possibilities into consideration before announcing that a change has not undergone lexical diffusion. Rudimentary logic tells us that it is impossible to prove a negative.

192 *Word Frequency and Lexical Diffusion*

Therefore, any statement that lexical diffusion does not play or has not played a role in the implementation of a change should at minimum be rephrased as not having been found in the data evaluated, however extensive that data may seem.

Meanwhile, as Ogura (1995: 32) suggests, what are considered to be neogrammarian or "regular" changes are most likely to be changes that diffuse so quickly through the lexicon that they only seem to affect all the words at the same time. Ogura and Wang (1998: 322) make this position even clearer in their distinction between "W-diffusion," which is "diffusion from word to word in a single speaker or at a single site" and "S-diffusion," which is "diffusion from speaker to speaker, or from site to site of a single word." They add that "[o]ne cannot say either W-diffusion or S-diffusion is always faster. It probably depends on the particular phonetic and societal parameters involved." Neogrammarian regularity, however, they define as "W-diffusion . . . proceed[ing] so fast that it is difficult to observe it" (p. 324). Under this view, the real question becomes: Why do some changes proceed through the lexicon so quickly while others operate so slowly?

Berg's (1998: 243) appeal to ease of articulation and the fact that Labov (1994: 541) sees neogrammarian change in low-level phonetic output rules might lead one to hypothesize that such shifts in allophonic variants are especially susceptible to rapid spread through the lexicon. Certainly, our discussion of the lexical diffusion of such changes in Chapter 3 found that many affect the most frequent words first, which also of necessity are the most likely words to be heard and noted by investigators. Labov's characterization of this type of change as being below the level of conscious awareness proves problematic, however, since it has been shown that speakers encode much phonetic detail and make use of it, especially in perception, but also in the gradual restructuring of their own phonological representations – word by word. What is meant by "below the level of consciousness" and where that level might be located, then, becomes difficult to determine.

Certainly the notion of salience must play a role here. And yet, judging from the number of different ways in which it has been invoked, a unified definition of salience has clearly not been settled upon. Kerswill and Williams's (2002: 81) provisional definition is perhaps as useful as any, namely, "a property of a linguistic item or features that makes it in some way perceptually and cognitively prominent." Yet they warn that although they "take the view that salience offers sufficient insights for it to be a potential explanatory factor, . . . without careful argumentation on the linguist's part, the concept all too easily lapses into circularity

Conclusions, Connections, and Implications 193

and mere labelling" (p. 82). One thing that is clear is that phonetic salience need **not** be tied to phonemic distinctiveness in the traditional, minimal-pair sense. Not only are there many ways in which subphonemic differences are meaningful to speakers, but it has long been recognized that in the case of phonemic split, the rule assigning allophones based on phonetic conditioning must already be no longer operable in order for phonemes to split after the conditioning environment has been lost. Janda (2003: 417) strongly emphasizes how important this understanding is:

> When such quantitative documentation of socially motivated exaggeration is deftly combined with psychophonetic research on the origins of phonological change in another kind of exaggeration, and viewed in the light of existing psycholinguistic studies of categorization (especially concerning phonemes versus allophones), the solidity of the conclusion that phonemicization/phonologization of an allophone can precede loss of its conditioning environment can hardly be exaggerated.

Aski's (2001a, b) work on the development of Latin /tj/ and /kj/ has led her to the conclusion that neogrammarian regularity is to be found below the level of the phoneme as a prototype categorization. The pertinent data involve the shift in some dialects of Italian, of Latin /tj/ and /kj/ to /(t)ts/ and /(t)tʃ/, respectively, with, however, "numerous exceptions of the opposite development: /kj/ > /(t)ts/ and /tj/ > /(t)tʃ/" (2001b: 205). She suggests

> that prototype categorization is the cognitive dynamic underlying the process of (lexically conditioned) lexical diffusion, and that sound change is a phonetically and lexically gradual phenomenon. It is phonetically gradual in that... a range of allophonic variants is produced, perceived and processed by language users.... It is lexically gradual, since the items affected are dictated by linguistic, cognitive and social factors. (p. 207)

Significantly, prototype or exemplar phonemes need not meet the minimal-pair requirement of classical phonemics. Aski separates sound change into "innovation" (or "actuation") and "propagation" (what we would call "implementation") and places neogrammarian change in the "innovation" category. That is, in her Multivariant Reanalysis

194   *Word Frequency and Lexical Diffusion*

theory, lexical diffusion does not begin until speakers interpret as prototype/exemplar phonemes the allophonic variants they hear. But even extremely low-level variants have been shown to be influenced by word frequency; witness, for example Lociewicz's (1992) findings, as reported in Bybee (2001: 78), "that on average the *-ed* suffix on low frequency verbs is 7 msec. longer than on high frequency verbs" (as well as other evidence presented in Chapter 3). And if all the allophonic variants were equally likely in all words, then one would expect completely random outcomes for Latin /tj/ and /kj/; that is, if the innovative affrications were truly uninfluenced by lexical item and so close to each other phonetically that some words developed one way and some another, one would expect speakers' categorizations to be either uniform for both or at least to be lexically random. The fact that in most words /tj/ did become /(t)ts/ and /kj/ become /(t)tʃ/ and that only in a minority of words did the opposite results obtain suggests that the phonetic details of the words in question always differed to some extent from lexeme to lexeme. Thus, again, the lexical diffusion becomes more obvious and perhaps is slowed by the prototype or exemplar categorization of the sounds in question, but lexical differences must have existed from the beginning.

Cheng and Wang (1977: 99) suggest that what they call "phonetic strength" and which others might call "naturalness" could cause some changes to proceed faster than others:

> It is our conjecture that perhaps a notion which we may call *phonetic strength* is relevant here. A change such as nasalization of vowels before nasal stops has a lot of phonetic strength. Such a change is consummated rapidly, perhaps with an S-type chronological profile. Changes like tone shift (and perhaps, vowel shift to a lesser degree), on the other hand, are phonetically weak changes and may well proceed slowly, linearly, and characteristically leave a large residue. The notion of phonetic strength must have independent meaning in terms of phonetic observation, either from the point of view of articulatory ease or perceptual distinctness.

Their suggestion is echoed in Labov's (1994: 531–2) limitation of lexically diffused changes to complex articulations of "abstract" classes. Similarly, Côté (1997: 240–1) uses salience in this sense in her discussion of the acoustic salience of final segments, where "phonetic salience" seems to equal number of acoustic cues that would allow a segment to be identified. In the same way, Andersen (2003: 21), discusses how

Conclusions, Connections, and Implications 195

the High German Consonant Shift involves "protensity," a phonological feature which Andersen notes requires "the coordinated interaction of the three valves – glottal, velopharyngeal, and oral – that serve to implement the distinctive differences in timing," yet which "cannot be reduced to any single such gesture (combination)." Such a feature would be considered highly salient acoustically. As for the change at the heart of the neogrammarian–lexical diffusion debate, the raising or tensing of [æ] to [Æ] in such cities as Philadelphia, perhaps the extra salience of lengthened + raised + tensed vowels accounts for its slower progress and hence more obvious lexical diffusion. Kerswill and Williams's (2002) study of salience in dialect leveling in England, however, finds that such phonetic factors "remain useful [only] so long as they are seen as interacting with extra-linguistic factors" (p. 91). Indeed, they find that "salience, however defined and however caused, will be different for different social groups" (p. 101).

Even though social salience, then, may be more responsible for influencing the speed of a change, it too proves difficult to define and to link to specific paths of change. Hock and Joseph (1996: 151–2), for instance, suggest that the change of /u:/ to /ʊ/ in words such as *good, look, foot* has been slow to change (witness lexical exceptions such as *food, mood, groom, groove*) because of its lack of social connotations: "At best we can say that [rūt] [for *root*] may strike some people as perhaps a little too formal, while others consider [rut] a little too informal" (p. 151). The centralization of the /ay/ and /aw/ diphthongs on Martha's Vineyard, on the other hand, had strong social connotations, which, they claim, caused it to be adopted rapidly, affecting many lexical items simultaneously. That is, "The fact that centralization took place quite rapidly reflects the strong social motivation of the change, while the slow-moving nature of *oo*-shortening is explained by its weak social motivation" (pp. 151–2). In a similar vein, Hickey (1998: 100) suggests that the Dublin Vowel Shift affecting allophonic variants of diphthongs is regular among "motivated participants – fashionable Dubliners" but lexically diffused among "detached participants – socially conscious urbanites from outside Dublin."

Other socially salient changes might spread very slowly, however. Labov's (1994: 542) observation that lexical diffusion is "most characteristic of the late stages of an internal change" that "has developed a high degree of social awareness or of borrowings from other systems" gives us a clue about what causes some changes to proceed slowly enough for their lexical diffusion to be noticeable. That is, lexical diffusion does often seem more obvious on the geographical peripheries of a

196 Word Frequency and Lexical Diffusion

change – where the pronunciation in question has developed salience as a regional dialect marker – and on the chronological peripheries – where the pronunciation is particularly salient as an innovative form or as an "old-fashioned" form, hence the typical S-diagram depicting the progression of most sound changes. It is particularly interesting that hypercorrections, which were once thought to indicate the completion of a change, in fact can exist throughout the diffusion of a sound change, even in its earliest stages, as exemplified in the Old English raising of /æ/ (Toon 1983: 145). Such hypercorrections indicate that a change can be salient in some sense throughout its progression. In contrast, the geographical and chronological center of the change is more likely to be a relatively homogeneous dialect area, within which speakers imitate or replicate each other's pronunciations. The less consciously this is done, i.e. the less salient the difference in features or the social associations, the more chance that a sound change once introduced will spread rapidly to all of the lexemes – hence the rapid spread of most reductive changes. In this view, the more social salience a pronunciation has developed, the more likely it is that the change will progress more slowly, leaving some lexical items untouched.

It is not difficult to see that the preceding views of the influence of social and phonetic salience on the rate at which a sound change spreads are often contradictory. The differing views are included here to emphasize how much remains to be done in this field. That is, the role of salience and its effect on the speed at which a sound change spreads areally and socially remains an open and intriguing field of study.

7.6 Conclusion

The primary aims of this book have been to provide extended examples of sound changes which have diffused through the lexicon based on word frequency and to provide an explanation for why some of those changes affect the most frequent words first and others the least frequent first. Of course, word frequency is but one factor affecting the diffusion of change through the lexicon and through populations of speakers. Phonological, morphological, semantic, social, pragmatic, and cognitive factors all influence which words are affected when. A usage-based model inherently recognizes the need to incorporate all of these factors. However, any model of the lexicon which aims to incorporate plausible diachronic developments must address the differences between those changes which affect the most frequent words first and those which affect the least frequent words first.

Appendix A
Stress Patterns and the Suffix -*ate*

Table A.1   British English trisyllabic verbs in (C)V(C)\$CVC\$C-*ate*

Verb	Frequency	1755	1780	1824	1872	1917	1937	1988	2003
concentrate	1084	–	–	–	–	+	+	+	+
demonstrate	821	–	–	–	–	+	+	+	+
illustrate	557	–	–	–	–	+	+	+	+
contemplate	319	–	–	–	–/+	+	+	+	+
compensate	217	–	–	–	+/–	+	+	+	+
designate	129		+	+	+	+	+	+	+
alternate	124	–	–	–	+/–	+	+	+	+
infiltrate	73					–	–	+/–	+
devastate	67		–	–	+	+		+	+
masturbate	66								+
elongate	56	–	–	–	–	+		+	+
confiscate	55	–	–	–	–/+	+	+	+	+
orchestrate	41					+	+	+	+
impregnate	36	–	–	–	–	+/–	+/–	+/–	+/–
inundate	27				–/+	+	+	+	+
remonstrate	25	–	–	–	–	–/+	–/+	+/–	+/–
inculcate	19	–	–	–	–	+/–	+/–	+/–	+/–
hibernate	17				+	+	+	+	+
promulgate	16	–	–	–	–	+	+	+	+
enervate	12	–	–	–	–	+	+	+	+
demarcate	9					+	+	+	+
obfuscate	8			–	–	+	+	+	+
incarnate	7	–	–	–	–	–/+	+/–	+/–	+/–
adumbrate	5	–	–	–	–	+	+	+	+
coruscate	2			–	–/+	+	+	+	+
commentate	2							+	+
bifurcate	2					+	+	+	+
consternate	1					+	+	+	+
altercate	0				+	+	+	+	+
auscultate	0						+	+	+
condensate	0	–	–	–	–				
defalcate	0	–	–	–	–	–/+	–/+	+/–	+/–
eructate	0			–	–	–	–	–	
exculpate	0	–	–	–	–	+	+	+	–/+
expurgate	0			–	–/+	+	+	+	+
extirpate	0	–	–	–	–	+	+	+	+

198

Table A.1 (Continued)

Verb	Frequency	1755	1780	1824	1872	1917	1937	1988	2003
fecundate	0				+	+	+	+	+
fenestrate	0							−/+	−/+
inculpate	0				−	+/−	+/−	+/−	+/−
incurvate	0	−	−	−	−	+	+	+	+
objurgate	0	−	−	−		+	+	+	+
prolongate	0				−				
sequestrate	0	−	−	−	−	−/+	−/+	−/+	−/+

+ = antepenultimate stress (*'concentrate*); − = penultimate stress (*con'centrate*).

Table A.2   American English trisyllabic verbs in (C)V(C)\$CVC\$C-*ate*

Verb	Frequency	1806	1828	1909	1953	1993	2004
concentrate	1084	−	−	−/+	+	+	+
demonstrate	821	+	+	+/−	+	+	+
illustrate	557	−	−	−	+/−	+/−	+/−
contemplate	319	+	+	+/−	+/−	+	+
compensate	217	+	+	+/−	+/−	+	+
designate	129		+	+	+	+	+
alternate	124	+	+	+/−	+	+	+
infiltrate	73	−	−	−	−	−/+	−/+
devastate	67		+	+	+	+	+
masturbate	66					+	+
elongate	56	−	−	−	−	−/+	−/+
confiscate	55	+	+	+/−	+/−	+	+
orchestrate	41				+	+	+
impregnate	36	−	−	−	−	−/+	−/+
inundate	27		−	−	+/−	+	+
remonstrate	25	−	−	−	−	+/−	+/−
inculcate	19	−	−	−	+/−	−/+	−/+
hibernate	17		+	+	+	+	+
promulgate	16	−	−	−	−	+/−	+/−
enervate	12	+	+	−/+	+	+	+
demarcate	9			−	−/+	−/+	−/+
obfuscate	8	−	−	−	−/+	+/−	+/−
incarnate	7	−	−	−	−	−/+	−/+
adumbrate	5	+	−	−	−/+	+/−	+/−
coruscate	2		+	+/−	+	+	+
commentate	2			+		+	+
bifurcate	2			−	+/−	+/−	+/−
consternate	1				+	+	+
altercate	0	+	+	+	+	+	+
auscultate	0			+	+	+	+

condensate	0	–	–	–	–		
defalcate	0	–	–	–	–	–/+	–/+
eructate	0	–					
exculpate	0	–	–	–	+/–	+/–	+/–
expurgate	0		+	+/–	+	+/–	+
extirpate	0		+	+/–	+/–	+	+
fecundate	0	+	+	+	+	+	+
fenestrate	0						
inculpate	0			–	–/+	–/+	–/+
incurvate	0	–	–	–	–	+/–	+/–
objurgate	0	–	–	–	+/–	+	+
prolongate	0	–	–	–	–	–	
sequestrate	0	–	–	–	–	+/–	+/–

+ = antepenultimate stress ('*concentrate*); – = penultimate stress (*con'centrate*).

Appendix B
Prenasal /a/-Raising in the Old English *Pastoral Care*

Data for function words include prepositions, conjunctions, pronouns, articles, and adverbs (which in Old English are difficult to distinguish from function words). Spellings in «a» are used in the tables, unless no such spellings were found in the *Pastoral Care*.

Table B.1   Percentage of «on, om» spellings in OE *Pastoral Care*: function words

Function words	Frequency in *PC*	% of «on, om» Spellings
gemang	1	0
hwonon	3	100
ærðon(ðe)	4	100
hwane	5	80
same	6	33
tosomne	7	100
ætsomne	8	100
hwanne	11	82
ongemang	18	56
ðonan	20	95
ðon	21	100
forðon	55	95
from	86	95
ðone	382	99
ðonne	1400	99
on	1536	99
ond	2552	100

Table B.2   Percentage of «on, om» spellings in OE *Pastoral Care*: nouns

Nouns		
anga, forwanan, gamene, gebanne, gespann, mancessan	1	0
longunge, orðonc, sconca, somrædenne	1	100
lambe, pannan	2	0
gemanges, gesamhiwena	2	50
swongornesse, wong	3	100

gespan, hwammas, rammas	4	0
sang	6	33
wana	6	50
gesomnung	12	100
nama	13	31
scand	19	21
wamb	19	21
land	27	44
scame	29	7
anda	33	3
hand	40	68
lichoma	71	99
ðonc	77	91
monn*	745	93

*_monn_ can also be used as an indefinite pronoun, similar to Modern English "one".

Table B.3   Percentage of «on, om» spellings in OE _Pastoral Care_: verbs

Verbs	Frequency in _PC_	% of «on, om» Spellings
afandon, astandan, aswand, dranc, gelamp, mangige, oncann, sang	1	0
gesomnode, ofstong, ðonciað, understondan	1	100
wandrian	2	0
befangne, spannað	2	50
begongað	2	100
geman, spane	3	0
gestrangod	3	67
hangian	4	0
nam, onfangen	4	25
gefangen	5	0
underfange	6	17
wiðstandan	7	71
wanað	8	0
ganganne	13	77
fandian	14	7
cann	15	46
scamað	18	22
wandað	21	0
standan	27	70
manian	242	26

202

Table B.4 Percentage of «on, om» spellings in OE *Pastoral Care*: adjectives

Adjectives	Frequency in *PC*	% of «on, om» Spellings
foreðancula, wanhale, widgangule	1	0
iongum	1	100
won	8	100
grambæra	10	0
strang	17	35
lang	25	60
manðwæran	27	78
manig	113	67

Appendix C
Unrounding of OE Long and Short /ø(ː)/ in the *Ormulum*

Table C.1   Percentage of ≪e≫ spellings for OE long /øː/ in the *Ormulum* (Phillips 1984: 328)

Word class	Base forms	Frequency	% ≪e≫	Average % ≪e≫
Adverbs and	*sket*	12	100	
function words	*newenn*	26	100	
(average % ≪e≫ = 100)	*bitwenenn*	51	100	100
Nonnumerical	*seoc*	2	50	
adjectives	*freo*	3	67	
(average % ≪e≫ = 70)	*dreoriȝ*	5	60	
	neow	8	88	66
	deop	21	62	
	deore	28	68	
	leof	36	97	76
Verbs	*beodeþþ*	2	50	
(average % ≪e≫ = 67)	*forrbedeþþ*	2	100	
	secnedd	2	100	
	nedenn	3	100	
	chesenn	4	100	
	fleȝhenn	4	100	
	cneolenn	6	83	
	wex	6	100	
	freollsenn	7	14	
	forrleosenn	8	63	
	(bi)reowenn	9	0	
	steorenn	9	22	
	dreȝhenn	10	100	
	forrseon	10	40	69
	leȝhenn	11	100	
	cneow	12	25	
	fell	13	100	
	fleon	15	47	
	heold	18	89	
	ȝede	26	100	
	streonenn	47	13	68
	seon	69	52	52
	beon	355	41	41
Nouns	*breostlin*	1	0	
(average % ≪e≫ = 28)	*derrlinng*	1	100	
	þeos	1	0	

204

Table C.1 (Continued)

Word class	Base forms	Frequency	% «e»	Average % «e»
	leo	2	0	
	fend	3	100	
	wheol	5	20	
	heowe	6	67	
	fe(hh)	7	100	
	freond	8	50	49
	deor	21	14	
	leom	23	0	
	treo	26	12	
	streon	27	0	
	leod	47	4	6
	preost	68	3	
	þeod	82	4	4
	deofell	158	1	1
Numerals	*feorþe*	17	0	0
(average % «e» = 0)	*þreo*	45	0	0

Table C.2 Percentage of «e» spellings for OE short /ø/ in the *Ormulum* (Phillips 1984: 329)

Word class	Base forms	Frequency	% «e»	Average % «e»
Function words	*binepenn*	1	100	
(average % «e» = 100)*	*sellf*	137	100	
	hemm	347	100	
Verbs	*clepenn*	3	100	
(average % «e» = 85)	*herrcnenn*	3	100	
	werrpenn	6	100	
	ȝerrnde	9	11	
	berrȝhenn	10	100	
	forrweorrpenn	39	97	
Nonnumerical	*feorr*	2	50	
adjectives	*þeorrf*	3	67	
(average % «e» = 72)	*fele*	15	100	
Nouns	*berrhless*	1	100	
(average % «e» = 55)	*deorrf(like)*	1	0	
	berrne	2	100	
	sede(full)	2	100	76
	weorrc	26	62	
	weorelld	42	2	
	heorrte	90	73	46
	heofenn	154	6	6
Numerals	*seofenntiȝ*	2	0	
(average % «e» = 10)	*seoffnde*	5	20	
	seofenn	46	9	

*Omitting *he(o)re* 'her.'

Appendix D
Vowel Lengthening before Voiced Homorganic Consonant Clusters in the *Ormulum*

Table D.1 Vowel lengthening before voiced homorganic consonant clusters in the *Ormulum* (Phillips 1983b: 495–8)

Doubled consonants indicate a preceding short vowel, single consonants a preceding long vowel. Only one form per lexeme is listed, but the frequency count, in parentheses, may include additional inflectional forms, derivatives, and compounds.

Environment	Word class	With lengthened vowels	Variable	With unlengthened vowels
-ld	Noun	*child* (160), *dæpshildiʒnesse* (5), *dwilde* (12), *elde* (31), *faldess* (2), *feld* (3), *ʒeldess* (1), *gold* (9), *hald* (14), *kald* (1), *mildheorrtnesse/-leʒʒc* (9), *þild* (11), *walde* (61)		*wullderr* (8)
	Verb	*be(o)ldenn*, (10), *bihaldenn* (1), *childenn* (14), *cwaldenn* (2), *dwalde* (2), *eldenn* (2), *ʒeldenn* (3), *ʒoldenn* (1), *haldenn* (87), *oferrgildedd* (1), *saldenn* (6), *shildenn* (3), *tald* (18), *weldenn* (3)		
	Adjective	*ald* (39), *allwældennd* (8), *bald* (1), *childlæs* (1), *dæpshildiʒ* (2), *-fald [an-, twa-/twi-, þre-, fif-, sefenn-]* (14), *gildene* (1), *hold* (3), *milde* (39), *wilde* (10)		

205

206

Table D.1 (Continued)

Environment	Word class	With lengthened vowels	Variable	With unlengthened vowels
	Adverb	*aldeliʒ/-like* (2), *baldeliʒ* (2), *hunndreddfald* (1), *seldenn* (2), *þildiliʒ* (1), *wald* (1)		
	Auxiliary	*wollde* (338), *sollde/shollde* (412)		
-nd	Noun	*band* (18), *fandinng* (4), *forrswundennleʒʒc/-nesse* (4), *grund* (12), *hund* (4), *kind* (138), *land* (119), *lende* (3), *minde* (2), *sand* (2), *sanderrmann* (7), *shande* (1), *strande* (3), *stund* (6), *sund* (2), *wand* (1), *wind* (2), *wunde* (12)	*ende* (112)/ *ennde* (1), *hand* (24)/ *hannd* (24)	*unnderrn* (1), *winndell* (3), *wunnderr* (12)
	Verb	*attwindenn* (1), *bindenn* (19), *blendeþþ* (13), *bundenn* (12), *endenn* (25), *fandenn* (61), *fundenn* (55), *grindesst* (2), *lendenn* (2), *wand* (2), *wundenn* (19)	*findenn* (74)/ *finndeþþ* (1), *shendenn* (5)/ *shennd* (3), *wendenn* (13)/ *wenndenn* (34)	*brennd* (8), *senndenn* (68), *stanndenn* (58), *unnderrstanndenn* (177), *wiþþstanndenn* (5)
	Adjective	*blind* (7), *endelæs* (1), *findiʒ* (5), *kindelæs* (1)		
	Adverb			*ʒonnd* (3), *wunnderr* (2)
	Auxiliary		*sindenn* (2)/ *sinndenn* (81)	*munndenn* (30)
	Conjunction			*annd* (13+, usually abbreviated "7")
	Preposition			*biʒonndenn* (3), *bihinndenn* (3), *unnderr* (87)
-mb	Noun	*camb* (1), *lamb* (39), *wambe* (27)		
	Verb	*climbenn* (1)		

207

	Adjective	*crumb* (2), *dumb* (4)		
	Adverb		*umbe* (1)/ *ummbe* (13)	
	Preposition			*ummbenn* (1)
-ng	Noun	*ange* (3), *gang* (4), *genge* (31), *king* (225), *offspring* (3), *sang* (12), *swinginng* (1), *tunge* (10), *þing* (133), *þwang* (6), *wengess* (2)		*enngell* (72), *hunngerr* (12)
	Verb	*biþrungenn* (2), *forrclungenn* (1), *forrlangedd* (1), *gengenn* (12), *langenn* (3), *ringenn* (5), *singeþþ* (1), *sprang* (2), *springenn* (3), *sprungenn* (2), *stingenn* (1), *strengenn* (5), *stungenn* (3), *sungenn* (5), *swingenn* (1), *þingenn* (2), *unnderr-/onnfengenn* (8)	*unnderfangenn* (1)/*fanngenn* (11), *heng* (1)/ *henngedd* (3)	*brinngenn* (51), *ganngenn* (11), *sinnʒheþþ* (1)
	Adjective	*ʒung* (14), *lang* (2), *strang* (20), *wrang* (2)		
	Adverb	*wrang* (14)		*forrlannge* (13), *lannge* (13)
	Preposition	*(a)mang* (55), *bilenge* (1), *lang* (1)		
-rd	Noun	*ærd* (106), *birde* (29), *bord* (9), *brerd* (7), *ferd* (3), *flærd* (5), *hirde* (31), *hord* (12), *ord* (7), *re(o)rd* (6), *swerd* (7)	*word* (255)/ *worrd* (1)	*girrdell* (2), *ʒerrde* (3)
	Verb	*hordenn* (1), *we(o)rdenn* (8)		*birrdenn* (27), *ferrdenn* (5), *sperrd* (3)
	Adjective			*harrd* (22), *innwarrd* (11), *wiþerrwarrd* (1)
	Adverb			*harrde* (2), *-warrd [affterr-, dunn-, forrþ-,heþenn-, upp-,wheþenn-, whiderr-]* (38)
	Auxiliary			*wurrdenn* (1)
	Conjunction			
	Preposition			*affterrwarrd* (2), *frawarrd* (6), *towarrd* (55)
-rþ	Noun	*e(o)rþe* (238)		
	Verb	*forþenn* (61)		*forrwurrþenn* (5), *wurrþenn* (28)

208

Table D.1 (Continued)

Environment	Word class	With lengthened vowels	Variable	With unlengthened vowels
	Adjective	*e(o)rþliȝ/-lic/-like* (84)	*wurþi* (1)/ *wurrþi(ȝ)* (20)	*derewurrþe* (5)
	Adverb			*forrþenn* (13), *forrþerr* (1)
	Auxiliary			*wurrþenn* (229)
-rn	Noun	*ærn* (7), *bærn* (1), *corn* (10), *hirne* (3), *le(o)rninngcnihhtess* (65)	*ste(o)rne* (3)/ *ste(o)rrne* (34)	*barrness* (3), *berrne* (1), *þorrness* (2)
	Verb	*bærnenn* (7), *eornenn* (17), *ȝe(o)rnenn* (39), *le(o)rnenn* (22)		*turrnenn* (119)
	Adjective	*dærne* (29), *irnene* (1), *stirne* (1)	*unnorne* (8)/ *unnorrne* (1)	
	Adverb	*dærneliȝ/-like* (8), *unnorneliȝ* (5)	*ȝe(o)rne* (22)/ *ȝerrne* (3)	*forrnonn* (1)
	Auxiliary			*arrn* (2)
-rl	Noun	*cherl* (1), *eorless* (1)		*barrliȝ* (1), *birrless* (4)
	Verb			*birrlenn* (5)

Appendix E
Spellings in «a» versus «o» before Nasals in the *Pastoral Care*

In the table below, the «a» spelling occurs in the left-hand column for a word group unless the only spellings were in «o». Word forms included in one word group could be related to the stem through inflection, derivation, or compounding; e.g. under "man", get *man, mann, mannes, mannum, manna, mannan, mandædum, ealdorman, ðeningmannum*. Words listed in the -an- column have only that spelling, and those in the -on- column only «o». In the variable column, the percentage of «on» spellings is given in parentheses for each word; thus, of the three tokens of *gestrangod/gestrongiað*, two contained «o», yielding 67 percent.

Table E.1 Spellings in «a» versus «o» before nasals in the *Pastoral Care*

Word group frequency	-an-	-an- ~ -on- (% -on-)	-on-
1	afandon, anga, astandan, aswand, dranc, foreðancula, forwanan, gamene, gebanne, gelamp, gemang, gespann, mancessan, mangige, oncann, sang, wanhale, widgangule		gesomnode, iongum, longunge, ofstrong, orðonc, sconce, somrædenne, ðonciað, understondan
2	lambe, pannan, wandrian	befangne/ befongne (50), gemanges/ gemonnge (50), spannað/ gesponnene (50), gesamhiwena/ gesomhiwan (50)	begongað, ingong
3	geman, spane	gestrangod/ gestrongiað (67)	hwonon, swongornesse, wong
4	gespan, hangian, hwammas, rammas,	genam/genom (25), onfangne/ onfongne (25)	ærðon

209

210

Table E.1   (Continued)

Word group frequency	-an-	-an- ~ -on- (% -on-)	-on-
5	gefangen	hwane/hwone (80)	
6		underfangne/ underfongne (17), (swā) same/some (33), sang/song (33), wana/wona (50)	
7		wiðstande/ wiðstonde (71)	tosomne
8	wanað		ætsomne, won
10	grambæra		
11		hwanne/hwonne (82)	gesomnung
13		nama/noma (31),	
14		fandian/fondian (07), ganganne/gongað (79)	
15		can/con (46)	
17		strang/strong (35)	
18		scamað/scomað (22), ongemang/ ongemong (56)	
19		scand/scond (21), wamb/womb (21)	
20		ðanon/ðonon (95)	
21	wandað		ðon
25		lang/long (60)	
27		land/lond (44), standan/stondan (70), manðwæran, monðwæran (78)	
29		scame/scome (07)	
33		anda/onda (03)	
40		hand/hond (68)	
55		forðan/forðon (95)	
71		lichaman/ lichoman (99)	
77		ðance/ðonc (91)	
86		fram/from (95)	
113		manige/monige (67)	
242		manian/monian (26)	
382		ðane/ðone (99)	
745		mann/monn (93)	
1400		ðanne/ðonne (99)	
1536		an/on (99)	
2552			ond

Notes

1 Word Frequency and the Neogrammarian Controversy

1. A fuller version of Osthoff and Brugman's statement is translated by Lehmann (1967: 204) as

> First, every sound change, inasmuch as it occurs mechanically, takes place according to laws that admit no exception. That is, the direction of the sound shift is always the same for all the members of a linguistic community except where a split into dialects occurs; and all words in which the sound subjected to the change appears in the same relationship are affected by the change without exception.

2. The original reads:

> La vraie question est de savoir si les changements phonétiques atteignent les mots ou seulement les sons; la réponse n'est pas douteuse: dans *néphos, méthu, ánkhō,* etc., c'est un certain phonème, une sonore aspirée indo-européenne qui se change en sourde aspirée, c'est l's initial du grec primitif qui se change en *h,* etc., et chacun de ces faits est isolé, indépendant des autres événements du même ordre, indépendant aussi des mots où il se produit. Tous ces mots se trouvent naturellement modifiés dans leur matière phonique, mais cela ne doit pas nous tromper sur la véritable nature du phonème. (Saussure 1916 [1967]: 133)

3. "Le système de nos phonèmes est l'instrument dont nous jouons pour articuler les mots de la langue: qu'un de ces éléments se modifie, les conséquences pourront être diverses, mais le fait en lui-même n'intéresse pas les mots, qui sont, pour ainsi dire, les mélodies de notre répertoire" (Saussure 1916 [1967]: 134).
4. There is also clear lexical diffusion of [æ]-lengthening in British RP, as summarized by MacMahon (1998: 407).
5. Guy (1997) compares Optimality Theory (OT) with the Variable Rule (VR) model developed by Labov (1969) and Cedergren and Sankoff (1974). He notes that the main difference between the two approaches is that the VR model takes no stance on the universality of constraints (p. 37), that whereas in OT modeling of different varieties and registers of English is accomplished through different constraint rankings, in VR the input probability is calculated, which not only allows for differences between speakers but also for stylistic variations expressed by one and the same speaker. As Guy points out,

> No English speaker has been found who reliably reverses the community order by deleting coronal stops more after sonorants than after obstruents or more past tense forms than monomorphemes, but speakers vary widely

211

212 *Notes*

in overall rates. OT cannot explain either finding. Difference of any sort should [in OT] involve different constraint orders, and differences of pure frequency of use cannot be modeled at all. (pp. 338–9)

2 The Lexical Diffusion of Phonetically Abrupt Changes

1. The connection between type frequency and productivity has been demonstrated, for example, in Baayen and Lieber (1991), Bybee (1985, 2001), Moder (1992) and Wang and Derwing (1994).
2. The 2003 revision of that dictionary (Roach et al.) notes further changes, which may, however, be a result of the change of their model from *Received Pronunciation* to *BBC English. Mandate* still has variable stress, but *mandáte* is now listed first (which usually indicates the more common pronunciation); *gestate* has acquired a variable pronunciation, with *gestáte* listed first; and *pulsate, fixate, lactate, palpate,* and *filtrate* are now listed with initial stress only.
3. The British dictionaries start with Samuel Johnson's (1755) *Dictionary of the English Language.* Although Johnson's attitude toward usage is "ambivalent" (Landau 1984 [1989]: 53) – at one point claiming it is the lexicographer's task "to correct or proscribe ... improprieties and absurdities" and at another stating it is not his job to "form, but register the language" (quoted by Landau p. 53) – one can assume at least some uniformity from a dictionary primarily assembled by one person. Landau (p. 57) comments that "it was not until the publication of Thomas Sheridan's *A General Dictionary of the English Language* in 1780 that a major advance was made in the dictionary treatment of pronunciation," so his pronunciations are included in the data even though his stress patterns of the words under study were almost identical with those of Johnson. This is particularly encouraging since "Sheridan was the first major lexicographer to note variations from 'established, correct forms', based on his understandings of actual pronunciation usages of educated speakers" (Bronstein 1986: 24). The third dictionary, published in 1824, was an edition of Johnson revised by Henry John Todd. Apparently it "was esteemed the best of dictionaries in both England and America until well into the nineteenth century" (Landau p. 56). To fill the time gap between (Todd-)Johnson (1824) and the earliest twentieth-century dictionary in the study *Chamber's English Dictionary,* published in 1872, was consulted. Daniel Jones's *An English Pronouncing Dictionary,* published first in 1917, limits itself to RP (Received Pronunciation), which is advantageous, since it precludes the problem of mixing different dialects and registers. Jones himself writes (in the 1937 edition):

The pronunciation represented in this book is that which I believe to be most usually heard in everyday speech in well educated families of the South of England. The pronunciation is in the main that which I use myself. I have, however, put my pronunciation in a secondary place in all cases where another form appears to me to be in more frequent use. (p. ix)

Notes 213

The research reported below includes data from Jones's 1917, 1937, and 1988 editions, the last of which was edited by A.C. Gimson and revised by Susan Ramsaran. This latest edition still attempts to reflect RP speech, although the editors "widen[ed] its application" (p. vii). As they describe it,

> the speech-style now recorded, while retaining its underlying South-Eastern English characteristics, is applicable to a wider sample of contemporary speakers, especially those of the middle generations. . . . As a result of this relaxation of definition, the ordering of pronunciation variants has frequently been modified and certain new variants have been included. (p. vii)

4. For American English, the earliest dictionary in this study is Noah Webster's 1806 *A Compendious Dictionary of the English Language* and the enlarged 1828 *An American Dictionary of the English Language*. As Landau (1984 [1989]: 61) points out, "Webster's provinciality showed through markedly in his pronunciations, which were those of New England. The rest of the country was ignored or was considered to speak incorrectly." Merriam-Webster's 1909 *New International Dictionary* undoubtedly retains "Webster's eastern, conservative bias," as Landau says the 1934 edition did (p. 64), but there again is an advantage in a dictionary having this narrow a pronunciation focus. In 1953, Kenyon and Knott published their *Pronouncing Dictionary of American English*, stating their purpose as "to give (unless otherwise indicated) only pronunciations that are in general cultivated use – to give none that need be avoided as incorrect or substandard" (p. xxvii). They do list first "what is believed to be the most usual colloquial pronunciation" but warn that "not too much importance should be given to the order" (p. xxvii). Of *Webster's Third New International Dictionary* (1961), Landau claims its "full coverage of pronunciation can be interpreted as its substitute for a revision of Kenyon and Knott ([also] originally published by G. & C. Merriam)" (p. 98). Since Landau says that Merriam Webster's 8th and 9th Collegiate Dictionaries contain "more accurate [pronunciations] than those of any other American dictionary," I have chosen their latest edition, Webster's 11th (2004), as my most recent source for American English.
5. Minkova and Stockwell (2005: 274) provide a list that includes these and more, some of which are not as obviously frequent among the general population, but sometimes a reduced pronunciation develops among a select social group and spreads from there, just as the word *boatswain* is still pronounced by many today as /bosən/, based on the pronunciation by rowers who do use it frequently.
6. Levelt (2002) finds that the evidence, reviewed in detail in Levelt (1999), supports "on-line" computation of word stress, at least in Dutch, and concludes, "It is probably the case that only irregularly stressed words carry metrical information in their stored phonological codes" (p. 90). Compare Pepperkamp's (2004) study of lexical exceptions to stress rules and speakers' perception of stress, which suggests that "the encoding of stress in the phonological representation of words depends on the surface observability of stress" (p. 120).

214 *Notes*

3 The Lexical Diffusion of Phonetically Gradual Changes

1. Murray (2000: 640) interprets Orm's spellings as indicating a difference between smoothly cut syllables (e.g. *wreȝenn*) and abruptly cut syllables (e.g. *eȝȝe*), with ambisyllabicity being "a derivative property of the abruptly cut syllable."
2. Ogura includes *icicle* as having the same phonetic environment as these words, but I have omitted it because it has more than one syllable.
3. An investigation of parallel environments for /iː/ was inconclusive, except for /iː/ before /s/, already discussed. Ogura's data include no reflexes of ME [iː] before /θ/, and the influence of word frequency of /iː/ before /x/ was indeterminate because of the variety of word classes represented: *sight* (n.), *fight* (n. or v.), *might* (n. or v.), *night* (n.), *right* (n., v., adj., adv.), *light* (n., v, adj.). Since Orton's *Survey of English Dialects* was not always recording nouns, for instance, the influence of word class could not be discounted. See Chapter 4 for further discussion of the role of word class on the course of lexical diffusion.
4. The discovery by Yaeger-Dror (1996) of part of a chain shift in Montreal French Vernacular that appears to affect frequent words such as *père*, *mère*, *frère* offers an interesting contrast to the pattern Ogura (1987) found in the English Great Vowel Shift. Yaeger-Dror (1996: 281) suspects associative semantic links to be the cause of the hesitance of these forms to undergo the shift.
5. In their study of change in real time, Nahkola and Saanilahti (2004: 90) conclude,

> If a speaker acquires a feature with little or no variation in it no major changes are likely to take place during the speaker's lifetime. . . . If, however, a speaker acquires a feature as a variable one with two (or more) truly competing variants, it is possible – even likely – that the balance of the variants will change during the speaker's lifetime. The more equal the proportions of the rivalling variants are, the more likely it is that one of the variants will increase its proportion and gain dominancy during the speaker's life. . . . All this also gives support to the idea that the rate of a language change follows the shape of the S-curve: the phase of maximal variation is passed quickly.

Their finding is consonant with our study here of apparent time.
6. The number of words beginning with /du-, nu-/ is not greater than the number of words beginning with /dju-, nju-/, according to a count of one-syllable words from the *Random House Unabridged Dictionary*, assembled by Brett Kessler at http://www.artsci.wustl.edu/~bkessler/SensPhonotactic/dictAlign. But vowels have been found always to associate themselves more strongly with codas than with onsets (Booij 1983; Fudge 1969, 1987; Selkirk 1982); therefore the more important comparison for our study seems to be the onset /t, d, n/ or /tj, dj, nj/.
7. Jones (1989: 271–5) investigates /h/ loss in Henry Machyn's diary (1550–63), finding that the etymological word-initial /h/ is most often omitted in less

Notes 215

frequent words. The motivation behind this loss or behind Machyn's spellings is unclear, however.

8. See Hogg (1992b: 104) for a discussion of an alternate view of the short diphthongs as "centralized and monophthongized allophones of the front vowels."

9. Compare, however, Lass and Laing's (2005: 289) suggestion that

> The standard story in which /e(:)o/ first monophthongised to a mid front rounded vowel which remained in the West is unnecessarily complex. ... All we need to account for subsequent orthographic and phonological developments is a variable split of the diphthongs in which some reflexes merged with those of /e(:)/ and others merged with those of /o(:)/.

Of particular interest in the support it lends to the lexical diffusion of such changes is their finding that in their LAEME (Linguistic Atlas of Early Middle English) corpus based on Southwest Midlands manuscripts, spellings are often lexically specific. The reflex of Old English /y/, for instance, is consistently written ≪i≫ in "king" and "church."

10. Hogg (1992a: 216) believes that occasional OE spellings in ≪e≫ or ≪o≫ for expected ≪eo≫ /ø(:)/ "no doubt reflect uncertainty over the most proper representation of the new sound, and preference for ≪e≫ over ≪o≫ need not be taken to imply monophthongization to /e(:)/." Orm's orderly distribution of ≪e≫ versus ≪eo≫, on the other hand, must indicate a true change in progress.

11. See Johannesson (1997) for a closer description of Orm's corrections and emendations. Johannesson notes that the extant version is clearly a copy of an earlier draft, since Orm clearly skips words at times. That he attempted to correct spellings in ≪eo≫ but not any of the spellings indicating diphthongization suggests that, as one might expect, the monophthongization of /ø(:)/ was a change of which he was consciously aware, whereas he was either not as aware of diphthongization or neither variant had attained a socially preferred status in his mind.

12. Luick (1914–21 [1964]: 474–5) suggests that this vowel lengthening probably actually began as early as the seventh century and that, although the vowels of low-stressed function words were never lengthened, some of the words in the *Ormulum* contain reshortened vowels (e.g. *senndenn* "send," *brinngenn* "bring," *harrd* "hard"). Yet, if we accept Luick's theory, we are left to explain why, if vowels are inherently longer before such clusters, an "unnatural" shortening would affect the more frequent words. The shortcomings of Ritt's (1994) account of quantitative shifts in Early Middle English are outlined in Bermúdez-Otero's (1997) review. One of Bermúdez-Otero's criticisms, however, turns out not to be true; that is, Bermúdez-Otero (1997: 623) claims, "There appears to be no compelling evidence that the synchronic grammars internalized by native speakers incorporate any sort of probabilistic device for computation." For evidence to the contrary, see, for instance, the papers in Bod et al.(2003).

13. Donka Minkova (personal communication) points out that "Hogg's explanation has the serious problem of predicting that the inflected forms of such words would have a light stressed syllable in the early verse and, therefore,

216 *Notes*

trigger resolution, which is not the case; they behave as heavy from the start. The clusters are always bisegmental; only the sonorant can be moraic. The phonetically most plausible account from a perceptual point of view would be a reanalysis of the sonorant mora into a mora associated with the vowel."

14. One exceptional spelling in Orm that is noted by Minkova and Stockwell (1992: 201) – *dwillde* – is listed by Holm (1922: xxxviii) as an error in Holt's edition. Minkova and Stockwell also note that modern *build* and *guild* retain a short vowel, but this resistance to "late-breaking" may be due to their rounded front vowels in Old English. According to the online edition of the *Oxford English Dictionary*, "'member of a guild, guild-brother' was expressed by OE. ʒylda and ʒeʒylda" (the initial hard /g/ of *guild* being due to Norse influence) and *build* goes back to an unattested OE form, *byldan*. The word *bieldan*, on the other hand, is attested in Modern English with the reflex of the long vowel, *bield*.

4 Lexical Diffusion and Word Class

1. Bell et al. (1999: 398) also find nonphonetic factors that influence the likelihood of reduction in function words: their place in the utterance ("Function words are more likely to be unreduced when they are turn-initial or utterance-final"); the sex of the speaker ("Female speakers are more likely to have long or unreduced function words; this effect is mostly but not completely due to their slightly slower speaking rate"); and the "effect of planning problems" ("[F]illed pauses (*uh* and *um*) are the strongest factor in predicting lengthening of a previous function word").

2. A similar table in Phillips (1983b: 493) is flawed. The current table corrects those errors.

3. *Stood* and *soot* both show innovative vowels in most of the dictionaries, while *root* does so in only one.

4. Sometimes a distinction is drawn between a lexeme and a word form – for example, the lexeme for the indefinite article in English has two word forms (*a* and *an*).

5. Jescheniak et al. (2003: 437) also note shortcomings in Bonin and Fayol's (2002) study, which might have led the latter not to find full frequency inheritance in homophones in French. Another recent study which questions the inheritance effect of homophones is Miozzo et al. (2004), whose evidence comes from a brain-damaged subject suffering from anomia.

5 Analogy, Borrowing, and Lexical Diffusion

1. The shortcomings of the radical underspecification approach Kiparsky uses to support his view of sound change are outlined in Goldsmith (1995: 13–18).

2. "Gehen wir davon aus, dass es nur Individualsprachen gibt, so können wir sagen, dass in einem fort Sprachmischung stattfindet, sobald sich überhaupt zwei Individuen miteinander unterhalten.... In diesem Sinne haben wir die Sprachmischung durch alle Kapitel hindurch berücksichtigen müssen, da sie etwas von dem Leben der Sprache unzertrennliches ist". (Paul 1880: 390, as quoted by Chen 1972: 463)

Notes 217

3. The *Rushworth Gospels* have traditionally been described as North Mercian, but Coates (1997) locates the scriptorium further south, in Lichfield. See Hogg (1998) for a discussion of dialect labels for Old English.
4. The dates for these manuscripts are those assigned by Hogg (1992a: 5–6).
5. http://www-users.york.ac.uk/~lang22/YCOE/info/YcoeTextInfo.htm#cocura. o2
6. The «a» spelling appears very frequently before «ng», and it was shown above that even in the Corpus Glossary, «a» was retained most often before the velar nasal, so it is possible that in the dialect area of *Rushworth 1*, the change to /ɔ/ had not reached completion in that environment. Certainly there is no reason to suppose that the change had progressed as far as it had in the *Vespasian Psalter*. Even though both manuscripts are generally regarded as Mercian, Campbell (1959: §11) observes that "the *Vespasian Psalter* and the *Rushworth Gospels* represent in many respects highly divergent dialects." Spellings in «a» are also fairly frequent in unstressed syllables, where it occurs on average 16 percent of the time. But Toon includes in this category also unstressed words: "*on* is spelled *an* only once out of 95 occurrences; *þone* is spelled *þane* 8% of the time. In 22 of 94 cases, *þonne* is found as *þanne*" (p. 117). Why *þonne* 'then; therefore; than' should have so many «a» spellings is not clear. In the *Pastoral Care* it was spelled with «o» 99 percent of the time. In stressed syllables, the verb *gelamp* 'succeeded' (3×) versus usual *gelomp* (19×) is the only word with «a» before /m/ (*-a-* being the typical pattern for the past tense of class III strong verbs). Before /n/, «a» also occurs in three class III verbs: *bewand* 'surrounded' (1×), *blan* 'ceased' (1×) and *ongan* 'began' (1×) (cf. *ongon* 1×]). Otherwise there is only one instance of «a», in *standende* 'standing' (cf. *stondende* 3×, *stondan* 'to stand' 9×), and all other verbs have exclusively «o»: *conn* 'knew' (4×), *gebond* 'bound,' *ingonn* 'to enter' (5×), *monade* 'warned'. Thus there is not enough variation among the verbal forms for word frequency effects to be noticeable.

6 Applications of Lexical Diffusion

1. A fourth paper, "Æ-Raising in the *Peterborough Chronicle*" (Phillips 2004), traces the diffusion of the raising of [æ] in Old English, from early Mercian glosses (*c.* 700) through the *Ormulum* (*c.* 1180) and additionally demonstrates how exemplar theory helps in understanding spelling evidence for the later stages of the change.
2. Although all of the tallies are based on my own search through the pertinent years of the *Peterborough Chronicle*, using Clark (1970), the "Index Verborum" contained in Clark's thesis (1952) proved extremely helpful as a starting point and as a check on my own counts.
3. This is the stance taken, for instance, in Lass (1992a), who also argues that "the spelling of these early glosses and the like is not 'irregular' or full of 'mistakes' (though there are plenty of those, of course, which can usually be spotted because of their lack of principle). Rather it is the real thing, properly to be taken as a variation-sample at (imagined) utterance level, more or less as if it were speech."

218 *Notes*

4. Clark coalesces forms from the Interpolations into the copied annals and forms from the First Continuation, because "in general they show similar developments" (1970: xlvi). I have disregarded forms from the Interpolations because they seem to have been copied from earlier, albeit Anglian, sources.

5. The word *nedes* (1×) 'of necessity' was omitted from the tally, since it was unclear whether it should be considered a noun or an adverb. The word *se* 'the' (from OE masc. *sē/sĕ* and OE fem. *sēo*) was also not included, because Clark (1970: lix) finds evidence of "almost complete effacement of the Old-English gender system"; but before OE feminine nouns it is always *se* (6×), and there is one inverse spelling before a masculine noun, *seo ærcebiscop*. The inclusion of both of these in a category of "function words" with the prepositions would not change the overall percentage of ≪e≫ forms; it would still be 100 percent.

6. Included in this calculation are spellings which Clark emended by adding the final *m*: *hem* (8×)/*heom* (22x). Not included was the word *seoueniht* 'week' (2×), since the decision would be arbitrary whether to list it under nouns or under numerals.

7. If one accepts spellings in ≪ea≫ and ≪æ≫ as equivalent to those in ≪e≫, only one percentage is significantly affected: verbs with short vowels are spelled with ≪e≫, ≪ea≫, or ≪æ≫ 72 percent of the time compared to 54 percent in Table 6.3. Other, nonsignificant differences are that long-vowel verbs are spelled with ≪e≫, ≪ea≫, or ≪æ≫ 88 percent of the time, short-vowel nonnumerical adjectives 75 percent, and short-vowel nouns 26 percent. All other percentages remain the same.

8. The spellings in ≪ag≫ seem to indicate the velar consonant: *agen(e)* 'own' (5×), *dragen* 'dragged/drawn' (1×), *ofslagen* 'slain' (1×).

9. I have included proper nouns in order to show all the data available. I leave it to the reader to decide whether to consider them on the same level of evidence as the common nouns.

10. See Rusch (1992: 100–5) for "a case for structured variation" of ≪æ≫, ≪a≫, and ≪ea≫.

11. Many thanks go to Robert Stockwell, Donka Minkova, and an anonymous reviewer, all of whom had comments and suggestions that made this section immeasurably better. Shortcomings, of course, remain strictly my own.

12. I will use the term "laxing" as a cover term to refer to the change in vowel quality involved in this shift. I realize that the appropriateness of the term "lax" has long been questioned, as in Lindau's (1978: 557–8) discussion of the difficulty of defining the phonetic correlates of tenseness. Lindau concludes that a feature distinguishing tense versus lax vowels "is probably not required for classificatory purposes, because it never seems to occur without concomitant differences in length" and that "the difference between tense and lax vowels is best labeled by a feature Peripheral," which is an acoustically defined feature first used by Stockwell, as in his (1973) interpretation of the Great Vowel Shift. The question posed in the current section, however, is not what feature is best for "classificatory purposes" or which feature best describes the acoustic properties of the sounds in question, but whether the motivation behind the change is a quantitative adjustment or a qualitative assimilation.

13. Ogura (1987: 200–1) accounts for the relengthened vowel by appealing to homonymic clash with the word *fud* 'buttocks.' Similarly, Barber (1997: 124)

Notes 219

claims there is evidence "for the existence of all three pronunciations of the word *foot*, namely [fuːt], [fʊt], and, [fʌt] although the third was possibly vulgar."

14. Carroll et al. (1971) list the frequency per million tokens of *food* as 467.35, *root* as 58.060, and *boot* as 5.6262. The word *soot* is described as short in half of the late seventeenth-century sources, but its frequency is not listed in Spevack's (1973) Shakespeare concordance (Ogura 1987: 146, 200); Carroll et al. (1971) give the frequency per million tokens as 1.8513. One might speculate that it must have been a frequent word in Shakespeare's time, despite its absence in his works.

15. Although Labov (1994: 543) and Kiparsky (1995) both recognize lexically diffused sound changes, neither addresses the difference between lexically diffused changes which affect the most frequent words first and those which affect the least frequent words first. See Phillips (1984, 1998b) and Ogura (1995) for further discussion. For a Gilliéronian's perspective on Labov (1994), see Kretzschmar's (1996) review.

16. For more on the parallel development of ME /ɛː/, see Labov (1994: 304–5, 528–9). The similarity of the changes may be gauged by Labov's description of how members in this class in the seventeenth century "were either shortened to /e/ or rose to high position and merged with the *ē* class, except those beginning with initial clusters of consonant plus /r/, which merged with the *ā* class" (p. 306); "shortening" also occurred before dentals, as in "*head, dead, breath,* and *sweat*" (p. 528). Ogura (1987: 173) states that "before dentals [d], [θ], and [s], it seems that shortening [of ME [ɛː]] took place earlier in the more frequent words than in the less frequent ones, but before [t] no such tendency can be found."

7 Conclusions, Connections, and Implications

1. See Phillips (2004) for how exemplar theory informs our understanding of scribal practice in Old English and its reflection of sound change and reorganization of the emergent phonemic system.

References

Abd-el-Jawad, H. R., and Saleh M. Suleiman. 1990. "Lexical conditioning of phonological variation." *Language Sciences* 12: 291–330.

Aitchison, Jean. 2003. *Words in the Mind: an Introduction to the Mental Lexicon*, 3rd edn. Oxford: Blackwell.

Alario, F.-Xavier, and Laurent Cohen. 2004. "Closed-class words in sentence production: evidence from a modality-specific dissociation." *Cognitive Neuropsychology* 21 (8): 787–819.

Alba, Matthew C. 2003. "¿Cómo se llega a l'escuela?: a study of usage effects on hiatus resolution in New Mexican Spanish." Paper presented at New Ways of Analyzing Variation (NWAV) 31. Stanford University, Palo Alto, CA. Oct. 10–13.

Albright, Adam, and Bruce Hayes. 2003. "Rules vs. analogy in English past tenses: a computational/experimental study." *Cognition* 90: 119–61.

Andersen, Henning. 1973. "Abductive and deductive change." *Language* 49: 765–93.

———. 2001. "Actualization and the (uni)directionality of change." *Actualization: Linguistic Change in Progress*, edited by Henning Andersen, pp. 225–48. Amsterdam: John Benjamins.

———. 2003. "On bifurcations and the Germanic consonant shifts." *Language in Time and Space: a Festschrift for Werner Winter on the Occasion of his 80th Birthday*, edited by Brigitte L. M. Bauer and Georges-Jean Pinault, pp. 19–33. Berlin: Mouton de Gruyter.

Anderson, A. H., E. G. Bard, C. Sotillo, A. Newlands, and G. Doherty-Sneddon. 1997. "Limited visual control of the intelligibility of speech in face-to-face dialogue." *Perception and Psychophysics* 39: 580–92.

Antonsen, Elmer. 1961. "Germanic umlaut anew." *Language* 37: 215–30.

Anttila, Raimo. 1972. *An Introduction to Historical and Comparative Linguistics*. New York: Macmillan.

Aski, Janice M. 2001a. "Multivariable reanalysis and phonological split." *Historical Linguistics 1999: Selected Papers from the 14th International Conference on Historical Linguistics*, Vancouver, 9–13 August 1999, edited by Laurel J. Brinton, pp. 31–47. Amsterdam: John Benjamins.

———. 2001b. "Prototype categorization and phonological split." *Diachronica* 18: 205–39.

Baayen, R. Harald, and Rochelle Lieber. 1991. "Productivity and English derivation: a corpus-based study." *Linguistics* 29: 801–43.

Bailey, Todd M., and U. Hahn. 2001. "Determinants of wordlikeness: phonotactics or lexical neighborhoods." *Journal of Memory and Language* 44: 568–91.

Bakken, Kristin. 2001. "Patterns of restitution of sound change." *Actualization: Linguistic Change in Progress*, edited by H. Andersen, pp. 59–78. Amsterdam: John Benjamins.

Balota, D. A., and J. I. Chumbley. 1984. "Are lexical decisions good measures of lexical access? The role of word frequency in the neglected decision

References 221

stage." *Journal of Experimental Psychology: Human Perception and Performance* 10: 340–57.

——. 1985. "The locus of word-frequency effects in the pronunciation task: lexical access and/or production?" *Journal of Memory and Language* 24: 89–106.

Barber, Charles. 1997. *Early Modern English*. Edinburgh: Edinburgh University Press. First published André Deutsch [1976].

Barinova, G. A. 1971. "Redukcija vypadenie intervokal'nych soglasnych v razgovornoj reči." *Fonologič eskie podsistemy*, edited by S. S. Vygotskiu et al., pp. 117–27. Moscow: Nauka.

Barnhart, Clarence, ed. 1947. *The American College Dictionary*. New York: Random House.

Barrack, Charles. 1976. "Lexical diffusion and the High German consonant shift." *Lingua* 40: 151–75.

——. 1998. *Sievers' Law in Germanic* (Berkeley Insights in Linguistics and Semiotics, vol. 22). New York: Peter Lang.

Barry, Christopher, Catriona M. Morrison, and Andrew W. Ellis. 1997. "Naming the Snodgrass and Vanderwart pictures: effects of age of acquisition, frequency, and name agreement." *The Quarterly Journal of Experimental Psychology* 50A: 560–85.

Beal, Joan. 1999. *English Pronunciation in the Eighteenth Century. Thomas Spence's "Grand Repository of the English Language."* Oxford: Clarendon Press.

Becker, Thomas. 2002. "Zur neuhochdeutschen Dehnung in offener Tonsilbe." *Sounds and Systems: Studies in Structure and Change: a Festschrift for Theo Venneman*, edited by David Restle and Dietmar Zaefferer, pp. 35–58. Berlin: Mouton de Gruyter.

Beckman, Mary E., and Jan Edwards. 2000. "Lexical frequency effects on young children's imitative productions." *Papers in Laboratory Phonology V: Acquisition and the Lexicon*, edited by Michael B. Broe and Janet B. Pierrehumbert, pp. 208–18. Cambridge: Cambridge University Press.

Beddor, Patrice Speeter, Rena Arens Krakow, and Luis M. Goldstein. 1986. "Perceptual constraints and phonological change: a study of nasal vowel height." *Phonology Yearbook* 3 (1986): 197–218.

Bell, Alan et al. 1999. "Forms of English function words – effects of disfluencies, turn position, age and sex, and predictability." *Proceedings of ICPHS-99*, vol. 1. 395–8.

Bennett, Jack A. W., and G. V. Smithers, eds. 1968. *Early Middle English Verse and Prose*. Oxford: Clarendon.

Berg, Thomas. 1993. "The phoneme through a psycholinguist's looking-glass." *Theoretical Linguistics* 19: 39–76.

——. 1995. "Sound change in child language: a study of inter-word variation." *Language and Speech* 38 (4): 331–63.

——. 1998. *Linguistic Structure and Change: an Explanation from Language Processing*. Oxford: Oxford University Press.

——. 1999. "Stress variation in British and American English." *World Englishes* 18: 123–43.

——. 2000. "The position of adjectives on the noun–verb continuum." *English-Language and Linguistics* 4: 269–93.

Berg, Thomas, and Ulrich Schade. 2000. "A local connectionist account of consonant harmony in child language." *Cognitive Science* 24: 123–49.

222 *References*

Bergen, Dick van. 1995. "Acoustic and lexical vowel reduction". PhD Dissertation, University of Amsterdam.

Berko, Jean. 1958. "The child's learning of English morphology." *WORD* 14: 150–77.

Bermúdez-Otero, Ricardo. 1997. Review of Nikolaus Ritt, *Quantity Adjustment: Vowel Lengthening and Shortening in Early Middle English* (Cambridge Studies in Linguistics: supplementary volume). Cambridge: Cambridge University Press, 1994. *Journal of Linguistics* 33: 620–5.

Blevins, Juliette and Andrew Garrett. 1998. "The origins of consonant–vowel metathesis." *Language* 74: 508–56.

——. 2004. "The evolution of metathesis." *Phonetically Based Phonology*, edited by Bruce Hayes, Robert Kirchner, and Donca Steriade, pp. 117–56. Cambridge: Cambridge University Press.

Bloomfield, Leonard. 1933. *Language*. New York: Holt, Rinehart and Winston.

Boberg, Charles, and Stephanie M. Strassel. 2000. "Short-a in Cincinnati: a change in progress." *Journal of English Linguistics* 28: 108–26.

Bock, J. Kathryn. 1999. "Language production." *MIT Encyclopedia of the Cognitive Sciences*, edited by R. Wilson and F. Keil, pp. 453–6. Cambridge, MA: MIT Press.

Bod, Rens, Jennifer Hay, and Stefanie Jannedy, eds. 2003. *Probabilistic Linguistics*. Cambridge, MA: MIT Press.

Boersma, Paul. 1998. *Functional Phonology: Formalizing the Interactions between Articulatory and Perceptual Drives*. Netherlands Graduate School of Linguistics. The Hague: Holland Academic Graphics.

Boersma, Paul, and Bruce Hayes. 2001. "Empirical tests of the Gradual Learning Algorithm." *Linguistic Inquiry* 32: 45–86.

Bolinger, Dwight. 1963. "Length, vowel, juncture." *Linguistics* 1: 5–29.

——. 1975. *Aspects of Language*, 2nd edn. New York: Harcourt Brace Jovanovich.

Bolla, Kálmán, and I. Valaczkai. 1986. *Német Beszédhangok Atlasza* (A Phonetic Conspectus of German). Magyar Fonetikai Füsetek (Hungarian Papers in Phonetics) 16. Budapest: Hungarian Academy of Sciences.

Bonin, Patrick, and N. Fayol. 2002. "Frequency effects in written and spoken production of homophonic picture names." *European Journal of Cognitive Psychology* 14: 289–313.

Booij, Geert. 1983. "Principles and parameters in prosodic phonology." *Linguistics* 21: 249–80.

——. 2004. "Reflections on usage-based phonology." (Review article of Joan Bybee, *Phonology and Language Use*. Cambridge: Cambridge University Press, 2001.) *Studies in Language* 28: 225–37.

Borowsky, Ron, and Besner, D. 1993. "Visual word recognition: a multistage activation model." *Journal of Experimental Psychology: Learning, Memory, and Cognition* 19: 813–40.

Bradlow, Ann R. 2002. "Confluent talker- and listener-oriented forces in clear speech production." *Laboratory Phonology 7*, edited by Carlos Gussenhoven and Natasha Warner, pp. 241–73. Berlin: Mouton de Gruyter.

Braine, Martin D. S. 1974. "On what might constitute learnable phonology." *Language* 50: 270–99.

Brink, Lars. 1977. "On sound laws." Paper given at the Society for Nordic Philology, Copenhagen.

References 223

Brink, Lars, and Jørn Lund. 1975. *Dansk Rigsmål I-II. Lydudviklingen siden 1840 med særligt henblink på sociolekterne i København.* Copenhagen: Akademisk Forlag og Gyldendal.

Bronstein, Arthur J. 1986. "The history of pronunciation in English-language dictionaries." *The History of Lexicography*, edited by R. K. K. Hartmann, pp. 23–33. Amsterdam: John Benjamins.

Bronstein, Arthur J., and Esther K. Sheldon. 1951. "Derivatives of Middle English ō in eighteenth- and nineteenth-century dictionaries." *American Speech* 26: 81–9.

Browman, Catherine, and Louis Goldstein. 1991. "Gestural structures: distinctiveness, phonological processes, and historical change." *Modularity and the Motor Theory of Speech Perception*, edited by Ignatius G. Mattingly and Michael Studdert-Kennedy, pp. 313–38. Hillsdale, NJ: Lawrence Erlbaum.

Brown, Edward Miles. 1891. *Die Sprache der Rushworth Glossen zum Evangelium Matthäus und der mercische Dialekt* (I. *Vokale*). Göttingen: W. Fr. Kästner.

Brown, Leslie, ed. 1993. *The New Shorter Oxford English Dictionary on Historical Principles.* 2 vols. Oxford: Clarendon.

Brunner, Karl. 1965. *Altenglische Grammatik nach der angelsächsischen Grammatik von Eduard Sievers*, 3rd edn. Tübingen: Max Niemeyer.

Bunger, Ann. 2002. "Spoken word recognition, acoustic-phonetic variation, and grammatical category." Manuscript. Longer version of paper presented at the annual meeting of the Linguistic Society of America, San Francisco, January 5, 2002.

Burchfield, R. W. 1956. "The language and orthography of the *Ormulum* MS." *Transactions of the Philological Society* 1956: 56–87.

Burnage, Gavin. 1990. *CELEX: a Guide for Users.* Nijmegen: Celex-Centre for Lexical Information.

Bush, Nathan. 2001. "Frequency effects and word-boundary palatalization in English." *Frequency and the Emergence of Linguistic Structure*, edited by Joan Bybee and Paul Hopper, pp. 255–80. Amsterdam: John Benjamins.

Bybee, Joan. 1985. *Morphology: a Study of the Relation between Meaning and Form.* Amsterdam: John Benjamins.

———. 1995. "Regular morphology and the lexicon." *Language and Cognitive Processes* 10: 425–55.

———. 1999. "Usage-based phonology." *Functionalism and Formalism in Linguistics.* Vol. I: *General Papers*, edited by Michael Darnell et al., pp. 211–42. Amsterdam: John Benjamins.

———. 2000a. "Lexicalization of sound change and alternating environments." *Papers in Laboratory Phonology V: Acquisition and the Lexicon*, edited by Michael B. Broe and Janet B. Pierrehumbert, pp. 250–68. Cambridge: Cambridge University Press.

———. 2000b. "The phonology of the lexicon: evidence from lexical diffusion." *Usage-Based Models of Language*, edited by Michael Barlow and Suzanne Kemmer, pp. 65–86. Stanford: CSLI (Center for the Study of Language and Information).

———. 2001. *Phonology and Language Use.* Cambridge: Cambridge University Press.

———. 2002a. "Lexical diffusion in regular sound change." *Sounds and Systems: Studies in Structure and Change: a Festschrift for Theo Vennemann*, edited by David Restle and Dietmar Zaefferer, pp. 59–74. Berlin: Mouton de Gruyter.

224 *References*

——. 2002b. "Word frequency and context of use in the lexical diffusion of phonetically conditioned sound change." *Language Variation and Change* 14: 261–90.

Bybee, Joan, and Joanne Scheibman. 1999. "The effect of usage on degree of constituency: the reduction of *don't* in American English." *Linguistics* 37: 575–96.

Campbell, A(listair). 1959. *Old English Grammar*. Oxford: Clarenden Press.

Caramazza, Alfonso, A. Costa, M. Miozzo, and Y. Bi. 2001. "The specific-word frequency effect: implications for the representation of homophones in speech production." *Journal of Experimental Psychology: Learning, Memory, and Cognition* 27: 1430–50.

Carr, Philip. 1991. "Lexical properties of postlexical rules: postlexical derived environment and the elsewhere condition." *Lingua* 85: 41–54.

Carroll, John B., Peter Davies, and Barry Richman. 1971. *The American Heritage Word Frequency Book*. Boston: Houghton Mifflin.

Carterette, E., and M. H. Jones. 1974. *Informal Speech: Alphabetic and Phonetic Texts with Statistical Analyses and Tables*. Berkeley: University of California Press.

Cavalli-Sforza, Luigi. 1994. "An evolutionary view in linguistics." *In Honor of William S-Y Wang: Interdisciplinary Studies on Language and Language Change*, edited by Matthew Chen and Ovid J. L. Tzeng, pp. 17–28. Taipei: Pyramid Press.

Cedergren, Henrietta, and David Sankoff. 1974. "Variable rules: performance as a statistical reflection of competence." *Language* 50: 333–55.

Center for Lexical Information. 1993. *CELEX Lexical Database*. Nijmegen: Max Planck Institute for Psycholinguistics.

Chambers, J. K. 1995. *Sociolinguistic Theory*. Oxford: Blackwell.

Chambers, William. 1872 . *Chamber's English Dictionary: Pronouncing, Explanatory, and Etymological*. London: W. & R. Chambers.

Chen, Matthew Y. 1970. "Vowel length variation as a function of the voicing of the consonant environment." *Phonetica* 22: 129–59.

——. 1972. "The time dimension: contribution toward a theory of sound change." *Foundations of Language* 8: 457–98.

——. 2000. *Tone Sandhi: Patterns across Chinese Dialects*. Cambridge: Cambridge University Press.

Chen, Matthew, and William S-Y Wang. 1975. "Sound change: actuation and implementation." *Language* 51: 255–81.

Cheng, Chin-Chuan, and William S-Y Wang. 1977. "Tone change in Chao-Zhou Chinese: a study in lexical diffusion." *The Lexicon in Phonological Change*, edited by William S-Y Wang, pp. 86–100. The Hague: Mouton.

Chomsky, Noam. 1986. *Knowledge of Language*. New York: Praeger.

Chomsky, Noam, and Morris Halle. 1968. *The Sound Pattern of English*. New York: Harper and Row.

Clark, Cecily. 1952. "An edition of annals 1070 to 1154 of the *Peterborough Chronicle* with introduction, grammar, commentary, and glossary." Unpublished B. Litt. thesis, Oxford University.

——, ed. 1970. *The Peterborough Chronicle: 1070–1154*, 2nd edn. Oxford: Clarendon.

Cleary, Miranda, and David B. Pisoni. 2001. "Speech perception and spoken word recognition: research and theory." *Blackwell Handbook of Perception*, edited by E. Bruce Goldstein, pp. 499–534. Oxford: Blackwell.

Coates, Richard. 1997. "The scriptorium of the Mercian Rushworth Gloss: a bilingual perspective." *Notes & Queries* 242 [New Series vol. 44] (no. 2): 453–8.

Cohn, Abby, Johanna Brugman, Clifford Crawford, and Andrew Joseph. 2005. "Phonetic duration of English homophones: an investigation of lexical frequency effects." Paper presented at the 79th LSA (Linguistic Society of America) meeting, Oakland, CA, 7 January 2005.

Cole, P., C. Beauvillain, and J. Segui. 1989. "On the representation and processing of prefixed and suffixed derived words: a differential frequency effect." *Journal of Memory and Language* 28: 1–13.

Coles, E. 1674. *The Compleat English Schoolmaster*. London: Peter Parker.

Cook, Albert S. 1894. *A Glossary of the Old Northumbrian Gospels*. Halle: Max Niemeyer.

Cooley, Marianne. 1978. "Phonological constraints and sound changes." *Glossa* 12: 125–36.

Cooper, C. 1685 [1953]. *Grammatica Linguæ Anglicanæ*. Rpt. in B. Sundby, *Christopher Cooper's English Teacher*. Lund: Gleerup.

——. 1687 [1953]. *The English Teacher*. Rpt. in B. Sundby, *Christopher Cooper's English Teacher*. Lund: Gleerup.

Côté, Marie-Hélène. 1997. "Phonetic salience and consonant cluster simplification." *MIT Working Papers in Linguistics* 30: 229–62.

Cutler, Anne. 1984. "Stress and accent in language production and understanding." *Intonation, Accent and Rhythm*, edited by Dafydd Gibbon and Helmut Richter, pp. 77–90. Berlin: Walter de Gruyter.

Cutler, Anne, and S. Butterfield. 1992. "Rhythmic cues to speech segmentation: evidence from juncture misperception." *Journal of Memory and Language* 31: 218–36.

Daines, S. 1640. *Orthoepia Anglicana*. London: Robert Young and Richard Badger for the Company of Stationers.

Danielsson, Bror. 1948. *Studies on the Accentuation of Polysyllabic Latin, Greek, and Romance Loan-words in English*. Stockholm: Almqvist & Wiksell.

Dell, Gary S. 1985. "Positive feedback in hierarchical connectionist models: applications to language production." *Cognitive Science* 9: 3–23.

——. 1986a. "Effects of frequency and vocabulary type on phonological speech errors." *Language and Cognitive Processes* 5: 313–49.

——. 1986b. "A spreading activation model of retrieval in sentence production." *Psychological Review* 93: 283–321.

——. 1988. "The retrieval of phonological forms in production: tests of predictions from a connectionist model." *Journal of Memory and Language* 27: 124–42.

——. 1990. "Effects of frequency and vocabulary type on phonological speech errors." *Language and Cognitive Processes* 5: 313–49.

Dell, Gary, and P. G. O'Seaghdha. 1991. "Mediated and convergent lexical priming in language production: a comment on Levelt et al. (1991)." *Psychological Review* 98: 604–14.

——. 1992. "Stages of lexical access in language production." *Cognition* 42: 287–314.

Dell, Gary S., and P. A. Reich. 1981. "Stages in sentence production: an analysis of speech error data." *Journal of Verbal Learning and Verbal Behavior* 20: 611–29.

Dell, Gary S., M. F. Schwarts, N. Martin, E. Saffran, and D. A. Gagnon. 1997. "Lexical access in aphasic and nonaphasic speakers." *Psychological Review* 104: 801–38.

226   *References*

D'Introno, Francisco, and Juan Manuel Sosa. 1986. "Elisión de la /d/ en el español de Caracas: aspectos sociolingüísticos e implicaciones teóreticas." *Estudios Sobre la Fonología de Español del Caribe,* edited by Rafael A. Núñez Cedeño, Iraset Páez Urdaneta, and Jorge Guitart, pp. 135–63. Ediciones La Casa de Bello.

Dobson, E. J. 1968. *English Pronunciation 1500–1700.* 2 vols. Oxford: Clarendon.

Dogil, Grzegorz, and Bernd Möbius. 2001. "Towards a model of target oriented production of prosody." *Proceedings of the European Conference on Speech Communication and Technology* (Aalborg, Denmark), vol. 1, 665–8.

Dolby, James, and H. L. Resnikoff. 1964. *English Word Speculum,* 5 vols. The Hague: Mouton.

Donegan, Patricia, and David Stampe. 1979. "The study of natural phonology." *Current Approaches to Phonological Theory,* edited by David Dinnsen, pp. 126–73. Bloomington: Indiana University Press.

Dressler, Wolfgang U. 1984. "Explaining natural phonology." *Phonology Yearbook* 1: 29–50.

Faber, Alice. 1992. "Articulatory variability, categorical perception, and the inevitability of sound change." *Explanation in Historical Linguistics,* edited by Garry W. Davis and Gregory Iverson, pp. 59–75. Amsterdam: John Benjamins.

Fay, William. 1966. *Temporal Sequence in the Perception of Speech.* The Hague: Mouton.

Fenk-Oczlon, Gertraud. 1989a. "Geläufigkeit als Determinante von phonologischen Backgrounding-Prozessen." *Papiere zur Linguistik* 40: 91–103.

——. 1989b. "Word frequency and word order in freezes." *Linguistics* 27: 517–56.

——. 2001. "Familiarity, information flow, and linguistic form." *Frequency and the Emergence of Linguistic Structure,* edited by Joan Bybee and Paul Hopper, pp. 431–48. Amsterdam: John Benjamins.

Ferguson, Charles. 1972. " 'Short *a*' in Philadelphia English." *Studies in Linguistics: In Honor of George L. Trager,* edited by M. Estellie Smith, pp. 259–74. The Hague: Mouton.

Ferguson, Charles, and Carol B. Farwell. 1975. "Words and sounds in early language acquisition: English initial consonants in the first fifty words." *Language* 51: 419–30.

Fidelholz, James. 1975. "Word frequency and vowel reduction in English." *Papers from the Eleventh Regional Meeting of the Chicago Linguistic Society,* edited by Robin E. Grossman, L. James San, and Timothy J. Vance, pp. 200–13. Chicago: Chicago Linguistic Society.

Fintoft, K. 1961. "The duration of some Norwegian speech sounds." *Phonetica* 7: 19–36.

Fischer-Jørgensen, Eli. 1964. "Sound duration and place of articulation." *Zeitschrift für Phonetik, Sprachwissenschaft und Kommunikationsforschung* 17: 175–207.

Fodor, J. A. 1983. *The Modularity of Mind.* Cambridge, MA: MIT Press.

Fowler, Carol A., and Jonathan Housum. 1987. "Talkers' signaling of 'new' and 'old' words in speech and listeners' perception and use of the distinction." *Journal of Memory and Language* 26: 489–504.

Francis, W. Nelson, and Henry Kučera. 1982. *Frequency Analysis of English Usage.* Boston: Houghton Mifflin.

Frisch, Stefan. 2004. "Language processing and segmental OCP effects." *Phonetically-Based Phonology,* edited by Bruce Hayes, Robert Kirchner, and Donka Steriade, pp. 346–71. Cambridge: Cambridge University Press.

Fudge, E. C. 1969. "Syllables." *Journal of Linguistics* 5: 253–86.
——. 1987. "Branching structure within the syllable." *Journal of Linguistics* 23: 359–77.
Gąsiorowski, Piotr. 1997. "Words in *-ate* and the history of English stress." *Studies in Middle English Linguistics*, edited by Jacek Fisiak, pp. 157–80. Berlin: Mouton de Gruyter.
Gattel, Claude-Marie. 1819 [1797]. *Dictionnaire universel de la langue française.* Paris: Les Belles Lettres.
Gerhand, Simon, and Christopher Berry. 1998. "Word frequency effects in oral reading are not merely age-of-acquisition effects in disguise." *Journal of Experimental Psychology: Learning, Memory, and Cognition* 24 (2): 267–83.
——. 1999. "Age of acquisition, word frequency, and the role of phonology in the lexical decision task." *Memory and Cognition* 27: 592–602.
Gerritsen, Marinel, and Frank Jansen. 1980. "Word frequency and lexical diffusion in dialect borrowing and phonological change." *Dutch Studies* 4: 31–54.
Gess, Randall. 2003. "Constraint re-ranking and explanatory adequacy in a constraint-based theory of phonological change." *Optimality Theory and Language Change* (Studies in Natural Language and Linguistic Theory), edited by D. Eric Holt, pp. 67–90. Dordrecht: Kluwer Academic Publishers.
Giegerich, Heinz J. 1999. *Lexical Strata in English: Morphological Causes, Phonological Effects* (Cambridge Studies in Linguistics 89). Cambridge: Cambridge University Press.
Gierut, Judith. 2001 "A model of lexical diffusion in phonological acquisition." *Clinical Linguistics and Phonetics* 12: 481–99.
Gierut, Judith, and Michele L. Morrisette. 1998. "Lexical properties in implementation of sound change." *Proceedings of the 22nd Annual Boston University Conference on Language Development*, edited by A. Greenhill, M. Hughes, H. Littlefield, and H. Walsh, pp. 257–68. Somerville, MA: Cascadilla Press.
Gierut, Judith, and Holly L. Storkel. 2002. "Markedness and the grammar in lexical diffusion of fricatives." *Clinical Linguistics and Phonetics* 16 (2): 115–34.
Gilbert, John H., and Virginia J. Wyman. 1975. "Discrimination learning of nasalized and non-nasalized vowels by five-, six- and seven-year-old children." *Phonetica* 31: 65–80.
Gilhooly, K. J., and R. H. Logie. 1980. "Age of acquisition, imagery, concreteness, familiarity, and ambiguity measures for 1,944 words." *Behavior Research, Methods, and Instrumentation* 12: 395–427.
Gilliéron, Jules. 1902–10. *Atlas linguistique de la France.* 13 vols. Paris: Champion.
——. 1918. *Pathologie et thérapeutique verbale.* Paris: Champion.
Gimson, A. C., ed. 1988 [1991]. *English Pronouncing Dictionary*, 14th edn. Reprint of 1977 edition with Revisions and Supplement by Susan Ramsaran. Cambridge: Cambridge UP, 1991.
Godfrey, J., J. McDaniel, and J. Holliman. 1992. *SWITCHBOARD: a Telephone Speech Corpus for Research and Development.* San Francisco: ICASSP Proc.
Goeman, A. C. M., and P. Th. van Reenen. 1985. "Word-final t-deletion in Dutch dialects." *VU-Working Papers in Linguistics* 16: 157–208.
Goeman, A. C. M., P. Th. van Reenan, and E. Wattel. 1993. "The diphthongization of West Germanic î and its relation to West Germanic û in Modern Dutch dialects: a quantitative approach." *Verhandlungen des Internationalen Dialektologenkongresses: Bamberg, 29.7–4.8.1990*, edited by W. Viereck, pp. 76–97. Stuttgart: Franz Steiner.

228 References

Goldinger, Stephen D. 1992. "Words and voices: implicit and explicit memory for spoken words." *Research on Speech Perception Technical Report No. 7.* Bloomington, IN: Indiana University.

Goldsmith, John A. 1990. *Autosegmental and Metrical Phonology.* Oxford: Blackwell.

——. 1995. "Phonological theory." *The Handbook of Phonological Theory,* edited by J. A. Goldsmith, pp. 1–23. Oxford: Blackwell.

Gordon, Barry, and Alfonso Caramazza. 1985. "Lexical access and frequency sensitivity: frequency saturation and open/closed class equivalence." *Cognition* 21: 95–115.

Görlach, Manfred. 1991. *Introduction to Early Modern English.* Cambridge: Cambridge University Press.

Gove, Philip, ed. 1961. *Webster's Third New International Dictionary of the English Language.* Springfield, MA: G. & C. Merriam.

——, ed. 1963. *Webster's Seventh Collegiate Dictionary.* Springfield, MA: G. & C. Merriam.

Guion, Susan. 1995. "Word frequency effects among homonyms." *Texas Linguistic Forum* 35: 103–16.

Guy, Gregory. 1997. "Violable is variable: optimality theory and linguistic variation." *Language Variation and Change* 9: 333–48.

Hale, Mark. 2003. "Neogrammarian sound change." *The Handbook of Historical Linguistics,* edited by Brian Joseph and Richard Janda, pp. 343–68. Oxford: Blackwell.

Hammond, Michael. 1998. "Is phonology irrelevant? How and why frequency can be modelled in phonology." *Literary and Linguistic Computing* 13: 165–75.

——. 1999a. "Lexical frequency and rhythm." *Functionalism and Formalism in Linguistics,* edited by M. Darnell et al., pp. 329–58. Amsterdam: John Benjamins.

——. 1999b. *The Phonology of English: a Prosodic Optimality-Theoretic Approach.* Oxford: Oxford University Press.

Hansen, Anita Berit. 2001. "Lexical diffusion as a factor of phonetic change: the case of Modern French nasal vowels." *Language Variation and Change* 13: 209–52.

Harley, T. 1984. "A critique of top-down independent level models of speech production: evidence from non-plan-internal speech errors." *Cognitive Science* 8: 191–219.

Harris, John. 1985. *Phonological Variation and Change: Studies in Hiberno-English.* Cambridge: Cambridge University Press.

——. 1989. "Towards a lexical analysis of sound change in progress." *Journal of Linguistics* 25: 35–56.

Henaff Gonon, M, R. Bruckert, and F. Micel. 1989. "Lexicalization in an anomic patient." *Neuropsychologia* 27: 391–407.

Hickey, Raymond. 1998. "The *Dublin Vowel Shift* and the historical perspective." *Advances in English Historical Linguistics (1996),* edited by Jacek Fisiak and Marcin Krygier, pp. 79–105. Berlin: Mouton de Gruyter.

——.1999. "Dublin English: current changes and their motivation." *Urban Voices: Accent Studies in the British Isles,* edited by Paul Foulkes and Gerard Docherty, pp. 265–81. London: Arnold.

Hindle, Donald. 1978. "Approaches to vowel normalization in the study of natural speech." *Linguistic Variation: Models and Methods,* edited by David Sankoff, pp. 161–72. New York: Academic Press.

References 229

Hinskens, Frans. 1998. "Variation studies in dialectology and three types of sound change." *Sociolinguistica* 12: 155–93.

Hock, Hans Henrich. 1985. "Regular metathesis." *Linguistics* 23: 529–46.

Hock, Hans Henrich, and Brian D. Joseph. 1996. *Language History, Language Change, and Language Relationship: an Introduction to Historical and Comparative Linguistics.* Berlin: Mouton de Gruyter.

Hogaboam, Thomas W., and Charles A. Perfetti. 1975. "Lexical ambiguity and sentence comprehension." *Journal of Verbal Learning and Verbal Behavior* 14: 265–74.

Hogg, Richard. 1982. "Was there ever an /ɔ/ phoneme in Old English?" *Neuphilologische Mitteilungen* 83: 225–9.

——. 1992a. *A Grammar of Old English.* Vol. 1: *Phonology.* Oxford: Blackwell.

——. 1992b. "Phonology and morphology." *The Cambridge History of the English Language.* Vol. 1: *The Beginnings to 1066*, edited by R. Hogg, pp. 67–167. Cambridge: Cambridge University Press.

——. 1998. "On the ideological boundaries of Old English dialects." *Advances in English Historical Linguistics*, edited by Jacek Fisiak and M. Krygier, pp. 107–18. Berlin: Mouton de Gruyter.

Hogg, Richard, and C. B. McCully. 1987. *Metrical Phonology: a Coursebook.* Cambridge: Cambridge University Press.

Holder, Maurice. 1990. "Lexical diffusion and word frequency in phonological borrowing: *o/ou* and *ais/ois* in the history of French." *Papers from the Fourteenth Annual Meeting of the Atlantic Provinces Linguistic Association*, edited by Jim Black, pp. 69–82. Canada: Atlantic Provinces Linguistic Association.

Holes, C. 1983. "Patterns of communal language variation in Bahrain." *Language in Society* 12: 433–57.

Holm, Sigurd. 1922. *Corrections and Additions in the Ormulum Manuscript.* Uppsala: Almqvist & Wiksell.

Holt, D. Eric, ed. 2003a. *Optimality Theory and Language Change.* Dordrecht: Kluwer Academic Publishers.

——. 2003b. "Remarks on Optimality Theory and language change." *Optimality Theory and Language Change*, edited by D. Eric Holt, pp. 1–30. Dordrecht: Kluwer.

Hooper, Joan. 1976. "Word frequency in lexical diffusion and the source of morphophonological change." *Current Progress in Historical Linguistics: Proceedings of the Second International Conference on Historical Linguistics, Tucson, Arizona, 12–15 January 1976*, edited by W. M. Christie, pp. 95–106. Amsterdam: North-Holland.

——. 1981. "The empirical determination of phonological representation." *The Cognitive Representation of Speech*, edited by Terry Myers, John Laver, and John Anderson, pp. 347–57. Amsterdam: North-Holland.

Hopper, Paul J., and Elizabeth Closs Traugott. 1993. *Grammaticalization.* Cambridge: Cambridge University Press.

Hotopf, W. H. N. 1980. "Semantic similarity as a factor in whole-word slips of the tongue." *Errors in Linguistic Performance: Slips of the Tongue, Ear, Pen, and Hand*, edited by Victoria A. Fromkin, pp. 97–109. New York: Academic Press.

Hume, Elizabeth. 2004. "The indeterminacy/attestation model of metathesis." *Language* 80: 203–37.

Jaeger, Jeri J. 1997. "How to say 'Grandma': the problem of developing phonological representations." *First Language* 17: 1–29.

230 References

Janda, Richard D. 2003. "'Phonologization' as the start of dephoneticization – or, on sound charge and its aftermath: of extension, generalization, lexicalization, and morphologization." *A Handbook of Historical Linguistics*, edited by Brian D. Joseph and Richard Janda, pp. 401–22. Oxford: Blackwell.

Janda, Richard D., and Brian D. Joseph. 2003a. "On language, change, and language change – or, of history, linguistics, and historical linguistics." *A Handbook of Historical Linguistics*, edited by Brian D. Joseph and Richard Janda, pp. 3–180. Oxford: Blackwell.

——. 2003b. "Reconsidering the canons of sound change: towards a Big Bang theory." *Historical Linguistics 2001: Selected Papers from the International Conference on Historical Linguistics*, Melbourne, 13–17 August 2001, edited by Barry Blake and Kate Burridge, pp. 205–19. Amsterdam: John Benjamins.

Janson, Tore. 1977. "Reversed lexical diffusion and lexical split: loss of -d in Stockholm." *The Lexicon in Phonological Change*, edited by William S-Y Wang, pp. 252–65. The Hague: Mouton.

——. 1983. "Sound change in perception and production." *Language* 59: 18–34.

Jescheniak, Jörg D., and Willem J. M. Levelt. 1994. "Word frequency effects in speech production: retrieval of syntactic information and phonological form." *Journal of Experimental Psychology: Learning, Memory, and Cognition* 20 (4): 824–43.

Jescheniak, Jörg D., Willem J. Levelt, and A. S. Meyer. 2003. "Specific word frequency is not all that counts in speech production. Reply to Caramazza et al." *Journal of Experimental Psychology: Learning, Memory, and Cognition* 29: 432–8.

Jespersen, Otto. 1909–49. *A Modern English Grammar on Historical Principles*. Heidelberg: Carl Winter; Copenhagen: Munksgaard.

Johannesson, Nils-Lennart. 1997. "Overwriting, deletion and erasure: exploring the changes in the *Ormulum* manuscript." *Jestin' (Journal of English Studies in Norway)* 2: 21–9.

Johanson, Lars. 2002. "Contact-induced change in a code-copying framework." *Language Change: the Interplay of Internal, External and Extra-Linguistic Factors*, edited by Mari C. Jones and Edith Esch, pp. 285–313. Berlin: Mouton.

Johnson, Keith. 1997. "Speech perception without speaker normalization: an exemplar model." *Talker Variability in Speech Processing*, edited by Keith Johnson and John W. Mullennix, pp. 145–65. San Diego, CA: Academic Press.

Johnson, Samuel. 1755. *A Dictionary of the English Language*. London: W. Strahan.

——. 1824. *A Dictionary of the English Language: In Which the Words are Deduced from their Originals, Explained in their Different Meanings, and Authorized by the Names of the Writers in Whose Works They are Found*. Abridged from the Rev. H. J. Todd's Corrected and Enlarged Quarto Edition, by Alexander Chalmers. London: C.& J. Rivington; J. Scatcherd; J. Cuthell [and others].

Jones, Charles. 1989. *A History of English Phonology*. London: Longman.

Jones, Daniel. 1917. *English Pronouncing Dictionary*. London: J. M. Dent.

——. 1937. *English Pronouncing Dictionary*, 4th edn. New York: E. P. Dutton.

——. 1977. *Everyman's English Pronouncing Dictionary*. Revised and edited by A. C. Gimson. 14th edn. London: Dent.

Jong, E. D. de. 1979. *Spreektaal, Woordfrequenties in gesproken Nederlands*. Utrecht: Bohn, Scheltema & Holkema.

Josselson, H. 1953. *The Russian Word Count*. Detroit: Wayne University Press.

References 231

Jurafsky, Dan. 2003. "Probabilistic modeling in psycholinguistics: linguistic comprehension and production." *Probabilistic Linguistics*, edited by Rens Bod, Jennifer Hay, and Stefanie Jannedy, pp. 39–95. Cambridge, MA: MIT Press.

Jurafsky, Daniel, Alan Bell, and Cynthia Girand. 2002. "The role of the lemma in form variation." *Laboratory Phonology 7*, edited by Carlos Gussenhoven and Natasha Warner, pp. 3–34. Berlin: Mouton de Gruyter.

Jurafsky, Daniel, Alan Bell, Michelle Gregory, and William D. Raymond. 2001. "Probabilistic relations between words: evidence from reduction in lexical production." *Frequency and the Emergence of Linguistic Structure*, edited by Joan Bybee and Paul Hopper, pp. 229–54. Amsterdam: John Benjamins.

Jusczyk, P. W., P. Luce, and J. Charles-Luce. 1994. "Infants' sensitivity to phonotactic patterns in the native language." *Journal of Memory and Language* 33: 630–45.

Just, M. A., and P. A. Carpenter. 1980. "A theory of reading: from eye fixations to comprehension." *Psychological Review* 87: 329–54.

Karlgren, Bernhard. 1954. "Compendium of phonetics in ancient and archaic Chinese." *BMFEA (Bulletin of the Museum of Far Eastern Antiquities, Stockholm)* 26: 211–367.

Katamba, Francis. 1993. *Morphology*. New York: St. Martin's.

Keller, Frank, and Ash Asudeh. 2002. "Probabilistic learning algorithms and optimality theory." *Linguistic Inquiry* 33: 225–44.

Kelly, Michael H., and J. Kathryn Bock. 1988. "Stress in time." *Journal of Experimental Psychology: Human Perception and Performance* 14: 289–403.

Kenrick, William. 1773. *A New Dictionary of the English Language*. London: John and Francis Rivington, William Johnston et al.

Kenyon, John, and Thomas Knott. 1953. *A Pronouncing Dictionary of American English*. Springfield: Merriam.

Kerswill, Paul. 1983. "Social and linguistic aspects of Durham (e:)." *Cambridge Papers in Phonetics and Experimental Linguistics* 2: 3–22.

Kerswill, Paul, and Ann Williams. 2002. " 'Salience' as an explanatory factor in language change: evidence from dialect leveling in urban England." *Language Change: the Interplay of Internal, External and Extra-Linguistic Factors*, edited by Mari C. Jones and Edith Esch, pp. 81–110. Berlin: Mouton de Gruyter.

Kim, Suksan. 1973. "A collation of the Old English MS Hatton 20 of King Alfred's *Pastoral Care*." *Neuphilologische Mitteilungen* 74: 425–42.

King, J. W., and Marta Kutas. 1995. "A brain potential whose latency indexes the length and frequency of words." *Newsletter of the Center for Research in Language* 10 (2): 3–9.

———. 1998. "Neural plasticity in the dynamics of human visual word recognition." *Neuroscience Letters* 244: 61–4.

Kiparsky, Paul. 1968. "Linguistic universals and linguistic change." *Universals in Linguistic Theory*, edited by Emmon Bach and Robert T. Harms, pp. 170–202. New York: Holt, Rinehart and Winston.

———. 1982. "From cyclic phonology to lexical phonology." *The Structure of Phonological Representations*, Vol. 1, edited by H. van der Hulst and N. Smith, pp. 131–75. Dordrecht: Foris.

———. 1995. "The phonological basis of sound change." *The Handbook of Phonological Theory*, edited by John Goldsmith, pp. 640–70. Oxford: Blackwell.

———. 2000. "Opacity and cyclicity." *The Linguistic Review* 17: 351–65.

232 *References*

Kirchner, Robert. 1999. "Preliminary thoughts on 'phonologization' within an exemplar-based speech processing system." *UCLA Working Papers in Linguistics*, no. 1. (Papers in Phonology 2), edited by Matthew K. Gordon, pp. 207–31. Los Angeles: UCLA Linguistics Dept.

Kloeke, G. G. 1927. *De Hollandsche expansie*. The Hague: Martinus Nijhoff.

Kniezsa, Veronika. 1988. "Accents and digraphs in the Peterborough Chronicle." *Studia Anglica Posnaniensia* 21: 15–23.

Kretzschmar, William. 1996. "A glass half empty, a glass half full." *American Speech* 71: 198–205.

Kreuz, Roger J. 1987. "The subjective familiarity of English homophones." *Memory and Cognition* 15: 154–68.

Krishnamurti, Bh. 1998. "Regularity of sound change through lexical diffusion: a study of *s* > *h* > Ø in Gondi dialects." *Language Variation and Change* 10: 193–220.

Kučera, H., and W. Francis. 1967. *Computational Analysis of Present-day American-English*. Providence, RI: Brown University Press.

Kurath, Hans, and Sherman M. Kuhn, eds. 1956–. *Middle English Dictionary*. Ann Arbor: University of Michigan Press.

Kurath, Hans, and Raven I. McDavid, Jr. 1961. *The Pronunciation of English in the Atlantic States*. Ann Arbor: University of Michigan Press.

Kutas, Marta, and Bernadette M. Schmitt. 2003. "Language in microvolts." *Mind, Brain, and Language: Multidisciplinary Perspectives*, edited by Marie Banich and Molly Mack, pp. 171–209. Mahwah, NJ: Lawrence Erlbaum Associates.

Labov, William. 1969. "Contraction, deletion, and inherent variability of the English copula." *Language* 45: 715–62.

——. 1972. "The internal evolution of linguistic rules." *Linguistic Change and Generative Theory*, edited by Robert P. Stockwell and R. K. S. Macaulay, pp. 101–71. Bloomington: Indiana University Press.

——. 1975. "The quantitative study of linguistic structure." *Pennsylvania Working Papers on Linguistic Change and Variation, I* (3).

——. 1980. "The social origins of sound change." *Locating Language in Time and Space*, edited by William Labov, pp. 251–65. New York: Academic Press.

——. 1981. "Resolving the neogrammarian controversy." *Language* 57: 267–308.

——. 1991. "The three dialects of English." *New Ways of Analyzing Sound Change*, edited by Penelope Eckert, pp. 1–44. New York: Academic Press.

——. 1992. "Evidence for regular sound change in English dialect geography." *History of Englishes: New Methods and Interpretations in Historical Linguistics*, edited by Matti Rissanen et al., pp. 42–71. Berlin: Mouton de Gruyter.

——. 1994. *Principles of Linguistic Change*. Vol. 1: *Internal Factors*. Oxford: Blackwell.

Labov, William, Sharon Ash, and Charles Boberg, eds. 2005. *Atlas of North American English: Phonetics, Phonology and Sound Change*. Berlin: de Gruyter.

Labov, William, Mark Karen, and Coery Miller. 1991. "Near-mergers and the suspension of phonemic contrast." *Language Variation and Change* 3: 33–74.

Labov, William, Malcah Yaeger, and Richard Steiner. 1972. *A Quantitative Study of Sound Change in Progress*, Vol. 1. Philadelphia: US Regional Survey.

Lachs, Lorin, Kipp McMichael, and David B. Pisoni. 2003. "Speech perception and implicit memory: evidence for detailed episodic encoding." *Rethinking Implicit Memory*, edited by J. Bowers and C. Marsolek, pp. 215–35. Oxford: Oxford University Press.

References 233

Ladefoged, Peter, and Ian Maddieson. 1996. *The Sounds of the World's Languages*. Oxford: Blackwell.

Laferriere, Martha. 1977. "Boston short *a*: social variation as historical residue." *Studies in Language Variation*, edited by Ralph Fasold and Roger Shuy, pp. 100–7. Washington, DC: Georgetown UP.

Landau, Sidney. 1984 [1989]. *Dictionaries: the Art and Craft of Lexicography*. Cambridge University Press.

Lass, Roger. 1984. *Phonology*. Cambridge: Cambridge University Press.

——. 1992a. "Front rounded vowels in Old English." *Evidence for Old English*, edited by Fran Colman, pp. 88–116. Edinburgh: John Donald.

——. 1992b. "Phonology and morphology." *Cambridge History of the English Language*. Vol. 2: *1066–1476*, edited by Norman Blake, pp. 23–155. Cambridge: Cambridge University Press.

——. 1997. *Historical Linguistics and Language Change*. Cambridge University Press.

——. 1999. "Phonology and morphology." *The Cambridge History of the English Language*. Vol. 3: *1476–1776*, edited by Roger Lass, pp. 56–186. Cambridge: Cambridge University Press.

Lass, Roger, and Margaret Laing. 2005. "Are front rounded vowels retained in West Midland Middle English?" *Rethinking Middle English*, edited by Nikolaus Ritt and Herbert Schendl, pp. 280–90. Berlin: Peter Lang.

Laubstein, Ann Stuart. 1999. "Lemmas and lexemes: the evidence from blends." *Brain and Language* 68: 135–43.

Laver, John. 1994. *Principles of Phonetics*. Cambridge: Cambridge University Press.

Lavoie, Lisa. 2002. "Some influences on the realization of *for* and *four* in American English." *JIPA* (Journal of the International Phonetic Association) 32: 175–202.

Lehiste, Ilse. 1970. *Suprasegmentals*. Cambridge MA: MIT Press.

Lehmann, Winfred P., ed. and trans. 1967. *A Reader in Nineteenth-Century Historical Indo-European Linguistics*. Bloomington: Indiana University Press.

Leskien, August. 1876. *Die Declination im Slavisch-Litauischen und Germanischen*. Leipzig: S. Hirzel.

Leslau, Wolf. 1969. "Frequency as determinant of linguistic change in the Ethiopian languages." *Word* 25: 180–9.

Levelt, Willem J. M. 1999. "Producing spoken language: a blueprint of the speaker." *The Neurocognition of Language*, edited by P. Hagoort and C. M. Brown, pp. 94–122. Oxford: Oxford University Press.

——. 2001. "Spoken word production: a theory of lexical access." *Proceedings of the National Academy of Sciences* 98 (23): 13464–71.

——. 2002. "Phonological encoding in speech production: comments on Jurafsky et al., Schiller et al., and van Heuven & Haan." *Laboratory Phonology 7*, edited by Carlos Gussenhoven and Natasha Warner, pp. 87–99. Berlin: Mouton de Gruyter.

Levelt, Willem J. M., A. Roelofs, and A. S. Meyer. 1999. "A theory of lexical access in speech production." *Behavioral and Brain Sciences* 22: 1–75.

Levelt, Willem J. M., H. Schriefers, D. Vorgerg et al. 1991. "The time course of lexical access in speech production: a study of picture naming." *Psychological Review* 98: 122–42.

Levins, Peter. 1570 [1867]. *Manipulus Vocabulorum: a Dictionarie of English and Latine Words* (London). Reprint (= EETSOS 27) edited by H. B. Wheatley. London: Oxford.

234 References

Li, Ping, and Michael C. Yip. 1996. "Lexical ambiguity and context effects in spoken word recognition: evidence from Chinese." *Proceedings of the 18th Conference of the Cognitive Science Society*, edited by G. Cottrell, pp. 228–32. Hillsdale, NJ : Lawrence Erlbaum.

Lieberman, Philip. 1963. "Some effects of semantic and grammatical context on the production and perception of speech." *Language and Speech* 6: 172–87.

Lindau, Mona. 1978. "Vowel features." *Language* 54: 541–63.

Lindblom, Björn. 1990. "Explaining phonetic variation: a sketch of the H and H theory." *Speech Production and Speech Modeling*, edited by W. Hardcastle and A. Marchal, pp. 403–39. Dordrecht: Kluwer.

Lippi-Green, Rosina. 1989. "Social network integration and language change in progress in a rural alpine village." *Language in Society* 18: 213–34.

Lively, S. E., D. B. Pisoni, R. A. Yamada, Y. Tohkura, and T. Yamada. 1992. "Training Japanese listeners to identify English [r] and [l]: III. Long-term retention of the new phonetic categories." *Research on Speech Perception Progress Report No. 18*, pp. 185–216. Bloomington, IN: Indiana University.

Lociewicz, B. L. 1992. "The effect of frequency on linguistic morphology." PhD Dissertation, University of Texas, Austin.

Luick, Karl. 1914–21 [1964]. *Historische Grammatik der englischen Sprache*, Vol. 1, part 1. Oxford: Blackwell.

Lutz, Angelika. 1988. "On the historical phonotactics of English." *Luick Revisited*, edited by Dieter Kastovsky and Gero Bauer, pp. 221–41. Tübingen: Gunter Narr Verlag.

——. 1991. *Phonotaktisch gesteuerte Konsonantenveränderungen in der Geschichte des Englischen*. Tübingen: Max Niemeyer.

——. 1993. "Lautwandel und Paläographische Evidenz: die Wiedergabe von /h/ (<Germ. /x/) in der Lindisfarne-Glosse." *Anglia* 111, 3 (4): 285–309.

MacDonald, M. C., N. J. Perlmutter, and M. S. Seidenberg. 1994. "The lexical nature of syntactic ambiguity resolution." *Psychological Review* 101: 676–793.

MacMahon, Michael K. C. 1998. "Phonology." *The Cambridge History of the English Language*, Vol. IV: *1776–1997*, edited by Suzanne Romaine, pp. 373–535. Cambridge: Cambridge University Press.

MacWhinney, Brian. 1995. *The CHILDES Project: Tools for Analyzing Talk*. Hillsdale, NJ: Lawrence Erlbaum.

Malkiel, Yakov. 1967. "Every word has its own history." *Glossa* 1: 137–49.

Mańczak, Witold. 2000. Review of Damaris Nübling, *Prinzipien der Irregularisierung. Eine kontrastive Analyse von zehn Verben in zehn germanischen Sprachen* (Linguistische Arbeiten 415), Tübingen: Niemeyer, 2000. *Folia Linguistica Historica* 21: 265–71.

——. 2004. Review of Joan Bybee and Paul Hopper (eds), *Frequency and the Emergence of Linguistic Structure* (Typological Studies in Language 45), Amsterdam: John Benjamins, 2001. *Folia Linguistica Historica* 25: 299–302.

Marchand, Hans. 1969. *The Categories and Types of Present-Day English Word Formation. A Synchronic–Diachronic Approach*, 2nd edn. Munich: Beck.

Martin, N., R. W. Weisberg, and E. M. Saffran. 1989. "Variables influencing the occurrence of naming errors: implications for a model of lexical retrieval." *Journal of Memory and Language* 28: 462–85.

Martinet, André. 1955. *Économie des Changements Phonétiques: Traité de Phonologie Diachronique*. Berne: A. Francke.

References 235

Melinger, Alissa. 2003. "Morphological structure in the lexical representation of prefixed words: evidence from speech errors." *Language and Cognitive Processes* 2003: 335–62.

Menn, Lise, and Brian MacWhinney. 1984. "The repeated morph constraint: toward an explanation." *Language* 60: 519–41.

Merlo, Pietro. 1885. "Cenni sullo stato presente della grammatica ariana istorica e preistorica a proposito d'un libro di G. Curtius." *Rivista de filologie e d'istruzione classica* 14: 145–78.

Meunier, Fanny, and Juan Segui. 1999. "Morphological priming effect: the role of surface frequency." *Brain and Language* 68: 54–60.

Meyer, E. 1903. *Englische Lautdauer*. Uppsala: Akademiska bokhandeln.

Milroy, James. 1980. "Lexical alternation and the history of English: evidence from an urban vernacular." *Papers from the Fourth International Conference on Historical Linguistics, Stanford, March 26–30, 1980*, edited by Elizabeth C. Traugott, R. La Brum, and S. Shepherd, pp. 355–62. Amsterdam: John Benjamins.

———. 1992a. *Linguistic Variation and Change: On the Historical Sociolinguistics of English*. Oxford: Blackwell.

———. 1992b. "Middle English dialectology." *Cambridge History of the English Language*, Vol. 2: *1066–1476*, edited by Norman Blake, pp. 156–206. Cambridge: Cambridge University Press.

———. 1992c. "A social model for the interpretation of language change." *History of Englishes: New Methods and Interpretations in Historical Linguistics*, edited by Matti Rissanen et al., pp. 72–91. Berlin: Mouton de Gruyter.

———. 1993. "On the social origins of language change." *Historical Linguistics: Problems and Perspectives*, edited by Charles Jones, pp. 215–36. London: Longman.

———. 1999. "Toward a speaker-based account of language change." *Language Change: Advances in Historical Sociolinguistics*, edited by E. Jahr, pp. 21–36. Berlin: Mouton.

———. 2003a. "On the role of the speaker in language change." *Motives for Language Change*, edited by Raymond Hickey, pp. 143–57. Cambridge: Cambridge University Press.

———. 2003b. "When is a sound change?" *Social Dialectology: In Honour of Peter Trudgill*, edited by David Britain and Jenny Cheshire, pp. 209–21. Amsterdam: John Benjamins.

Milroy, James, and Lesley Milroy. 1985. "Linguistic change, social network, and speaker innovation." *Journal of Linguistics* 21: 339–84.

Milroy, Lesley. 2003. "Social and linguistic dimensions of phonological change: fitting the pieces of the puzzle together." *Social Dialectology: In Honour of Peter Trudgill*, edited by David Britain and Jenny Cheshire, pp. 155–71. Amsterdam: John Benjamins.

Minkova, Donka. 1997. "Constraint ranking in Middle English stress-shifting." *English Language and Linguistics* 1: 135–75.

———. 2003. *Alliteration and Sound Change in Early English*. Cambridge: Cambridge University Press.

Minkova, Donka, and Robert P. Stockwell. 1992. "Homorganic clusters as moric busters in the history of English: the case of *-ld, -nd, -mb*." *History of Englishes: New Methods and Interpretations in Historical Linguistics*, edited by Matti Rissanen et al., pp. 191–206. Berlin: Mouton de Gruyter.

236 *References*

——. 2003. "English vowel shifts and 'optimal' diphthongs: is there a logical link?" *Optimality Theory and Language Change*, edited by D. Eric Holt, pp. 169–90. Dordrecht: Kluwer Academic Publishers.

——. 2005. "Clash avoidance in morphologically derived words in ME: why [hʊd] but [dm]." *Rethinking Middle English*, edited by Nikolaus Ritt and Herbert Schendl, pp. 263–79. Berlin: Peter Lang.

Miozzo, M., and A. Caramazza. 1997. "Retrieval of lexical syntactic features in tip-of-the-tongue states." *Journal of Experimental Psychology: Learning, Memory, and Cognition* 23: 1410–23.

Miozzo, Michele, Melissa L. Jacobs, and Nicholas J. W. Singer. 2004. "The representation of homophones: evidence from anomia." *Cognitive Neuropsychology* 21 (8): 840–66.

Mish, Frederick, ed. 1993. *Merriam-Webster's Collegiate Dictionary*, 10th edn. Springfield, MA: Merriam Webster.

——, ed. 2004. *Merriam-Webster's Collegiate Dictionary*, 11th edn. Springfield, MA: Merriam Webster.

Mitchell, John Lawrence. 1974. "The language of the Peterborough Chronicle." *Computers in the Humanities*, edited by J. L. Mitchell, pp. 132–45. Minneapolis: University of Minnesota Press.

Moder, Carol. 1992. "Productivity and categorization in morphological classes." PhD Dissertation, State University of New York at Buffalo.

Morin, Yves-Charles, Marie-Claude Langlois, and Marie-Éve Varin. 1990. "Tensing of word-final [ɔ] and [o] in French: the phonologization of a morphophonological rule." *Romance Philology* 43: 507–28.

Morrisette, Michele. 1999. "Lexical characteristics of sound change." *Clinical Linguistics and Phonetics* 13 (3): 219–38.

Morton, J. 1969. "Interaction of information in word recognition." *Psychological Review* 76: 165–78.

Mossé, Fernand. 1952. *A Handbook of Middle English*. Translated by James A. Walker. Baltimore: Johns Hopkins.

Munson, Benjamin, and Nancy Pearl Solomon. 2004. "The effect of phonological neighborhood density on vowel articulation." *Journal of Speech, Language, and Hearing Research* 47 (5): 1048–58.

Murray, James et al., eds. 1888–1928. *A New English Dictionary on Historical Principles*. Oxford: The Clarendon Press.

Murray, Robert. 2000. "Syllable-cut prosody in Early Middle English." *Language* 76: 617–54.

Murray, Robert, and Theo Vennemann. 1983. "Sound change and syllable structure in Germanic phonology." *Language* 59: 514–28.

Myers, James T. 2003. "Frequency effects in Optimality Theory." MS.

Nahkola, Kari, and Marja Saanilahti. 2004. "Mapping language changes in real time: a panel study on Finnish." *Language Variation and Change* 16: 75–91.

Neu, Helene. 1980. "Ranking of constraints on /t,d/ deletion in American English: a statistical analysis." *Locating Language in Time and Space*, edited by William Labov, pp. 37–54. New York: Academic Press.

Niedzielski, Nancy, and Dennis Preston. 2000. *Folk Linguistics*. Berlin: Mouton de Gruyter.

Nielsen, Hans F. 1992. "Variability in Old English and the Continental Germanic languages." *History of Englishes: New Methods and Interpretations in Historical*

References 237

Linguistics, edited by Matti Rissanen et al., pp. 640–6. Berlin: Mouton de Gruyter.

Nygaard, L. C., and D. B. Pisoni. 1998. "Talker-specific learning in speech perception." *Perception and Psychophysics* 60 (3): 355–76.

Ogura, Mieko. 1987. *Historical English Phonology: a Lexical Perspective.* Tokyo: Kenkyusha.

——. 1995. "The development of Middle English ī and ū : a reply to Labov (1992, 1994)." *Diachronica* 12: 31–53.

Ogura, Mieko, and William S-Y. Wang. 1998. "Evolution theory and lexical diffusion." *Advances in English Historical Linguistics*, edited by Jacek Fisiak and M. Krygier, pp. 315–44. Berlin: Mouton de Gruyter.

Ohala, John. 1974. "Phonetic explanation in phonology." *Papers from the Parasession on Natural Phonology*, edited by Anthony Bruck, R. A. Fox, and M. W. LaGaly, pp. 251–75. Chicago: Chicago Linguistic Society.

Oldfield, R. C., and A. Wingfield. 1965. "Response latencies in naming objects." *Quarterly Journal of Experimental Psychology* 17: 273–81.

Oliveira, Marco Antonio de. 1991. "The neogrammarian controversy revisited." *International Journal of the Sociology of Language* 89: 93–105.

Onions, C. T., ed. 1944. *The Oxford Universal Dictionary on Historical Principles*, 3rd edn. London: Oxford.

Orton, Harold et al. 1962–69. *Survey of English Dialects.* 4 vols. Leeds: E. J. Arnold.

Osthoff, Hermann, and Karl Brugmann. 1878. *Morphologische Untersuchungen auf dem Gebiete der indogermanischen Sprachen I.* Leipzig: S. Hirzel.

Pandey, Pramod Kumar. 1997. "Optionality, lexicality and sound change." *Journal of Linguistics* 33: 91–130.

Parkes, Malcolm B. 1983. "On the presumed date and possible origin of the manuscript of the *Ormulum*: Oxford, Bodleian Library, MS Junius 1." *Five Hundred Years of Words and Sounds: a Festschrift for Eric Dobson*, edited by E. G. Stanley and Douglas Gray, pp. 114–27. Cambridge: D. S. Brewer.

Pater, Joe. 2000. "Non-uniformity in English secondary stress: the role of ranked and lexically specific constraints." *Phonology* 17: 237–74.

Patterson, David, and Cynthia M. Connine. 2001. "Variant frequency in flap production." *Phonetica* 58: 254–75.

Patterson, David, Paul C. LoCasto, and Cynthia M. Connine. 2003. "Corpora analyses of frequency of schwa deletion in conversational American English." *Phonetica* 60: 45–69.

Paul, Hermann. 1880 [1966]. *Prinzipien der Sprachgeschichte*, 7th unaltered edn. Tübingen: Max Niemeyer.

Penny, Ralph. 1984. "Esbozo de un atlas lingüístico de Santander." *Lingüística Española Actual* 6: 123–81.

——. 2000. *Variation and Change in Spanish.* Cambridge: Cambridge University Press.

Pepperkamp, Sharon. 2004. "Lexical exceptions in stress systems: arguments from early language acquisition and adult speech perception." *Language* 80: 98–126.

Petyt, K. M. 1985. *Dialect and Accent in Industrial West Yorkshire.* Amsterdam: Benjamins.

Phillips, Betty S. 1978. "A natural generative phonology of Old English based on King Alfred's translation of Gregory's *Pastoral Care*." PhD Dissertation, University of Georgia.

238 *References*

———. 1980. "Old English *an* ~ *on*: a new appraisal." *Journal of English Linguistics* 14: 20–3.

———. 1981. "Lexical diffusion and Southern *tune, duke, news*." *American Speech* 56: 72–8.

———. 1983a. "Constraints on syllables and quantitative changes in early English." *Linguistics* 21: 879–95.

———. 1983b. "Lexical diffusion and function words." *Linguistics* 21: 487–99.

———. 1983c. "ME diphthongization, phonetic analogy, and lexical diffusion." *WORD* 34: 11–23.

———. 1984. "Word frequency and the actuation of sound change." *Language* 60: 320–42.

———. 1989 [1993]. "The diffusion of a borrowed sound change." *Journal of English Linguistics* 22: 197–204.

———. 1994. "Southern English glide deletion revisited." *American Speech* 69: 115–27.

———. 1995. "Lexical diffusion as a guide to scribal intent: a comparison of ME <eo> vs. <e> spellings in the *Peterborough Chronicle* and the *Ormulum*." *Historical Linguistics 1993: Selected Papers from the 11th International Conference on Historical Linguistics, 16–20 August 1993*, edited by Henning Andersen, pp. 379–86. Amsterdam: John Benjamins.

———. 1997. "The *Peterborough Chronicle* diphthongs." *Studies in Middle English Linguistics*, edited by Jacek Fisiak, pp. 429–38. Berlin: Mouton de Gruyter.

———. 1998a. "British vs. American *-ate* and *-ator*: convergence, divergence, and the lexicon." *American Speech* 73: 160–77.

———. 1998b. "Lexical diffusion is NOT lexical analogy." *WORD* 49: 369–81.

———. 1998c. "Word frequency and lexical diffusion in English stress shifts." *Historical Linguistics 1995*. Vol. 2: *Germanic Linguistics*, edited by Richard Hogg and Linda van Bergen, pp. 223–32. Amsterdam: John Benjamins.

———. 2001. "Lexical diffusion, lexical frequency, and lexical analysis." *Frequency and the Emergence of Linguistic Structure*, edited by Joan Bybee and Paul Hopper, pp. 123–36. Amsterdam: John Benjamins.

———. 2002. "Lexical diffusion and competing analyses of sound change." *Studies in the History of the English Language: a Millennial Perspective*, edited by Donka Minkova and Robert Stockwell, pp. 231–43. Berlin: Mouton de Gruyter.

———. 2004. "Æ-raising in the *Peterborough Chronicle*." Paper presented at the International Conference on English Historical Linguistics, 24–8 August, Vienna, Austria. (To appear in the Proceedings.)

Pierrehumbert, Janet. 2001. "Exemplar dynamics: word frequency, lenition, and contrast." *Frequency and the Emergence of Linguistic Structure*, edited by Joan Bybee and Paul Hopper, pp. 137–57. Amsterdam: John Benjamins.

———. 2002. "Word-specific phonetics." *Laboratory Phonology 7*, edited by Carlos Gussenhoven and Natasha Warner, pp. 101–40. Berlin: Mouton de Gruyter.

———. 2003. "Probabilistic phonology." *Probabilistic Linguistics*, edited by Rens Bod, Jennifer Hay, and Stephanie Jannedy, pp. 177–228. Cambridge, MA: MIT Press.

Pisoni, David B. 1997. "Some thoughts on 'normalization' in speech perception." *Talker Variability in Speech Processing*, edited by Keith Johnson and J. W. Mullennix, pp. 9–32. San Diego: Academic Press.

Pisoni, D. B., H. C. Nusbaum, P. A. Luce, and L. M. Slowiaczek. 1985. "Speech perception, word recognition, and the structure of the lexicon." *Speech Communication* 4: 75–95.

References 239

Pitts, Ann. 1986. "Flip-flop prestige in American *tune, duke, news.*" *American Speech* 61: 131–8.

Porter, Noah, ed. 1909. *Webster's International Dictionary of the English Language.* Springfield, MA: G. & C. Merriam.

Potter, Simeon. 1948. "The Old English 'Pastoral Care.' " *Transactions of the Philological Society* 1947: 114–25.

Prince, Alan, and Paul Smolensky. 1993. *Optimality Theory: Constraint Interaction in Generative Theory.* Technical Report 2. New Brunswick, NJ: Rutgers University, Center for Cognitive Science.

Pyles, Thomas, and John Algeo. 1993. *The Origins and Development of the English Language,* 4th edn. Fort Worth: Harcourt Brace Jovanovich.

Reiss, Charles. 2003. "Language change without constraint reranking." *Optimality Theory and Language Change,* edited by D. Eric Holt, pp. 143–68. Dordrecht: Kluwer Academic Publishers.

Remez, R. E., J. M. Fellowes, and P. E. Rubin. 1997. "Talker identification based on phonetic information." *Journal of Experimental Psychology: Human Perception and Performance* 23 (5): 651–66.

Rhodes, Richard. 1996. "English reduced vowels and the nature of natural processes." *Natural Phonology: the State of the Art,* edited by Bernhard Hurch and Richard A. Rhodes, pp. 239–59. Berlin: Mouton de Gruyter.

Ritt, Nikolaus. 1994. *Quantity Adjustment: Vowel Lengthening and Shortening in Early Middle English.* Cambridge: Cambridge University Press.

——. 1997. "Early Modern English vowel shortenings in monosyllables before dentals: a morphologically conditioned sound change." *Language History and Linguistic Modelling: a Festschrift for Jacek Fisiak on his 60th Birthday,* Vol. 1: *Language History,* edited by Raymond Hickey and Stanislaw Puppel, pp. 65–71. Berlin: Mouton de Gruyter.

Rivierre, Jean-Claude. 1991. "Loss of final consonants in the north of New Caledonia." *Currents in Pacific Linguistics: Papers on Austronesian Linguistics and Ethnolinguistics in Honour of George W. Grace,* edited by Robert Blust, pp. 415–32. Canberra: Pacific Linguistics.

Roach, Peter, James Hartman, and Jane Setter, eds. 2003. *English Pronouncing Dictionary,* 16th edn. Cambridge: Cambridge University Press.

Rolland, J. F. 1809. *Nouveau vocabulaire, ou Dictionnaire portatif de la langue françoise,* 2nd edn. Paris: Didier.

Rusch, Willard J. 1992. *The Language of the East Midlands and the Development of Standard English.* New York: Peter Lang.

Saffran, Eleanor M. 2003. "Evidence from language breakdown: implications for the neural and functional organization of language." *Mind, Brain, and Language: Multidisciplinary Perspectives,* edited by Marie Banich and Molly Mack, pp. 251–81. Mahwah, NJ: Lawrence Erlbaum.

Salmons, Joseph, and Gregory Iverson. 1993. "Gothic *þl-* ~ *fl-* variation as lexical diffusion." *Diachronica* 10: 87–96.

Sapir, Edward. 1921. *Language: an Introduction to the Study of Speech.* New York: Harcourt.

Saussure, Ferdinand de. 1916 [1967]. *Cours de Linguistique Générale.* Paris: Payot.

——. 1916 [1959]. *Course in General Linguistics,* edited by Charles Bally and Albert Schehaye, in collaboration with Albert Riedlinger. Translated by Wade Baskin. New York: Philosophical Library.

240 *References*

Schachter, D. L. 1987. "Implicit memory: history and current status." *Journal of Experimental Psychology: Learning, Memory, and Cognition* 13: 501–18.

Scheibman, Joanne. 2000. "I dunno but . . . a usage-based account of the phonological reduction of *don't* in conversation." *Journal of Pragmatics* 32: 105–24.

Schirmunski, Viktor. 1956. "Schwachbetonte Wortformen in den deutschen Mundarten." *Fragen und Forschungen im Bereich und Umkreis der germanistischen Philologie*, edited by E. Karg-Gasterstädt, pp. 204–20. Berlin: Akademie Verlag.

Schogt, H. G. 1961. "La notion de loi dans la phonétique historique." *Lingua* 10: 79–92.

Schriefers, H., A. S. Meyer, and W. J. M. Levelt. 1990. "Exploring the time course of lexical access in production: picture–word interference studies." *Journal of Memory and Language* 29: 86–102.

Schuchardt, Hugo. 1885 [rpt. and trans. 1972]. "On sound laws: against the Neogrammarians." *Schuchardt, the Neogrammarians, and the Transformational Theory of Phonological Change*, edited by Theo Vennemann and Terence H. Wilbur, pp. 39–72. Frankfurt: Athenäum.

Schulman, R. 1983. "Vowel categorization by the bilingual listener." *PERILUS (Phonetic Experimental Research at the Institute of Linguistics University of Stockholm)* 3: 81–100.

Seebold, Elmar. 1972. *Das System der indogermanischen Halbvokale: Untersuchungen zum sogenannten "Sieversschen Gesetz" und zu den halbvokalhaltigen Suffixen in den indogermanischen Sprachen, besonders im Vedischen*. Heidelberg: Carl Winter.

Selkirk, E. O. 1982. "The syllable." *The Structure of Phonological Representations: Part II*, edited by H. van der Hulst and N. Smith, pp. 337–83. Dordrecht: Foris.

Sereno, Joan A. 1986. "Stress pattern differentiation of form class in English." *Journal of the Acoustical Society of America* 79: S36.

Sereno, Joan A., and Allard Jongman. 1995. "Acoustic correlates of grammatical class." *Language and Speech* 38: 57–76.

Sheridan, Thomas. 1780. *A General Dictionary of the English Language*. London: J. Dodsley, C. Dilly and J. Wilkie.

Sherman, Donald. 1975. "Noun–verb stress alternation: an example of the lexical diffusion of sound change in English." *Linguistics* 159: 43–71.

Silverstein, M. 1979. "Language structure and linguistic ideology." *The Elements: a Parasession on Linguistic Units and Levels*, edited by P. Clyne, W. Hanks, and C. Hofbauer, pp. 193–247. Chicago: Chicago Linguistic Society.

Simpson, G. B. 1981. "Meaning dominance and semantic context in the processing of lexical ambiguity." *Journal of Verbal Learning and Verbal Behavior* 20: 120–36.

Simpson, G. B., and C. Burgess. 1985. "Activation and selection processes in the recognition of ambiguous words." *Journal of Experimental Psychology: Human Perception and Performance* 11: 28–39.

Singh, Rajendra. 1996. "Natural phono(morpho)logy: a view from the outside." *Natural Phonology: the State of the Art*, edited by Berhard Hurch and Richard A. Rhodes, pp. 1–38. Berlin: Mouton de Gruyter.

Skousen, Royal. 1989. *Analogical Modeling of Language*. Dordrecht: Kluwer Academic.

——. 1992. *Analogy and Structure*. Dordrecht: Kluwer Academic.

Skousen, Royal, Deryle Lonsdale, and Dilworth B. Parkinson, eds. 2002. *Analogical Modeling: an Exemplar-based Approach to Language*. Amsterdam: John Benjamins.

Sommerfelt, A. 1962. *Diachronic and Synchronic Aspects of Language*. The Hague: Mouton.

Spevack, Marvin. 1973. *The Harvard Concordance to Shakespeare*. Cambridge, MA: Harvard University Press.

Stemberger, Joseph. 1981. "Morphological haplology." *Language* 57: 791–817.

——. 1984. "Structural errors in normal and agrammatic speech." *Cognitive Neuropsychology* 1 (4): 281–313.

——. 2004. "Neighbourhood effects on error rates in speech production." *Brain and Language* 90: 413–22.

Stemberger, Joseph, and Brian MacWhinney. 1986. "Frequency and the lexical storage of regularly inflected forms." *Memory and Cognition* 14 (1): 17–26.

Stephenson, Edward A. 1970. "Linguistic predictions and the waning of Southern [ju] in *tune, duke, news*." *American Speech* 45: 297–300.

Steriade, Donca. 2000. "Paradigm uniformity and the phonetics–phonology boundary." *Papers in Laboratory Phonology V: Acquisition and the Lexicon*, edited by Michael B. Broe and Janet B. Pierrehumbert, pp. 313–34. Cambridge: Cambridge University Press.

Stockwell, Robert. 1973. "Problems in the interpretation of the Great English Vowel Shift." *Studies in Linguistics: Papers in Honor of George L. Trager*, edited by M. Estellie Smith, pp. 344–62. The Hague: Mouton.

——. 2002. "How much shifting actually occurred in the historical English vowel shift?" *Studies in the History of the English Language: a Millennial Perspective*, edited by Donka Minkova and Robert Stockwell, pp. 267–81. Berlin: Mouton de Gruyter.

Stockwell, Robert, and Donka Minkova. 1988. "The English vowel shift: problems of coherence and explanation." *Luick Revisited*, edited by Dieter Kastovsky and Gero Bauer, pp. 355–94. Tübingen: Gunter Narr.

——. 1990. "The early modern English vowels, more o' Lass." *Diachronica* 7: 199–214.

Strang, Barbara. 1970. *A History of English*. London: Methuen.

Sweet, Henry. 1871–72 [1958]. *King Alfred's West-Saxon Version of Gregory's Pastoral Care*. Early English Text Society, Original Series, vols 45 and 50. London: Oxford University Press.

Thibadeau, R., M. A. Just, and P. A. Carpenter. 1983. "A model of the time course and content of reading." *Cognitive Science* 6: 157–203.

Thomas, Erik R. 2001. *An Acoustic Analysis of Vowel Variation in New World English*. PADS (Publication of the American Dialect Society) 85. Durham, NC: Duke University Press.

Thomason, Sarah Grey. 2003. "Contact as a source of language change." *The Handbook of Historical Linguistics*, edited by Brian Joseph and Richard Janda, pp. 687–712. Oxford: Blackwell.

Toon, Thomas. 1976a. "The actuation and implementation of an Old English sound change." *Proceedings of the Linguistic Association of Canada and the United States* 3: 614–22.

——. 1976b. "The variationist analysis of early Old English manuscript data." *Current Progress in Historical Linguistics: Proceedings of the Second International Conference on Historical Linguistics, Tucson, Arizona, 12–16 January 1976*, edited by William Christie, pp. 71–81. Amsterdam: North-Holland.

242 *References*

———. 1978. "Lexical diffusion in Old English." *Papers from the Parasession on the Lexicon*, edited by D. Farkas et al., pp. 357–64. Chicago: Chicago Linguistic Society.

———. 1983. *The Politics of Early Old English Sound Change.* New York: Academic Press.

———. 1986. "Old English dialects: what's to explain; what's an explanation?" *Explanation and Linguistic Change*, edited by Willem F. Koopman, Frederike van der Leek, Olga Fischer and Roger Eaton, pp. 275–93. Amsterdam: John Benjamins.

———. 1992. "Old English dialects." *The Cambridge History of the English Language.* Vol. 1: *The Beginnings to 1066*, edited by Richard M. Hogg, pp. 409–51. Cambridge: Cambridge University Press.

Trager, George L. 1940. "One phonemic entity becomes two: the case of 'short *a*'." *American Speech* 15: 255–8.

Trudgill, Peter. 1983. *On Dialect: Social and Geographical Perspectives.* Oxford: Basil Blackwell.

———. 1986. *Dialects in Contact.* Oxford: Blackwell.

Turennout, M. van, P. Hagoort, and C. M. Brown. 1998. "Brain activity during speaking: from syntax to phonology in 40 milliseconds." *Science* 280: 572–4.

Uit den Boogaart, P. C. 1975. *Woordfrequenties: in Geschreven en Gesproken Nederlands.* Utrecht: Oosthoek, Scheltema & Holkema.

Ultan, Russell. 1978. "A typological view of metathesis." *Universals of Human Language*, edited by Joseph Greenberg, pp. 367–402. Stanford: Stanford University Press.

Vennemann, Theo. 1972. "Hugo Schuchardt's theory of phonological change." *Schuchardt, the Neogrammarians, and the Transformational Theory of Phonological Change*, edited by Theo Vennemann and Terence H. Wilbur, pp. 116–74. Frankfurt: Athenäum.

———. 2000. "From quantity to syllable cuts: on so-called lengthening in the Germanic languages." *Italian Journal of Linguistics/Rivista di Linguistica* 12: 251–82.

Verner, Karl. 1876 [1967]. "An exception to Grimm's Law." *A Reader in Nineteenth-Century Historical Indo-European Linguistics*, edited and translated by Winfred P. Lehmann, pp. 132–63. Bloomington, IN: Indiana University Press.

Vestbøstad, Per, ed. 1989. *Nynorsk frekvensordbok.* Bergen: Alma Mater.

Vigliocco, Gabriella, Tiziana Antonini, and Merrill F. Garrett. 1997. "Grammatical gender is on the tip of Italian tongues." *Psychological Science* 8 (4): 314–17.

Viso, Susan del, José M. Igoa, and José E. García-Albea. 1991. "On the autonomy of phonological encoding: evidence from slips of the tongue in Spanish." *Journal of Psycholinguistic Research* 20: 161–85.

Vitevitch, Michael S. et al. 1997. "Phonotactics and syllable stress: implications for the processing of spoken nonsense words." *Language and Speech* 40: 47–62.

Vitevitch, Michael S., Jonna Armbrüstler, and Shinying Chu. 2004. "Sublexical and lexical representations in speech production: effects of phonotactic probability and onset density." *Journal of Experimental Psychology: Learning, Memory, and Cognition* 30 (2): 514–29.

von Essen, O. 1962. "Trubetzkoys fester und loser Anschluß in experimental phonetischer Sicht." *Proceedings of the Fourth International Congress of Phonetic Sciences*, edited by Antti Sovijärvi and Pentti Aalto, pp. 590–8. The Hague: Mouton.

References 243

Wang, H. Samuel, and Bruce L. Derwing. 1994. "Some vowel schemas in three English morphological classes: experimental evidence." *In Honor of William S-Y Wang: Interdisciplinary Studies on Language and Language Change*, edited by Matthew Chen and Ovid J. L. Tzeng, pp. 561–75. Taipei, Taiwan: Pyramid Press.

Wang, William S-Y. 1969. "Competing changes as a cause of residue." *Language* 45: 9–25.

———. 1979. "Language change – a lexical perspective." *Annual Review of Anthropology* 8: 353–71.

Wang, William S-Y, and Chin-Chuan Cheng. 1977. "Implementation of phonological change: the Shuāng-fēng case." *The Lexicon in Phonological Change*, edited by William S-Y Wang, pp. 148–58. The Hague: Mouton.

Wang, William S-Y, and Chinfa Lien 1993. "Bidirectional diffusion in sound change." *Historical Linguistics: Problems and Perspectives*, edited by Charles Jones, pp. 345–400. London: Longman.

Webster, Noah. 1806. *A Compendious Dictionary of the English Language.* A Facsimile of the First (1806), with introduction by Philip B. Gove. New York: Bounty.

———. 1828. *An American Dictionary of the English Language.* 2 vols. New York: S. Converse.

Weinreich, Uriel. 1974 [1953]. *Languages in Contact.* The Hague: Mouton.

Weinreich, Uriel, William Labov, and Marvin Herzog. 1968. "Empirical foundations for a theory of language change." *Directions for Historical Linguistics*, edited by W. Lehmann and Y. Malkiel, pp. 97–195. Austin: University of Texas Press.

Wells, J. C. 1982. *Accents of English.* 3 vols. Cambridge: Cambridge University Press.

White, R. M., and Robert Holt, eds. 1878. *The Ormulum.* 2 vols. Oxford: Clarendon.

Wingfield, A. 1968. "Effects of frequency on identification and naming of objects." *American Journal of Psychology* 81: 226–34.

Wolfram, Walt, and Natalie Schilling-Estes. 1996. "On the social basis of phonetic resistance: the shifting status of Outer Banks /ay/." *Sociolinguistic Variation: Data, Theory, and Analysis*, edited by Jennifer Arnold et al., pp. 69–82. Stanford, CA: CSLI Publications.

———. 2003. "Dialectology and linguistic diffusion." *The Handbook of Historical Linguistics*, edited by Brian D. Joseph and Richard D. Janda, pp. 713–35. Oxford: Blackwell.

Wright, Joseph. 1892. *A Grammar of the Dialect of Windhill.* London: Kegan Paul.

Wright, Richard. 2003. "Factors of lexical competition in vowel articulation." *Phonetic Interpretation: Papers in Laboratory Phonology VI*, edited by John Local, Richard Ogden, and Rosiland Temple, pp. 75–87. Cambridge: Cambridge University Press.

Yaeger-Dror, Malcah. 1994. "Phonetic evidence for sound change in Quebec French." *Phonological Structure and Phonetic Form*, edited by P. Keating, pp. 267–92. Cambridge: Cambridge University Press.

———. 1996. "Phonetic evidence for the evolution of lexical classes: the case of a Montreal French vowel shift." *Towards a Social Science of Language: Papers in Honor of William Labov.* Vol. 1: *Variation and Change in Language and Society*, edited by Gregory Guy, C. Feagin, J. Baugh, and D. Schiffrin, pp. 263–87. Amsterdam: John Benjamins.

244 References

Zimmermann, S., and S. Sapon. 1958. "A note on vowel duration seen crosslinguistically." *Journal of the Acoustical Society of America* 30: 152–3.

Zuraw, Kie. 2003. "Probability in language change." *Probabilistic Linguistics*, edited by Rens Bod, Jennifer Hay, and Stefanie Jannedy, pp. 139–76. Cambridge, MA: MIT Press.

Topic Index

actuation, 26–7, 41, 58, 126, 182, 193
æ-raising, **13–18**, 195–6
age of acquisition, 186–8
analogy/ analogical change, 2–3,
14–15, 29, 36, 81, 87, 92, **124–8**,
157, 177
apparent time, 182–3
areal diffusion, 27
assimilation, 29, 58, **67–70**, 86, 108,
151, 157, 175, 178–9, 190
-ate, -ator, 41–8, 52–5

borrowing, 2, 8, 14, 17, 25, 29, 68,
72–3, 78–9, 108, 124–5, **128–57**,
159, 195

child language, 5–6, 40, 86, 126,
182–6
connectionism/connectionist, 25–6,
29, 36, 40, 47, 52, 54–6, 75, 81,
94–5, 116, 118–19, 121, 125, 157,
181–2, 185–7
consonant shift, 1, 12, 108, 195

deletion/reduction, 9–10, 11–12, 22,
32, **58–67**, 69, 75, **76–84**, 96–8,
103–4, 108, 122, 127, 140,
175, 182
diphthongization, 11–12, **68–70**,
71–5, 93, **99–101**, 108–9, 127,
165–72, 175, 189
discourse, 20, 21, 22, 62, 67, **188–91**
dissimilation, 32, 33, 75
Dublin Vowel Shift, 143, 195
Dutch, 61, 63–5, 99–101, 108–9, 118,
120, 139

ease of articulation, 109, 189–90, 192
entrenched/entrenchment, 38, 41, 46,
52, 56, 81, 87, 112, 119, 121, 127,
128, 133, 157, 183, 186–8

see also strength, lexical
epenthesis, 32
exemplar, 18, **23–4**, 31, 123, 141–2,
150, 157, **186, 189,** 191,
193–4

flap, 32, 66, **74**
function words, 83, 99, 101, **102–12**,
151, 153

gang effect, 116, 182
generative, 126–7
Gothic, 158
gradience, 18, 20, 38–9, 40, 57, 84,
93–4
grammaticalization, 92
Great Vowel Shift, 71–5

High German Consonant Shift, 12,
108, 195
homophones, 33, 34–5, **120–3**
hypercorrection, 154, 164–5, 190, 196

implementation, 3, 6, **26–8**, 29, 32,
38, 47, **48–9, 55–6,** 58, 68, 75, 79,
81, 87, 93–4, 107, 121, **124–5**,
130, 132, 143, 156, 157, 182,
192, 193
innovation, 27, 39, 48, 75, 87, 94,
124–5, 129–32, 156–7, 193
-ity and k>s, 41

lengthening, *see* vowel lengthening
level of consciousness, 94, 192
lexical analysis, 29, 31, **46–9**, 52, 55,
76, 81, 90, 93, 175
lexical phonology, **7–9**, 20–1, 31,
52–5, 126
lexical strength, *see* strength, lexical
Lindisfarne Gospels, 82–4, 87, 164–5

246 *Topic Index*

memory, 23, 25, 27, 36–7, 48, 49, 51, 57, 81, 87, 94, 122, 127, 128, 142, 157, 186, 187–8, 191
Mercian, 82, 99, 148–9, 151, 153–5, 160, 164
metathesis, 5, 11, **32–3**
Middle English, *see Ormulum, Peterborough Chronicle, Rushworth 1*
motivation, **55–6**, 86, 121, **124–5**, 142–3, 151, 158, 173, 176–7, 179–80, 182, 185, 195

near–merger, 164, 182–3
neighbo(u)rs, lexical, 5, 25–6, 62, 142, 182
neogrammarian, 1–2, **4–8**, **10–12**, 13–18, 20, 32, 57, 115, 120, 125, 128, 131–2, 182, 185, 190, **191–6**
network, 7, 26, 27, 36, 47, 52, 75, 125, 182, 185, 190
Northern Cities Shift, **13–18**, 20, 79, 190

Old English, 10, 15, 33, 37, 58, 60, 67, 70, 74, 76, **81–4**, 86, **87–93**, 104, 107, 109, 111, 127, 143, **148–55**, 164–5, 175, 196
see also Lindisfarne Gospels, Pastoral Care, Vespasian Psalter
Optimality Theory, 2, 7, **18–22**, 31, 50, 74–5
Ormulum, 68–70, 85–6, 87–9, 105–7, 109–11, 159, 160, 163–4, 166–9, 170–2

Pastoral Care, 11, 104, 152–5
past tense, Modern English, 37, 40, 41, 63–4, 127, 177
perception, 7, 21, 23, 24, 25, 26, 38, 46, 74, 94, 103, 112, 117, 182–3, 192
Peterborough Chronicle, 99, **159–72**
phonetic analogy, 27, 93, 125, 127, **181**
phonologization, 92, 193
phonotactic constraints, 25, 54, 75, 80–1, 83–4, 90, 93, 95, 125, 128, 136, 157, 175, 181, 190

prefixes, 36, 37, **51–2**
production, 7, 19, 20, **24–6**, 38, 46, 47, **48–9**, 62, 63, 66, 74–5, 81, 87, **93–5**, 103, 112, **116–19**, 121–2, 123, 125, 128, 157, 175, **181–2**, 182–3, **183–5**, 188, 189–90
productivity, 1, 28, 32, 54, 81, 87, 116, 131, 135, 146, 147, 154
product-oriented schema, *see* schema

reanalysis, 5, 18, 92, 125, 193
reduction, *see* deletion/reduction
register, 19, 32, 131, 135, 152
reverse lexical diffusion, 135–7
Rhythm Rule, 18, **49–52**
Rushworth 1, 82–3, 148, 154–5, 164

salience, 143, **192–6**
schema, **39–41**, 48–9, 56
scribe, 84, 85, 87, 148, **149–50**, 154, 155, 159–60, 165, 166, 169
Siever's Law, 158
social diffusion, 27, 87, 125, 132, 139, 142, 143, 144, 147–8, 195–6
sporadic change, 17, 28–9, 131, 141, 156
spreading activation, 26, 119
strength, lexical, 24, 31, 41, 81, 84, 112, 118, 119, 121, 128, 157, 185, 194
stress shift, 29, 31, 32, **34–9**, **41–6**, **46–9**, 52, **53–6**, 121, 127, 175, 190, 191
string frequency, 21, 61–2
suffixes, 9, 36, 41, 45–6, 48, **51–2**, **52–5**
syllable, 12, 24, 33, 37–9, 49, 59, 75, 83, 90, 91, 93, 118, 123, 173, 175, 176, 181
syllable cut, 91–3

token frequency, 20, 23, **32**, 38, 41, 51, 59–60, 61, 63, 77, 99, 137, 141, 189
tone, 9, 32, 33–4, 121, 194
type frequency, 20, **32**, 33, 37, 38, 41, 81, 87, 191

/ū/>/ʊ/, 172–9
unrounding, 10, 58, 76, **84–7**, **160–3**, 170, 173

Topic Index 247

usage/usage–based phonology, 7, 9,
18, 20, 21, **22–6**, 28, 31, 36, 47–8,
50–1, 54, 55, 58, 66, 75, 113, 157,
182, 191, 196
uvular *r*, 32, 129, 130, 156

Vespasian Psalter, 148–9, 153
vowel laxing, 4, **113–14**, 135, 159,
173, **177–9**
vowel lengthening, 10, 11, 14, 58, 76,
87–93, 102, **109–11**, 130, 147

vowel raising, 10, 11, **14–17**, 57, 67,
115, 127, 133, 143, 147, **148–55**,
195, 196
vowel shift, 11, 57, 58, 149, 194
see also Dublin Vowel Shift, Great
Vowel Shift, Northern Cities
Shift
vowel shortening, 11, 14, 54, 88, 92,
126, 195
see also /ū/>/ʊ/

Author Index

Abd-el-Jawad, H., 137–8
Aitchison, J., 103, 116
Alario, F., 103
Alba, M., 61
Albright, A., 40
Algeo, J., 173
Andersen, H., 6, 131, 132, 139, 194–5
Anderson, A., 189
Antonsen, E., 86
Anttila, R., 81, 87
Ash, S., 151
Aski, J., 28, 193
Asudeh, A., 21

Baayen, R., 81, 212
Bailey, T., 20
Bakken, K., 2, 29, 136
Balota, D., 187
Barber, C., 218
Barinova, G., 59
Barnhart, C., 59
Barrack, C., 12, 13, 108, 158
Barry, C., 186, 187
Beal, J., 141, 144
Becker, T., 102
Beckman, M., 5, 6, 184
Beddor, P., 150
Bell, A., 216
Bennett, J., 159, 166, 172
Berg, T., 5, 47, 61, 111, 184, 185, 186, 189, 192
Bergen, D., 61
Berko, J., 40
Bermúdez-Otero, R., 215
Besner, D., 187
Blevins, J., 33
Bloomfield, L., 57, 129, 130, 135, 138
Boberg, C., 18, 151
Bock, J., 38, 111
Bod, R., 215
Boersma, P., 18, 20, 74

Bolinger, D., 102, 189
Bolla, K., 178
Bonin, P., 216
Booij, G., 24, 48, 214
Borowsky, R., 187
Bradlow, A., 189
Braine, M., 75
Brink, L., 11
Bronstein, A., 42, 113, 114, 212
Browman, C., 67, 69
Brown, E., 154
Brown, L., 42, 59
Brugmann, K., 1
Brunner, K., 154
Bunger, A., 112
Burchfield, R., 85
Burgess, C., 117
Burnage, G., 43
Bush, N., 69
Butterfield, S., 38
Bybee, J., 7, 9, 10, 12, 20, 21, 22, 23, 24, 27, 29, 36, 37, 39, 40, 41, 46, 48, 62, 63, 64, 65, 66, 78, 81, 104, 116, 119, 128, 175, 177, 180, 194, 212

Campbell, A., 33, 217
Caramazza, A., 113, 117, 119, 121
Carpenter, A., 113
Carr, P., 8, 123
Carroll, J., 4, 34, 71, 77, 145, 219
Carterette, E., 69
Cavalli-Sforza, L., 27
Cedergren, H., 211
Chambers, J., 75
Chambers, W., 43
Chen, M., 3, 7, 9, 90, 121, 123, 129, 184, 216
Cheng, C., 4, 32, 33, 194
Chomsky, N., 47, 127
Chumbley, J., 187

Author Index 249

Clark, C., 160, 161, 163, 166, 172, 217, 218
Cleary, M., 117
Coates, R., 82, 217
Cohen, L., 103
Cohn, A., 120
Cole, P., 36, 51
Coles, E., 144
Connine, C., 66
Cook, A., 84
Cooley, M., 80
Cooper, C., 14
Costa, A., 121
Côté, M., 194
Cutler, A., 38, 47

Daines, S., 144
Danielsson, B., 42
Dell, G., 25, 26, 94, 112, 116, 119, 120
Derwing, B., 81, 212
D'Introno, F., 66, 67
Dobson, E., 173, 176
Dogil, G., 48
Dolby, J., 34
Donegan, P., 188
Dressler, W., 188

Edwards, J., 5, 6, 184

Faber, A., 164
Farwell, C., 184
Fay, W., 33
Fayol, N., 216
Fenk-Oczlon, G., 59, 67, 188
Ferguson, C., 147, 184
Fidelholz, J., 58, 173, 175
Fintoft, K., 90
Fischer-Jørgensen, E., 178
Fodor, J., 120
Fowler, C., 21, 22, 67, 189
Francis, W., 59, 97, 187
Frisch, S., 26
Fudge, E., 214

Garrett, A., 33
Gaşiorowski, P., 45
Gattel, C., 91
Gerhand, S., 187
Gerritsen, M., 108

Gess, R., 19
Giegerich, H., 54
Gierut, J., 5, 184
Gilbert, J., 86
Gilhooly, K., 187
Gilliéron, J., 1, 3
Gimson, A., 42, 59, 213
Godfrey, J., 97
Goeman, A., 63, 64, 65, 99, 100, 104, 108
Goldinger, S., 23
Goldsmith, J., 53, 216
Goldstein, L., 67, 69
Gordon, B., 113
Görlach, M., 173, 175, 176
Gove, P., 34, 43
Guion, S., 122
Guy, G., 211

Hahn, U., 20
Hale, M., 5, 124, 126
Halle, M., 47
Hammond, M., 18, 19, 49, 50, 51
Hansen, A., 10, 57, 115
Harley, T., 119
Harris, J., 8, 155
Hayes, B., 18, 20, 40
Henaff, G., 117
Hickey, R., 143, 195
Hindle, D., 120
Hinskens, F., 27
Hock, H., 32, 195
Hogaboam, T., 117
Hogg, R., 33, 45, 82, 84, 85, 90, 148, 149, 215, 217
Holder, M., 79, 140
Holes, C., 138
Holm, S., 85, 216
Holt, D., 20, 85
Hooper, J., 22, 36, 59, 127, 173, 175, 177
Hopper, W., 92
Hotopf, W., 117, 119
Housum, J., 21, 22, 67, 189
Hume, E., 32, 33

Iverson, G., 158

Jaeger, J., 186
Janda, R., 2, 124, 193

250 Author Index

Jansen, F., 108
Janson, T., 32, 137
Jescheniak, J., 25, 113, 118, 120, 121, 216
Jespersen, O., 37, 58, 141
Johannesson, N., 215
Johanson, K., 130
Johnson, K., 23, 141
Johnson, S., 42, 212
Jones, C., 89, 90
Jones, D., 42, 59, 212
Jones, M., 69, 145
Jong, E., 101
Jongman, A., 37, 38, 39
Joseph, B., 2, 124, 195
Josselson, H., 59
Jurafsky, D., 94, 116, 122, 189
Jusczyk, P., 80
Just, M., 113

Karlgren, B., 3
Katamba, F., 53
Keller, F., 21
Kelly, M., 38, 111
Kenrick, W., 141
Kenyon, J., 43, 59, 145, 146
Kerswill, P., 12, 192, 195
Kim, S., 152
King, J., 113
Kiparsky, P., 30, 32, 52, 53, 57, 93, 124, 125, 128, 190, 219
Kirchner, R., 141
Kloeke, G., 139
Kniezsa, V., 166
Knott, T., 43, 59, 145, 146
Kretzschmar, W., 219
Kreuz, R., 188
Krishnamurti, B., 6, 10, 63
Kučera, H., 59, 97, 187
Kuhn, S., 105
Kurath, H., 78, 105, 131, 151
Kutas, M., 112, 113

Labov, W., 2, 4, 7, 10–17, 20, 23, 31, 57, 71, 72, 75, 76, 79, 94, 103, 120, 136, 141, 142, 147, 151, 164, 182, 190, 192, 194, 195, 211, 219
Lachs, L., 23, 57, 94, 117, 122, 123, 141

Ladefoged, P., 178, 179
Laferriere, M., 147
Laing, M., 215
Landau, S., 42, 212, 213
Lass, R., 6, 165, 166, 215, 217
Laubstein, A., 25, 117
Laver, J., 176, 177
Lavoie, L., 102
Lehiste, I., 177
Lehmann, W., 1, 211
Leskien, A., 1
Leslau, W., 127, 173, 175
Levelt, W., 25, 48, 94, 113, 116, 118, 119, 120, 121, 213
Levins, P., 34
Li, P., 117
Lieber, R., 81, 212
Lieberman, P., 189
Lien, C., 33, 129
Lindau, M., 218
Lindblom, B., 62, 189
Lippi-Green, R., 136
Lively, S., 23
Lociewicz, B., 9, 63, 194
Logie, R., 187
Luick, K., 166, 215
Lund, J., 11
Lutz, A., 83

MacDonald, M., 120
MacMahon, M., 211
MacWhinney, B., 40, 69, 119
Maddieson, I., 178, 179
Malkiel, Y., 1, 185
Mańczak, W., 3
Marchand, H., 53
Martin, N., 119
Martinet, A., 3
McCully, C., 45, 90
McDavid, R., 78, 131, 151
Menn, L., 40
Merlo, P., 6
Meunier, F., 36, 48
Meyer, A., 94
Meyer, E., 90
Milroy, J., 6, 27, 57, 79, 124, 128, 129, 130, 132–3, 156, 157, 172
Milroy, L., 27, 142, 147

Author Index

Minkova, D., 34, 37, 59, 60, 74, 84, 93, 173, 213, 215, 216
Miozzo, M., 117, 119, 216
Mish, F., 43, 59
Mitchell, J., 160
Möbius, B., 48
Moder, C., 81, 212
Morin, Y., 91, 96, 114
Morrisette, M., 5, 184
Morton, J., 94
Mossé, F., 165
Munson, B., 62
Murray, J., 41
Murray, R., 91, 92, 176, 214
Myers, J., 19, 50

Nahkola, K., 214
Neu, H., 103
Niedzielski, N., 78
Nielsen, H., 148
Nygaard, L., 23

Ogura, M., 4, 7, 12, 71, 72, 73, 127, 173, 174, 175, 176, 192, 214, 218, 219
Ohala, J., 178
Oldfield, R., 118, 189
Oliveira, M., 7
Onions, C., 34
Orton, H., 144
O'Seaghdha, P., 25, 26, 116, 119
Osthoff, H., 1

Pandey, P., 9
Parkes, M., 160, 166
Pater, J., 18, 19
Patterson, D., 60, 61, 66, 96, 97, 98
Paul, H., 129, 216
Penny, R., 139
Pepperkamp, S., 213
Perfetti, C., 117
Petyt, K., 123
Phillips, B., 10, 11, 20, 29, 34, 35, 41, 42, 43, 45, 46, 53, 55, 56, 59, 68, 75, 76, 77, 78, 79, 80, 85, 86, 90, 102, 104, 105, 107, 110, 127, 144–5, 152, 159, 160, 166, 167, 168, 170, 173, 175, 188, 216, 217, 219

Pierrehumbert, J., 20, 23, 24, 41, 46, 150, 182
Pisoni, D., 117
Pitts, A., 78
Porter, N., 43
Potter, S., 152
Preston, D., 78
Prince, A., 21
Pyles, T., 173

Ramsaran, A., 42, 213
Reich, P., 119
Reiss, C., 126
Remez, R., 23
Resnikoff, H., 34
Rhodes, R., 173
Ritt, N., 215
Rivierre, J., 156
Roach, P., 42, 212
Roelofs, A., 94
Rolland, J., 91
Rusch, W., 99, 218

Saanilahti, M., 214
Saffran, E., 120
Salmons, J., 158
Sankoff, D., 211
Sapir, E., 3
Sapon, S., 90
Saussure, F., 2
Schachter, D., 23
Schade, U., 186
Scheibman, J., 21, 62
Schilling-Estes, N., 132, 133–4
Schirmunski, V., 108
Schmitt, B., 112
Schogt, H., 155
Schriefers, H., 116
Schuchardt, H., 3, 6, 127, 129, 132, 172
Schulman, R., 183
Seebold, E., 158
Segui, J., 36, 48
Selkirk, E., 214
Sereno, J., 37, 38, 39, 46
Sheldon, E., 113, 114
Sherman, D., 34
Silverstein, M., 142
Simpson, G., 117

252 Author Index

Singh, R., 53
Skousen, R., 128
Smithers, G., 159, 166, 172
Smolensky, P., 21
Solomon, N., 62
Sommerfelt, A., 3
Sosa, J., 66, 67
Spevack, M., 174, 219
Stampe, D., 188
Stemberger, J., 26, 40, 119
Stephenson, E., 76
Steriade, D., 10
Stockwell, R., 59, 60, 74, 93, 173, 177, 213, 216
Storkel, H., 184
Strang, B., 177
Strassel, S., 18
Suleiman, S., 137–8
Sweet, H., 151, 152

Thibadeau, R., 113
Thomas, E., 151
Thomason, S., 131
Todd, H., 42
Toon, T., 68, 81, 115, 148, 149, 150, 151, 154, 155, 160, 164, 165, 196, 217
Trager, G., 14–15
Traugott, E., 92
Trudgill, P., 130–1, 144, 145
Turennout, M., 112

Uit den Boogaart, P., 64
Ultan, R., 32

van Reenen, P., 63, 64, 65, 104
Vennemann, T., 91, 92, 129, 176
Verner, K., 1
Vestbøstad, P., 137
Vigliocco, G., 117
Viso, S., 119
Vitevitch, M., 81
von Essen, O., 91

Wang, W., 3, 4, 6, 7, 31, 32, 33, 81, 115, 129, 130, 172, 192, 194, 212
Webster, N., 43
Weinreich, U., 125, 137
Wells, J., 123, 143, 145, 173
White, R., 85
Williams, A., 192, 195
Wingfield, A., 118, 189
Wolfram, W., 132, 133–4
Wright, J., 123
Wright, R., 62, 189
Wyman, V., 86

Yaeger-Dror, M., 10, 214
Yip, M., 117

Zimmermann, S., 90
Zuraw, K., 20